365 Ways to Cook Eggs

Elaine Corn

A JOHN BOSWELL ASSOCIATES BOOK

HarperCollins*Publishers*

For Ruby Magnolia, who ate eggs any way humans fixed them including in the ice cream she got on each of her fourteen birthdays

HarperCollins books may be purchased for educational, business, or sales promotional use. For information please write: Special Markets Department, HarperCollins Publishers, Inc., 10 East 53rd Street, New York, NY 10022.

FIRST EDITION

Series Editor: Susan Wyler
Design: Nigel Rollings
Index: Maro Riofrancos

Library of Congress Cataloging-in-Publication Data applied for.

ISBN 0-06-017138-3

96 97 98 99 00 DT/HC 10 9 8 7 6 5 4 3 2 1

Contents

Introduction: The Egg and I

I have reverence for the egg. When handled and used correctly, this simple ovoid packed with protein is responsible for some of the most pleasurable sensations of taste and texture in the culinary world. Eggs perform feats no other food can claim. Yolks emulsify and thicken. Whites give poof, puff, and fluff to an array of dishes, both savory and sweet.

As a whole, the protein in eggs is the source of coagulation. It is a phenomenon that is able to change a liquid from a fluid state to a curd. Coagulation is the moment when custard turns to scrambled eggs. Depending upon your intentions, this can be a benefit or a disaster.

The egg insists on being understood and treated gently. Under its fragile shell is a plethora of sensitivities. In the life of every culinary egg there comes a moment when it wants to say, "Enough!" It has endured too much whipping, too much heat, too much time in motion. And it lets you know in punishing ways. Too much heat, and coagulation becomes a curse known as curdling. This is an irreversible state. No amount of straining, whipping or wishing will make the egg smooth again. Or, the egg might separate. It can toughen, too. Or weep, seep, and fall.

The worst revenge is its inclination to incubate bacteria if not handled right. Be reassured, though, that using grade A eggs with clean, uncracked shells and keeping your eggs refrigerated except when you are cooking them will prevent practically all health problems.

The three functional properties of egg cookery are coagulation, emulsification, and foaming. Coagulation takes food from a liquid or gel state to a curdled state (custard, scrambled eggs). Emulsification bridges the domains of oil and water through the molecular attractions of yolks. It's what magically thickens egg and oil with a bit of liquid into mayonnaise. Foaming adds volume to food, cooked or not, from whipped egg whites.

In addition, eggs bind, leaven, thicken, glaze, and clarify. How egg protein is stretched, heated, and combined with fat is at the heart of egg performance. There are so many things to look for when you cook with an egg that one of the most important elements in your kitchen should be good light. The egg gives many clues about its status over the stages of a recipe, but you have to watch for the signs: gloss or sheen, peaks, ribbons, thickening, coating a metal spoon, the color of a lemon, and imminent curdling.

Eggs can be boiled without curdling, but only if the situation is right. A whole egg coagulates at 155°F. The yolk coagulates at various temperatures. If sugar and milk are present, the coagulation won't happen until 175° to 185°F. And if you add a starch like flour or cornstarch to the formula, the mixture can indeed be boiled without fear of curdling, as is evidenced in pastry cream, cream pie fillings, and some stove-top puddings.

Separating Eggs

Yolks separate best from whites when the eggs are cold. You can separate eggs directly in your hands, letting the whites slip through your fingers while capturing the yolk in your palm. If that's too messy, the usual way is to crack the egg gently in half, then pour the contents back and forth from shell to shell over a bowl, until the whites fall away and the yolk remains in one of the shells. Should you accidentally get some yolk into the whites you're intending to whip, scoop it out with the one tool that won't let the wayward yolk get away—a discarded egg shell. A small amount of yolk with its inherent fat prevents the whites from reaching their fullest volume.

Treating Egg Whites as They Deserve

Egg whites whip best when they are close to room temperature. If they're cold when you start, you can begin beating them over a pan of warm water, or set the bowl over the pilot light on your range if you have an old-fashioned gas stove. Whipped egg whites are really a foam of trapped air. When they are perfectly whipped to stiff peaks, they will hold their peak when the beaters are turned upside down, though the whites should still be glossy and supple. Overbeating causes the elasticity of the protein around the trapped air to stretch too far—and snap. At that point the whites will start to look dry; they will become brittle and break up when you try to fold them. On the other hand, underbeating won't give a pleasing result after baking.

The beating of egg whites is fraught with compromise. Sugar makes the whites very stable but limits their potential for greatest volume. An acid, such as cream of tartar, helps prevent a collapse but the whipping time will be longer.

To fold in beaten egg whites, I like to do a figure eight with a big rubber spatula. It's gentle but persuasive and quick.

Whites can keep up to a week if covered and refrigerated. They'll freeze with excellent quality for up to a year. Don't bother with the ice tray recommendation. This is the notion of pouring egg whites into ice trays and freezing them into cubes, which are transferred to zip-style storage bags, so we can use them in the future one at a time. In fact, egg whites are seldom used one at a time. If one egg white is called for, get a fresh one and use the single egg yolk in a few days. The best way to freeze egg whites is first to decide on how many egg whites you're comfortable freezing at a time. I like six. Freezer bags of egg whites in my freezer contain exactly six. A package defrosts easily in the microwave. If I freeze more, say twelve, which I know I can use in angel food batters, I'll write "12" on the container. As to such treatment, I've always believed egg whites enjoy torture. The older they are, the better they like a good whipping.

> *Always remember:*
> 1 egg white = 1 fluid ounce or 1 tablespoon
> 8 whites = 1/2 cup

Egg Safety: Hatching a New Outlook

In May 1995, the latest figures for the likelihood of eggs infected with salmonella were estimated. In tested flocks, 2 to 3 eggs out of 10,000 might be infected. Conservative scientists liberally estimate that nationally 1 out of 20,000 eggs might contain the bacteria. The total likelihood of finding an infected egg is .005 percent. If an egg does contain the salmonella organism, the number of them in a freshly laid egg will probably be small. And if the egg has an intact shell with no cracks and is properly refrigerated and handled, this number will not muliply enough to cause illness in a healthy person. Despite the minute possibility of salmonella entering the human digestive tract, cautionary advice is in place for the very young, the very old, people with compromised immune systems, and pregnant women. All in these groups should be wary of any recipes that contain raw eggs.

Raw No More

If a recipe calls for raw eggs but you'd prefer that they be cooked, here are the general guidelines from the American Egg Board:

Raw yolks—You'll need a minimum of 2 tablespoons of liquid *from the recipe per yolk,* blended together. Put the mixture into a heavy-bottomed saucepan over low heat, stirring constantly, until the mixture coats the back of a metal spoon. Then proceed with the recipe.

Raw whites (deemed low-risk)—First you'll combine the whites with the amount of sugar called for in the recipe in a heatproof bowl, using a minimum of 2 tablespoons of sugar per egg white. With a portable electric mixer on low speed (you don't want the whites to foam but you do want them to keep moving so they don't coagulate over the heat), insert a food thermometer and beat the egg whites over a pan recipe, you may add it during this step. Now transfer the heated whites to a mixing bowl and beat them to the desired consistency. This creates a very stable foam.

Egg Nutrition

There are nine essential amino acids. Eggs contain all nine: valine, leucine, isoleucine, threonine, histidine, tryptophan, phenylalanine, methionine, lysine. Because all nine are in a single egg, the egg is a complete protein. Protein is necessary for building body tissue. It regulates water balance within the body. It helps maintain the body's hydrogen ion concentration to that of water. Phenylalanine is required to synthesize adrenaline. Protein isn't a good thing to be without. Yet, protein has been overlooked in favor of complex carbohydrates on the bottom of our USDA food pyramid. But where there is growth of life, there must be, by definition, protein. The word comes from a Greek verb that means "to take first place." In fact, egg protein is so high that scientists use the egg as a worldwide standard in measuring the quality of protein in other foods. The Food and Agriculture Organization of the United Nations charts whole eggs as having a biological value of 93.7%. This rates eggs higher than milk (84.5%), fish (76%), and beef (74.3%).

One large egg contains:

75 calories
6 grams protein
5 grams fat
    1.5 grams saturated fat
    1.9 grams monounsaturated fat
    0.7 gram polyunsaturated fat
213 milligrams cholesterol
Vitamin A
Vitamin D
Vitamin E
Vitamin B_{12}
Choline
Folic acid
Vitamin B_3
Biotin
Inositol
Niacin
Vitamin B_6
Riboflavin
Thiamine

Cholesterol and the Egg

It's difficult to exonerate eggs for the alleged evils previously blamed on them. But let's try. Long ago and far away, eggs had a nutritional profile with a finding of 274 milligrams of cholesterol per egg and a total of 6 grams of fat. That was then; this is now. New testing methods and improved feeding and production of chickens and eggs has brought those numbers down to 213 milligrams cholesterol and 5 grams fat.

Now, the part about a difference of a single fat gram may be splitting hairs, but look closer. The saturated fat element in the *total fat* content is only 1.5 grams. And the reduction in cholesterol content is significant, as far as a number in measuring intake of dietary cholesterol. The numbers affixed to most amounts for dietary cholesterol must also take into account the cholesterol being manufactured constantly inside our bodies. If you don't take it in by food, your body will make its own. For those wishing to decrease or delete yolks from their diets, however, I have included an entire chapter on Egg White Cuisine page 151.

This book holds that the egg remains one of nature's most perfect gifts to the human diet. In *365 Ways to Cook Eggs*, you won't find any recipes that use egg substitutes or egg look-alikes, taste-alikes, or feel-alikes. The emphasis is on real eggs laid by hens.

You will discover new ways of making recipes you've always known, incorporating exciting new flavor combinations and ideas from all over the world. You'll find eggs boiled, fried, poached, baked, broiled, whipped into soufflés, and stirred into custards—sweet and savory, mild and spicy, firm and soft eggs.

The bottom line of egg cookery is that eggs are delicious and one of the most versatile foods we eat. I think it's swell that eggs are nutritious. But I eat them because I love them and they're simple to cook. And if you didn't know that already, you're about to find out.

Chapter 1

The Best of the Boiled

Properly hard-boiled eggs are not really boiled. To be precise, they are hard cooked. Eggs go into a pot, water is added to cover the eggs, the pot is covered, and it goes to the stove where the water is brought to a boil and the heat immediately turned off. This method always turns out an evenly cooked egg.

In this chapter, you'll find such so-called hard-boiled (and what would we do without the expression) eggs stuffed, mashed, mayonnaised and made into salad, sieved, chopped, diced, deviled, and added whole to an international array of recipes.

Much has been made about the greenish ring around the yolks and shells that won't peel—stumbling blocks that may annoy the cook but aren't worthy of vexation. Eggs aren't produced in factories. Like most things in nature, differences do occur, and not every egg behaves uniformly like every other.

Here are a few technical tips:

• To prevent a greenish ring from forming around the yolk, cool down the eggs in cold water and peel them as soon as they are cooked. They can be stored with the shells off in a bowl of cold water in the refrigerator for up to 3 days, though like most foods, hard-boiled eggs are best freshly cooked.

• To peel eggs easily, first roll the egg on the countertop to crackle it all over, then remove the shell. If should come off easily. A stubborn shell that sticks to the egg white may be the result of overcooking, or it can mean that the eggs are exceptionally fresh, which is nothing to complain about.

• An easy way to chop eggs into a small, even dice is to put them first lengthwise, then crosswise through a hand egg slicer. Or you can chop them with a large stainless steel knife. Or simply mash them in a bowl with a fork, preferably one with wide tines.

1   (HARD-BOILED EGGS)

Prep: none   Cook: 17 minutes   Serves: 1 per egg

Everyone knows these as hard-boiled eggs, but they are really not boiled at all, which would toughen the delicate protein. This is a surefire method, so you'11 never have to guess again. Be sure to peel the eggs as soon as they are cooked so they don't develop a green ring around the yolk. Once the shells are removed, the hard-boiled eggs can be stored in the refrigerator in a bowl of water for up to 3 days.

(Eggs)   (Cold water)

(1) Place eggs in a pot just large enough to hold them in a single layer. Add water to cover eggs by 1 inch.

(2) Bring to a boil over high heat. Immediately cover and turn off heat. Let eggs steep in hot water with lid on, 17 minutes.

(3) Transfer eggs to a colander. Run cold water over them until cool to touch.

(4) Immediately roll each egg on countertop until surface is crackled. Peel off shells.

---

2   DEVILED EGGS

Prep: 10 minutes   Cook: none   Makes: 12

It's a classic, but everyone loves them, as a substantial hors d'oeuvre or a picnic side dish. These are zesty but feel free to up the hot sauce, if you like.

6 hard-boiled eggs, peeled	½ teaspoon Tabasco sauce
1 teaspoon powdered mustard	¼ teaspoon salt
½ teaspoon distilled white or white wine vinegar	⅛ teaspoon pepper Paprika
3 tablespoons mayonnaise or salad dressing	

1. Halve eggs lengthwise and remove yolks. Set whites on a platter.

2. In a small bowl, mix powdered mustard with vinegar until dissolved to a paste. Stir in mayonnaise, Tabasco, salt, and pepper.

3. In another bowl, mash egg yolks with a fork. Add seasoned mayonnaise and blend well.

4. Mound filling into whites. Dust tops of eggs with paprika. Cover and refrigerate until ready to serve.

3   CAJUN DEVILED EGGS
Prep: 10 minutes   Cook: none   Makes: 12

This is a fiery filling worthy of any menu with other Louisiana favorites. Sprinkle on cayenne and Tabasco last, so the mixture is as tame or as wild as your taste.

6 hard-boiled eggs, peeled
2 tablespoons mayonnaise
2 tablespoons Dijon mustard
1½ tablespoons minced green
　　 bell pepper
2 tablespoons minced
　　 Andouille sausage or
　　 kielbasa

1 teaspoon lemon juice
⅛ teaspoon cayenne, or more
　　 to taste
2 drops of Tabasco sauce

1. Halve eggs lengthwise. Remove yolks and set whites on a platter.

2. Mash yolks in a bowl with a fork. Add remaining ingredients and blend until well mixed.

3. Mound filling into whites. Serve at once or cover and refrigerate.

4   CAJUN DEVILED EGGS WITH SHRIMP
Prep: 10 minutes   Cook: none   Makes: 12

If you prefer, 4 ounces of shredded crabmeat can be substitiuted for the shrimp.

6 hard-boiled eggs, peeled
2 tablespoons mayonnaise
2 tablespoons Dijon mustard
1½ tablespoons minced green
　　 bell pepper
2 tablespoons minced
　　 Andouille sausage or
　　 kielbasa

1 teaspoon lemon juice
⅛ teaspoon cayenne, or more
　　 to taste
2 drops of Tabasco sauce
¼ pound cooked bay shrimp,
　　 chopped

1. Halve eggs lengthwise. Remove yolks and set whites on a platter.

2. Mash yolks in a bowl with remaining ingredients until smooth.

3. Mound filling into whites. Cover and refrigerate until ready to serve.

5 DEVILED CURRY-SWIRL EGGS
Prep: 15 minutes   Cook: none   Makes: 24

You need a pastry bag with a star tip for the swirl effect. If you don't have one, just spoon the filling into the eggs.

12 **hard-boiled eggs, peeled**
⅓ **cup mayonnaise**
1 **tablespoon distilled white
  vinegar**

½ **teaspoon powdered
  mustard**
½ **teaspoon curry powder
  Seasoned salt or paprika**

1. Halve eggs lengthwise and scoop yolks into a mixing bowl. Set whites on a platter.

2. Mash yolks with a fork. Add mayonnaise, vinegar, mustard, and curry. Mix until very smooth. Transfer to a pastry bag with a medium star tip.

3. Pipe yolk mixture into whites, making swirls. Cover and refrigerate until serving time.

4. Just before serving, sprinkle with seasoned salt.

6 EGGS STUFFED WITH BLUE CHEESE, BACON, AND HERBS
Prep: 10 minutes   Cook: 5 to 7 minutes   Makes: 12

4 **strips of bacon**
6 **hard-boiled eggs, peeled**
¼ **cup crumbled blue cheese
  (American blue,
  Gorgonzola, Roquefort,
  Saga)**
1 **garlic clove, minced**

2 **tablespoons sour cream or
  yogurt**
1 **tablespoon minced fresh
  chives**
⅛ **teaspoon dried marjoram**
⅛ **teaspoon dried tarragon
  Dash of cayenne**

1. In a medium skillet, cook bacon over medium heat, turning a couple of times, until browned and crisp, 5 to 7 minutes. Drain on paper towels. Crumble when cool.

2. Halve eggs lengthwise and scoop yolks into a mixing bowl. Set whites on a platter.

3. Add cheese to yolks and mash with a fork until blended. Add garlic, sour cream, bacon, chives, marjoram, tarragon, and cayenne. Mix well, leaving filling a little chunky.

4. Mound filling into whites. Cover and refrigerate until ready to serve.

7   CRAB AND ARTICHOKE STUFFED EGGS
Prep: 15 minutes   Cook: none   Makes: 12

Depending on the size of the artichoke hearts you find in your area, you may have some filling left over, even after piling it high into the hollows of the egg whites. At least you should hope so: It's a great spread on crackers.

6 **hard-boiled eggs, peeled**	2 **tablespoons minced celery**
3 **to 4 artichoke hearts, fresh,**	2 **tablespoons minced onion**
frozen, or canned	1½ **tablespoons lemon juice**
1 **(7-ounce) can claw crabmeat**	1 **tablespoon olive oil**
or fancy Dungeness	1 **tablespoon mayonnaise**
crabmeat	

1. Halve eggs lengthwise and scoop yolks into a mixing bowl. Set whites on a platter.

2. Chop artichoke hearts coarsely by hand. Transfer to another bowl and toss with crabmeat just until it begins to flake.

3. Crumble yolks and add to artichoke-crab mixture. Add celery, onion, lemon juice, olive oil, and mayonnaise. Stir lightly, just until mixture binds. (If overmixed, it may turn an ugly green.)

4. Mound filling loosely in whites. Cover and refrigerate until ready to serve.

8   EGGS STUFFED WITH SPICY BUTTERED YOLKS
Prep: 15 minutes   Cook: none   Makes: 12

6 **hard-boiled eggs, peeled**	½ **teaspoon powdered**
2 **teaspoons lemon juice or**	**mustard**
distilled white vinegar	¼ **teaspoon salt**
2 **tablespoons mayonnaise**	⅛ **teaspoon cayenne**
3 **tablespoons melted butter**	¼ **cup bread crumbs**

1. Halve eggs lengthwise. Remove yolks and set whites on a platter.

2. In a medium bowl, mash yolks with a fork. Blend in lemon juice. Add mayonnaise, 2 tablespoons of the melted butter, mustard, salt, and cayenne. Stir and mash with fork until smooth.

3. Mound filling in whites. Cover and refrigerate until ready to serve.

4. In a small bowl, toss bread crumbs with remaining 1 tablespoon melted butter until evenly moistened. Just before serving, scatter buttered bread crumbs over eggs.

9   LIVER PÂTÉ–STUFFED EGGS
Prep: 8 minutes   Cook: none   Makes: 12

6 hard-boiled eggs, peeled
1 (4-ounce) can prepared liver
   pâté
1 tablespoon Cognac or sherry

3 tablespoons finely chopped
   parsley
Coarsely ground pepper

1. Halve eggs lengthwise. Scoop yolks into a mixing bowl. Set whites on a platter.

2. Mash egg yolks with a fork. Add liver pâté, Cognac, and 2 tablespoons of the parsley. Blend until smooth. Season with pepper to taste.

3. Mound filling into whites. Refrigerate, covered, until ready to serve.

4. Just before serving, sprinkle remaining parsley over eggs.

10   SUSHI-STYLE STUFFED EGGS WITH WASABI
Prep: 5 minutes   Cook: none   Makes: 12

Sushi is traditionally made with raw fish. Here I use canned tuna, but if you are in the habit of eating raw fish at home, you can substitute ¼ cup finely chopped *ahi* (tuna belly); it's delicious. Wasabi is a pungent green Japanese horseradish that always accompanies sushi. It is the consistency of stiff paste. A knife tip's worth is enough to make its eye-watering presence known. Wasabi comes in a tube or as powder, which must be reconstituted with a little water. The amount here refers to wasabi already in paste form.

6   hard-boiled eggs, peeled
3   tablespoons mayonnaise
1½ teaspoons rice vinegar
2   teaspoons soy sauce
¼   teaspoon wasabi paste

1   (6⅛-ounce) can water-
    packed tuna, drained
    and flaked
2   tablespoons salmon roe
    Soy or radish sprouts

1. Halve eggs lengthwise and remove yolks. Set whites aside on a platter.

2. In a bowl, mash yolks with mayonnaise, vinegar, soy sauce, and wasabi. Fold in tuna.

3. Mound whites with yolk mixture. Top decoratively with salmon roe and sprouts. Cover loosely with plastic and refrigerate until ready to serve.

11 RUSSIAN-STYLE STUFFED EGGS
Prep: 10 minutes   Cook: none   Makes: 12

6 hard-boiled eggs, peeled
3 tablespoons butter, softened
1 teaspoon Dijon mustard
1 teaspoon prepared white
    horseradish

1 tablespoon chopped fresh
    dill or 1 teaspoon dried
Salt and pepper
Romaine or butter lettuce
    leaves

1. Halve eggs lengthwise. Scoop yolks into a medium bowl. Set whites aside.

2. Mash yolks with butter until smooth. Add mustard, horseradish, and dill. Season with salt and pepper to taste.

3. Line a platter with lettuce leaves. Mound filling into egg white halves and set eggs on top. Refrigerate until ready to serve.

12 SMOKED SALMON–STUFFED EGGS
Prep: 10 minutes   Cook: none   Makes: 12

6 hard-boiled eggs, peeled
½ cup coarsely chopped
    smoked salmon (about 3
    ounces)
2 tablespoons mayonnaise

1 (3-ounce) package cream
    cheese
2 scallions, thinly sliced
2 tablespoons chopped black
    olives

1. Halve eggs lengthwise and scoop yolks into a mixing bowl. Set whites on a platter.

2. In a food processor, combine smoked salmon, mayonnaise, cream cheese, and scallions. Puree until smooth. Add to yolks.

3. Mash with a fork until mixture is mostly smooth but retains some chunks of egg yolk.

4. Mound filling into whites. Sprinkle with olives. Cover and refrigerate until ready to serve.

13 (SHRIMP AND AVOCADO STUFFED EGGS)
Prep: 10 minutes   Cook: none   Makes: 12

6 hard-boiled eggs, peeled
2 ripe avocados, pitted and
     peeled
1 small onion
2 garlic cloves
¼ cup lime juice

Salt and pepper
10 cooked and peeled medium
      shrimp, chopped
1 tablespoon finely chopped
      cilantro

1. Halve eggs lengthwise. Remove yolks and set whites on a platter.

2. In a food processor, combine egg yolks, avocados, onion, garlic, and lime juice. Puree until smooth. Season with salt and pepper to taste. Transfer to a bowl and mix in shrimp and cilantro.

3. Mound filling into whites. Cover and refrigerate until ready to serve.

14 HOMEMADE MAYONNAISE
Prep: 5 minutes   Cook: none   Makes: 1½ cups

Mayonnaise made from raw egg should be handled with care. Acid, such as lemon juice, added to the emulsion acts as a preservative as well as protection against bacterial growth. Nonetheless, be sure to store mayonnaise in refrigerator as soon as it is made.

1 egg
2 tablespoons lemon juice
¼ teaspoon salt

Pinch of cayenne
½ cup vegetable oil
½ cup olive oil

1. Place egg, lemon juice, salt, and cayenne in a blender or food processor. Process until blended.

2. Combine vegetable oil and olive oil in a measuring cup. With machine on, add oil very slowly. When about three-fourths of it is used, the mayonnaise will "catch" and begin to thicken. At that point, pour in remaining oil in a steady stream.

3. Use at once or cover and refrigerate for up to 5 days.

15 GARLIC MAYONNAISE WITH FRESH HERBS

Prep: 10 minutes   Cook: none   Makes: 1½ cups

1 whole egg
2 tablespoons lemon juice
2 garlic cloves, peeled
Small handful of fresh
  parsley
⅛ teaspoon dried thyme leaves

⅛ teaspoon dried oregano
¼ teaspoon salt
⅛ teaspoon pepper
Pinch of cayenne
½ cup vegetable oil
½ cup olive oil

1. Place egg, lemon juice, garlic, parsley, thyme, oregano, salt, pepper, and cayenne in a blender or food processor. Process until blended.

2. Combine vegetable oil and olive oil in a measuring cup. With machine on, add oil very slowly. When about three-fourths of it is used, the mayonnaise will "catch" and begin to thicken. At that point, pour in the rest of the oil in a steady stream.

3. Use at once or cover and refrigerate for up to 5 days.

16 HUNDRED-ISLAND DRESSING WITH HARD-BOILED EGGS

Prep: 5 minutes   Cook: none   Makes: 2 cups

A fine dip for crudités or for topping fish, this can be made with nonfat plain yogurt for a low-fat alternate to the mayonnaise inspiration. Without capers, the thousand-island variety is minus a number of islands, hence the name.

4 hard-boiled eggs, peeled
2 tablespoons tomato paste
3 tablespoons Dijon mustard
3 tablespoons distilled white
  vinegar
½ cup mayonnaise

6 tablespoons pickle relish
1 tablespoon Worcestershire
  sauce
Few dashes of Tabasco
  sauce
Freshly ground pepper

1. Halve eggs lengthwise and scoop out yolks. Set whites aside.

2. In a small bowl, mash 3 of the yolks with a fork. Add tomato paste, mustard, and vinegar. Mix well.

3. Press egg whites and remaining 1 egg yolk through a sieve into a bowl. Stir in mayonnaise, pickle relish, Worcestershire, and Tabasco. Season with pepper to taste. Refrigerate, tightly covered, for up to 1 week.

17   EGG SALAD FOR KIDS
Prep: 5 minutes   Cook: none   Serves: 2

Kids like a lot of mayonnaise, a little egg, and virtually no seasoning. The choice of mayonnaise or salad dressing is a highly personal one; it must be made individually by each family. Use whichever your child prefers.

2 hard-boiled eggs	**1½ tablespoons mayonnaise or salad dressing**

1. Be sure eggs are cooked until very firm. Add 1 or 2 minutes if in doubt. Peel eggs and mash in a small bowl with a fork until egg whites are broken into tiny squares and yolks are crumbled. Do not leave any large lumps.

2. Add mayonnaise and mix very well. Serve as a salad or between slices of bread for a sandwich.

18   AVOCADO-TOMATO EGG SALAD
Prep: 5 minutes   Cook: none   Serves: 3 to 4

This lush egg salad, piquant with garlic and lime juice and spiked with fresh herbs, is particularly good served with lavash crackers or in pita pockets.

2 ripe avocados, diced	**2 teaspoons minced garlic**
2 ripe plum tomatoes, diced	**1 tablespoon lime juice**
2 tablespoons minced fresh chives	**6 hard-boiled eggs, peeled**
1½ tablespoons chopped cilantro or parsley	**Salt and pepper**

1. In a medium bowl, combine avocados, tomatoes, chives, cilantro, garlic, and lime juice. Toss gently to mix.

2. Quarter eggs and fold into salad. Season with salt and pepper to taste.

19   BACON AND EGG SALAD
Prep: 10 minutes   Cook: 6 to 8 minutes   Serves: 3

6 slices of bacon	**1 tablespoon white wine vinegar or distilled white vinegar**
6 hard-boiled eggs, peeled	
¼ cup minced onion	
3 tablespoons mayonnaise	**Salt and pepper**
2 teaspoons Dijon mustard	

1. In a large skillet, cook bacon over medium heat, turning a couple of times, until browned and crisp, 6 to 8 minutes. Drain on paper towels. Crumble when cool.

2. In a medium bowl, mash eggs with a fork. Stir in bacon and onion.

3. In a small bowl, blend mayonnaise, mustard, and vinegar. Stir into egg salad. Season with salt and pepper to taste. Cover and refrigerate until ready to serve.

---

20   EGG-CAVIAR PLATTER
Prep: 10 minutes   Cook: none   Serves: 8 to 12

This is an elegant appetizer for a cocktail party or a serious before-dinner hors d'oeuvre. Instead of melba rounds, you could put out toasts points made from white bread or, if you want to go to the trouble, small buckwheat pancakes called blini.

8 hard-boiled eggs, peeled	1 cup minced onion
8 ounces fresh caviar or	2 lemons, cut into thin
2 (4-ounce) jars	wedges
pasteurized caviar	Melba toast rounds

1. Cut eggs in half lengthwise. Remove yolks and press through a sieve. Place in a small bowl. Coarsely chop egg whites.

2. Place caviar in a small serving bowl. Center caviar on a round platter. Arrange concentric rings of chopped egg whites, sieved egg yolks, and chopped onion around caviar.

3. Arrange lemon wedges and toast rounds around rim of platter. Serve with small spreader knives or spoons.

---

21   CHICKEN AND EGG SALAD
Prep: 10 minutes   Cook: none   Serves: 2

2 hard-boiled eggs, peeled	2 teaspoons chopped fresh
½ cup diced cooked chicken	parsley
¼ cup finely chopped onion or	3 tablespoons mayonnaise
scallion	Salt and pepper

1. In a small bowl, mash eggs with a fork. Add chicken, onion, parsley, and mayonnaise. Mix well.

2. Season chicken and egg salad with salt and pepper to taste. Serve immediately or cover and refrigerate until ready to serve.

22   EGG, ARTICHOKE, AND POTATO SALAD VINAIGRETTE

Prep: 15 minutes   Cook: 25 to 32 minutes   Serves: 6

This sounds French, but it's vintage Italian. You'll love the appearance of the eggs, which are left whole after peeling and are coated in the herbed vinaigrette.

3 large red potatoes (about 1¼ pounds), scrubbed
1 tablespoon olive oil
¼ pound mushrooms, sliced
6 hard-boiled eggs, peeled
6 to 8 canned artichoke hearts, sliced
1 teaspoon chopped fresh tarragon

1 tablespoon chopped parsley
¼ cup plus 2 tablespoons olive oil
2 tablespoons white wine vinegar
Salt and pepper

1. Place potatoes in a large saucepan and add enough cold salted water to cover by 1 inch. Bring to a boil. Reduce heat to medium and cook 20 to 25 minutes, until knife point slides easily into center of potato. Drain and rinse under cold running water. Peel potatoes, if desired, and cut into slices. Transfer potatoes to a large mixing bowl.

2. In a large skillet, heat oil over medium-high heat. Add mushrooms and cook, tossing, until lightly browned, 5 to 7 minutes. Add to potatoes.

3. Add eggs, artichoke hearts, tarragon, and parsley. Toss gently.

4. In a small bowl, slowly whisk oil into vinegar. Season with salt and pepper to taste. Pour vinaigrette over salad and toss to coat. Refrigerate until ready to serve. Serve chilled.

23   EGG SALAD WITH CHIVES

Prep: 5 minutes   Cook: none   Serves: 2

4 hard-boiled eggs, peeled
2 tablespoons mayonnaise
1 tablespoon minced fresh chives

Salt and pepper

1. Put eggs through an egg slicer twice, first crosswise, then lengthwise, to cut into small pieces. Or chop with a large stainless steel knife.

2. In a small bowl, mix eggs with mayonnaise and chives. Season with salt and pepper to taste. Eat directly from bowl or use in a sandwich.

24 EGG AND AVOCADO SALAD
Prep: 10 minutes   Cook: none   Serves: 1

Always one to find a way to sneak an avocado into a salad, I find this one of my favorite "on-hand" concoctions. That's right—an entire avocado, just for me . . . or you.

3 hard-boiled eggs, peeled
1 scallion, minced
¼ teaspoon minced fresh
  jalapeño pepper
2 tablespoons salad dressing,
  such as Miracle Whip

¼ teaspoon salt
⅛ teaspoon freshly ground
  pepper
1 ripe avocado, preferably
  Hass
1 tablespoon lemon juice

1. In a small bowl, mash eggs with a fork. Add scallion, jalapeño, salad dressing, salt, and pepper. Mix well.

2. Halve avocado around pit, twist to open, and remove pit. Score avocado into cubes, cutting to but not through skin. With a soup spoon, scoop cubes out of skin.

3. Fold avocado and lemon juice into egg salad. Eat immediately alone.

25 POTATO AND EGG SALAD
Prep: 10 minutes   Cook: 15 to 20 minutes   Serves: 6 to 8

4 white or red potatoes,
  scrubbed
3 celery ribs, chopped
1 medium onion, chopped
½ cup pickle relish
1 cup mayonnaise or salad
  dressing, such as
  Miracle Whip

2 teaspoons Dijon mustard
4 hard-boiled eggs, peeled
  Salt and pepper
  Paprika (optional)

1. Place potatoes in a large saucepan and add enough cold salted water to cover by 1 inch. Bring to a boil. Reduce heat to medium and cook 15 to 20 minutes, until knife point slides easily into center of potato. Drain and rinse under cold running water. Peel potatoes, if desired, and cut into ½- to ¾-inch dice. Transfer potatoes to a large mixing bowl.

2. Add celery, onion, relish, mayonnaise, and mustard. Mix well. Coarsely chop eggs and add to bowl. Fold into salad. Season with salt and pepper to taste.

3. Cover and refrigerate before serving. Dust with a light sprinkling of paprika before serving, if you like.

26 SPICED SHRIMP AND EGG SALAD
Prep: 10 minutes   Cook: 2½ to 3 minutes   Serves: 4 to 6

This salad is one of my favorite lunch box items from elementary school. My mom made it with leftover shrimp, which you can use, but the Spiced Boiled Shrimp that follow make it extra special.

Spiced Boiled Shrimp
  (recipe follows) or
  ½ pound cooked peeled
  shrimp
6 hard-boiled eggs, peeled
2 celery ribs, finely chopped

1 small onion, minced
1 tablespoon lemon juice
1 tablespoon creamy-style
  white horseradish
⅓ cup mayonnaise
Salt and pepper

1. Chop shrimp. Put eggs through an egg slicer twice, first crosswise, then lengthwise, to cut into small pieces. Or mash with a fork in a bowl.

2. In a medium bowl, combine shrimp, eggs, celery, onion, lemon juice, horseradish, and mayonnaise. Mix well.

3. Season with salt and pepper to taste. Serve immediately or cover and refrigerate until ready to serve.

SPICED BOILED SHRIMP
Makes: about 2 cups cooked shrimp

½ teaspoon whole cloves
1 teaspoon crushed hot red
  pepper
2 bay leaves
½ teaspoon dried thyme
½ teaspoon dried dill
¼ teaspoon cayenne

⅛ teaspoon turmeric
1 tablespoon coarse (kosher)
  salt
1 teaspoon whole black
  peppercorns
½ pound medium shrimp,
  shelled and deveined

1. Fill a large saucepan with water. Add all ingredients except shrimp. Cover and bring to a boil.

2. Add shrimp. Cook 2½ to 3 minutes, until shrimp are pink and loosely curled. (Water may not return to a boil.)

3. Immediately drain shrimp into a colander. Remove bay leaves before serving.

27 NEW YORK EGG SALAD
Prep: 10 minutes   Cook: none   Serves: 2

My friend Hilary's goal as a brave new cook was to make egg salad exactly the way her aunt in New York made it. Here it is.

4 hard-boiled eggs, peeled	**2 tablespoons mayonnaise**
¼ cup finely diced onion	**⅛ teaspoon salt**
1 celery rib, finely diced	**Pinch of white pepper**

1. Put eggs through an egg slicer twice, first crosswise, then lengthwise, to cut into small pieces. Or chop with a large stainless steel knife.

2. Add onion, celery, mayonnaise, salt, and white pepper. Eat directly from bowl or use in a sandwich.

28 SUNBURST SALAD
Prep: 5 minutes   Cook: none   Chill: 4 hours   Serves: 8

This is based on an old recipe called *oeufs marbrés*. The yolks and whites of hard eggs are riced, then layered in a beautiful yellow-and-white pattern. Serve with crackers.

12 hard-boiled eggs, peeled	**¼ cup finely minced onion**
¼ teaspoon salt	**1 to 2 anchovy fillets, minced,**
Freshly ground pepper	**or 1 tablespoon anchovy**
½ teaspoon Dijon mustard	**paste.**
½ cup plus 2 tablespoons mayonnaise	

1. Run 5 of the eggs through a ricer or press through a sieve, so eggs appear to have been grated. Place in a bowl and mix with salt, ¼ teaspoon pepper, mustard, and ¼ cup of the mayonnaise. Set aside.

2. Separate yolks and whites from remaining 7 eggs. Rice yolks and whites separately.

3. In a small bowl, combine riced egg whites with onion and 3 tablespoons of the mayonnaise. Mix to blend. In another small bowl, mash anchovies with remaining 3 tablespoons mayonnaise. Mix in yolks and season with pepper to taste.

4. In a small buttered dish, oval if possible, press half of egg white mixture over the bottom, tamping it firmly to make even. Top with all of egg yolk mixture, pressing evenly. Cover with all of whole egg salad, pressing firmly. Finally, cap with remaining whites. A good tool for pressing this mixture is a wide offset spatula.

5. Cover and refrigerate at least 4 hours, or overnight. Run knife around edge to loosen. If mold won't lift out whole, invert onto dish, then flip again onto a serving platter.

29 SON-IN-LAW EGGS
Prep: 15 minutes   Cook: 2 to 3 minutes   Serves: 6

A typical version has deep-fried hard-boiled eggs covered with a sauce containing tamarind water. Just as authentic—and far easier to duplicate—is the following sauce of brown sugar and fish sauce spiked with red chile and decorated with a confetti of crispy fried slices of shallot and garlic.

6 **hard-boiled eggs, peeled**
   Vegetable oil, for deep-
   frying
4 **shallots, thinly sliced**
2 **garlic cloves, thinly sliced**
2 **tablespoons brown sugar**

2 **tablespoons Asian fish**
   sauce*
½ **teaspoon crushed hot red**
   pepper
   Lettuce leaves
1 **tablespoon chopped cilantro**

1. Pat eggs dry with paper towels. In a deep-fat fryer or large saucepan, heat 3 inches of oil over medium-high heat until it reaches 350°F. Gently add eggs to hot oil and cook until golden brown and somewhat blistered, 1 to 2 minutes. Remove with a large strainer and drain on paper towels.

2. In same oil using strainer, dip shallot and garlic slices quickly into hot oil just until lightly browned, about 10 seconds. Drain on paper towels.

3. In a small saucepan, heat 2 tablespoons oil over medium heat. Add brown sugar, ¼ cup water, fish sauce, and hot pepper. Simmer 1 minute, stirring to dissolve brown sugar.

4. Cut eggs in half or quarters. Arrange on lettuce leaves. Pour sauce over eggs. Sprinkle fried shallots and garlic on top. Garnish with cilantro. Serve at room temperature.

* Available at Asian markets and in the Asian foods section of many supermarkets.

30 SCOTCH EGGS
Prep: 10 minutes   Chill: 1 hour   Cook: 12 to 16 minutes   Serves: 6

Served in the pubs of the British Isles or sold by the piece in quick-stop delis in the heart of London, sausage-wrapped Scotch eggs are the probable precursor of the classic meatloaf with hard-boiled eggs baked in the center. Serve with grainy mustard.

1 **pound bulk pork sausage**
2 **teaspoons Worcestershire**
   sauce
2 **tablespoons minced onion**
1 **tablespoon minced parsley**
6 **hard-boiled eggs, peeled**

   Flour, for dredging
2 **eggs, beaten**
1 **cup fine bread crumbs**
   Vegetable oil, for deep-
   frying

1. Combine ground pork, Worcestershire, onion, and parsley. Mix well.

2. Roll eggs lightly in flour to coat. Mold sausage around each egg. Dip in beaten eggs, then roll in bread crumbs. Pat crumbs in place, if necessary. Set on a plate, wrap with plastic, and refrigerate until well chilled, 1 to 8 hours.

3. In a deep-fat fryer or large saucepan, heat 3 inches of oil over medium-high heat until it reaches 350°F. Add the coated eggs, in 2 batches if necessary so they are not crowded, and fry, turning, until golden brown all over, 6 to 8 minutes per batch. Remove with a slotted spoon and drain on paper towels. Serve hot or cold.

---

31   EGGS BÉCHAMEL

Prep: 5 minutes   Cook: 12 to 19 minutes   Serves: 6

Back when no one questioned the pleasures of a creamy white sauce, this dish was a routine affair. It was usually spooned into puff pastry shells. Today, it is comfort food mostly for those with the memories. You can serve it over toast or English muffins.

4 tablespoons unsalted butter	¼ cup plus 2 tablespoons
2 tablespoons flour	grated Parmesan cheese
1 cup hot milk	Salt and pepper
Pinch of cayenne	6 hard-boiled eggs, peeled

1. Preheat oven to 350°F. Melt 2 tablespoons of the butter in a medium saucepan over medium-high heat. When bubbly, sprinkle in flour and cook, stirring, 1 minute. Slowly whisk in milk. Bring to a boil, stirring constantly, until sauce is smooth and thickened, 1 to 2 minutes. Remove from heat and add cayenne and ¼ cup of the Parmesan cheese. Season with salt and pepper to taste.

2. Quarter the eggs lengthwise and place in a small ovenproof casserole. Pour sauce over eggs. Sprinkle with remaining Parmesan cheese and dot with remaining butter.

3. Bake 10 to 15 minutes, until eggs and sauce begin to turn golden brown. Spoon out of dish at table.

Variation

---

32   EGGS BÉCHAMEL WITH SHRIMP AND CURRY

Prepare recipe as described above, but at end of step 1, blend 2 teaspoons curry powder into white sauce. In step 2, add 1 cup cooked peeled small shrimp along with eggs to casserole. Pour sauce over all and bake as directed.

33 SOUTHERN EGG SALAD
Prep: 10 minutes   Cook: none   Serves: 4

8 hard-boiled eggs, peeled
1 small onion, minced
2 celery ribs, finely diced
¼ cup salad dressing, such as
　　Miracle Whip

3 tablespoons pickle relish
¼ teaspoon salt
⅛ teaspoon pepper
　Paprika

1. Put eggs through an egg slicer twice, first crosswise, then lengthwise, to cut into small pieces. Place in a medium bowl. Or mash eggs in bowl with a fork.

2. Add onion, celery, salad dressing, relish, salt, and pepper and mix well.

3. Transfer to a serving bowl. Sprinkle paprika over top. Cover and refrigerate until ready to serve.

34 KEDGEREE
Prep time: 5 minutes   Cook: 5 minutes   Serves: 4 to 6

This British favorite is a fabulous excuse to make extra rice. If you don't have access to smoked haddock, this is equally delicious with smoked trout.

4 hard-boiled eggs
6 tablespoons butter
¾ pound smoked haddock,
　　flaked
2½ cups cooked long-grain
　　white rice, preferably
　　basmati

Salt
Cayenne
6 pimiento-stuffed olives,
　　sliced

1. Peel eggs; chop the whites and yolks separately. Reserve a third of the yolks for garnish. Combine remaining yolks with whites.

2. In a medium saucepan, melt butter over medium-high heat. When bubbly, add fish, chopped eggs, and rice.

3. Heat and stir kedgeree, adding salt and cayenne to taste, until very hot and somewhat thickened, about 5 minutes.

4. Transfer to a serving platter. Garnish with reserved yolks and sliced olives.

35 PICKLED BEETS AND EGGS
Prep: 10 minutes   Cook: 5 minutes   Chill: overnight   Makes: 12

This recipe is a family favorite from *Cincinnati Post* food editor Joyce Rosencrans, who has strains of Pennsylvania Dutch in her ancestry. Joyce prefers medium-size eggs to match the size of the canned beets. When she's ready to serve, she puts the eggs in a huge brandy snifter—cinnamon sticks and all. The bright purple eggs may be sliced over salad. Take them on picnics or just splash them with Worcestershire sauce and eat. These taste best the first or second day.

2 (16-ounce) cans beets (small whole, cut, or sliced), juices reserved
1 cup cider vinegar
1 to 1½ cups sugar
2 (3-inch) cinnamon sticks

2 whole cloves
2 black peppercorns
¼ teaspoon salt
12 medium eggs, hard-boiled and peeled
1 large onion, thickly sliced

1. Measure reserved beet juices and add enough water to make 2 cups. Place in a medium nonreactive saucepan. Add vinegar, sugar, cinnamon, cloves, peppercorns, and salt. Bring to a boil. Reduce heat to low and simmer 5 minutes.

2. In each of 2 wide-mouth 1-quart canning jars or in a 2-quart crock, layer whole eggs, beets, and onion slices. Pour in hot beet liquid. Let cool, cover, and refrigerate overnight.

3. To serve, halve eggs. Arrange on a platter and surround with beets and onions.

36 PICKLED EGGS WITH ORANGE SPICE
Prep: 2 minutes   Cook: 5 minutes   Makes: 8

1½ cups distilled white vinegar
½ cup (4 ounces) frozen orange juice concentrate

1 (3-inch) cinnamon stick
8 whole cloves
8 hard-boiled eggs, peeled

1. In a nonreactive medium saucepan, combine vinegar, orange juice concentrate, cinnamon stick, cloves, and ½ cup water. Bring to a boil. Reduce heat to low and simmer 5 minutes.

2. Carefully lower eggs into a wide-mouth 1-quart canning jar. Pour hot vinegar mixture over eggs. Cover tightly with lid.

3. Set on a wire rack and let cool 1 hour. Refrigerate up to 3 weeks. After opening, keep refrigerated and use within 1 week.

37   SPICED PICKLED EGGS
Prep: 10 minutes   Cook: 5 minutes   Chill: 1 week   Makes: 12

From her farm in southern Indiana, Maggie Oster writes books about food and gardening while tending her own kitchen, garden, and farm. This and the following are two of her best recipes for pickled eggs: one with spices, the other with herbs.

12 hard-boiled eggs, peeled
1 small onion, thinly sliced
3 cups red wine vinegar
1 (3-inch) cinnamon stick
1 tablespoon honey
1 teaspoon whole allspice

1 teaspoon whole cloves
½ teaspoon coriander seeds
1 quarter-size slice of fresh
    ginger
1 bay leaf

1. Place eggs and onion in each of 2 wide-mouth 1-quart canning jars or in a 2-quart crock.

2. In a nonreactive medium saucepan, combine all remaining ingredients. Bring to a boil over medium heat. Reduce heat to low and simmer 5 minutes.

3. Pour hot spiced vinegar over eggs. Let cool, cover tightly with lid, and refrigerate at least 1 week before serving. Refrigerate up to 2 months.

38   FRESH-HERB PICKLED EGGS
Prep: 10 minutes   Cook: none   Chill: 1 week   Makes: 12

12 hard-boiled eggs, peeled
¼ cup thinly sliced shallots
2 sprigs of fresh thyme or
    ½ teaspoon dried
2 sprigs of fresh marjoram or
    ½ teaspoon dried
2 sprigs of parsley

1 garlic clove
1 small dried red chile or
    1 teaspoon black
    peppercorns
1 tablespoon honey
3 cups white wine vinegar or
    rice vinegar

1. Place half of eggs, shallots, thyme, marjoram, parsley, garlic, and chile in each of 2 wide-mouth 1-quart canning jars or in a 2-quart crock.

2. Stir honey into vinegar and pour over eggs. Cover tightly with lids and refrigerate at least 1 week before serving. Refrigerate up to 2 months.

39 OPAL BASIL–ZINFANDEL PICKLED EGGS WITH STAR ANISE
Prep: 10 minutes   Cook: 10 minutes   Chill: 3 days   Makes: 12

Opal basil, which is a deep purple or mottled green, is known for its background spiciness. That's why it blends so well with the spicy flavor of Zinfandel wine, augmented here with even more spice from licorice-flavored star anise and cloves. If you can't find opal basil, use any purple or green basil or Thai basil.

12 hard-boiled eggs, peeled
 1 small onion, thinly sliced
1½ cups red wine vinegar
1½ cups Zinfandel or other full-bodied red wine
 ½ cup sugar
 5 star anise

 5 whole cloves
 2 sprigs of fresh thyme or
     ½ teaspoon dried
 1 cup fresh basil leaves, preferably opal basil or another purple variety

1. Place eggs and onion in 2 wide-mouth 1-quart canning jars or in a 2-quart crock.

2. In a medium nonreactive saucepan, combine all remaining ingredients. Bring to a boil over medium heat. Reduce heat to low and simmer 10 minutes.

3. Pour hot vinegar and spices over eggs. Let cool. Cover tightly with lids and refrigerate at least 3 days before serving. Refrigerate up to 2 months.

40 BEET CRACKLED EGGS
Prep: 5 minutes   Cook: 5 minutes   Makes: 12

12 hard-boiled eggs, in their shells
 3 cups juice from canned beets

 1 cup plain vinegar

1. Crackle shells by rolling eggs on countertop or tapping with back of a metal spoon, but do not peel. Place eggs in 2 wide-mouth 1-quart canning jars or in a 2-quart crock.

2. In a medium nonreactive saucepan, bring beet juice and vinegar to a boil. Reduce heat to low and simmer 5 minutes.

3. Pour hot beet juice over eggs. Cover tightly with lid. Set on a wire rack and let cool 1 hour. Refrigerate up to 3 weeks. After opening, keep refrigerated and use within 1 week. Peel at serving.

41   CHINESE TEA EGGS
Prep: 2 minutes   Cook: 1 hour   Stand: 30 minutes   Makes: 12

Once shelled, the crackled eggs simmered and soaked in tea water emerge with a beautiful marbling quality that looks very much like antique porcelain. They're best eaten the first or second day. Serve for breakfast or as a snack.

12 hard-boiled eggs, in their shells, cooking water reserved	3 tablespoons black tea leaves 2 tablespoons salt

1. Crackle shells by rolling eggs on countertop or tapping with back of a metal spoon, but do not peel.

2. Measure reserved egg cooking water. You should have 4 cups; if not, add water. Bring to a boil. Add tea, salt, and crackled eggs. Reduce heat to low, cover, and simmer 1 hour, until shells turn nut-brown.

3. Remove pan from heat. Let eggs stand in tea water, covered, 30 minutes. If desired, refrigerate in liquid up to 3 days.

4. When ready to eat, drain and remove shells. Quarter eggs.

42   EASTER EGGS
Prep: none   Cook: 6 minutes   Chill: overnight   Makes: 12

Have fun with these edible dyed eggs. They have a beautiful marbled appearance. If they are handled by many people or are used for play or are out of the refrigerator for any length of time, consider them just for show and don't eat them.

12 hard-boiled eggs, in their shells ½ small bottle each red, blue, and green food coloring	3 tablespoons distilled white vinegar

1. Crackle eggs by rolling on countertop or tapping with back of metal spoon, but do not peel.

2. Fill a small nonreactive saucepan with just enough water to cover 4 eggs at a time. Add red food coloring and 1 tablespoon vinegar to water. Heat to just under a boil, about 2 minutes.

3. Gently lower eggs into red water. Immediately remove from heat and transfer eggs and colored water to a heatproof bowl. Store eggs in water overnight in refrigerator. Repeat with 4 eggs in blue water and 4 eggs in green water.

4. Peel at serving. Color may begin to fade within 3 hours.

Chapter 2

Random Scramblers, Skillet Eggs, and Eggwiches

You'll find a mix of egg wizardry in this chapter. Scrambling eggs is one of the simplest, most pleasing, and most versatile ways to fix our favorite food.

The scrambler is the creative egg artist's easiest medium. Tasty additions can range from salami, to onions, to mushrooms and Brie. These are the improvised moments that make scrambled eggs a joy to make and eat.

You may like scrambled eggs soft and curdsy or hard. Here's how to get them the way you like: The softest curds are the result of gentle whipping and slow stirring in the pan. One of the best techniques for large soft curds is to draw a spatula or pancake turner across the eggs as they cook. A folding motion also yields soft eggs. At any rate, the faster you stir, the smaller and harder the cooked pieces will be.

Here you'll also find the simple fried egg and other creations carried out in a skillet, dishes that morning would not be the same without. And anyone who has carried an egg sandwich from hand to mouth would not want to be without some of the tasty ideas I've devised for putting an egg between two slices of bread.

43 SCRAMBLED EGGS

Prep: 2 minutes   Cook: 45 to 60 seconds   Serves: 1 to 2

I like my scrambled eggs on the soft side. By the time they're moved from skillet to plate (which, honestly, I don't have the foresight to warm in the oven) and make their journey to the table, residual heat cooks them even more. Overcooking while still in the pan can happen in a matter of seconds. The scrambled eggs seize up and become downright rubbery by the time you've put some of them on your fork. If you find the scrambled eggs in this recipe too soft, add extra cooking time in intervals of 15 seconds.

Eggs need salt, or they'll taste flat. In fact, even if salted before cooking, scrambled eggs often need a few shakes more at the table.

3 eggs
2 tablespoons milk (or cream)
¼ teaspoon salt

¼ teaspoon pepper
1 tablespoon butter

1. In a medium bowl, whisk eggs, milk, salt, and pepper just until blended but not bubbly.

2. In a small cast-iron or nonstick skillet, melt butter over high heat. When foamy, pour in eggs.

3. Immediately reduce heat to medium. Cook, pushing eggs gently around the skillet with the flat side of a spatula, bringing up set areas, then folding and stirring them into big, soft curds, until eggs are just set, creamy, and seem to glisten, 45 to 60 seconds. Immediately transfer to a plate and serve.

44 BUTTERED SCRAMBLED EGG FLUFF

Prep: 2 minutes   Cook: 13 minutes   Serves: 2 to 3

Six eggs may seem like a lot for two people, but they're so rich and delicious that including more partakers would wreak denial on all. The slow, gentle cooking in a double boiler produces the creamiest eggs ever.

6 eggs
2 tablespoons milk or heavy
   cream

½ teaspoon salt
¼ teaspoon pepper
3 tablespoons butter

1. Whisk eggs, milk, salt, and pepper until blended.

2. Melt butter in top of a double boiler over simmering water.

3. Pour in eggs. Cook, stirring from time to time but not constantly, until softly set for large, soft curds, about 13 minutes. Serve at once.

45 DOUBLE-CHEESE EGGS WITH MUSHROOMS AND SALSA

Prep: 5 minutes   Cook: 9 to 10 minutes   Serves: 2

6 ounces fresh mushrooms,
   sliced
1 tablespoon butter
3 eggs
⅓ cup shredded Swiss cheese
⅓ cup shredded sharp
   Cheddar cheese

Salt and pepper
2 or 3 slices of toast
1 tablespoon picante sauce or
   other salsa

1. In a medium nonstick skillet, sauté mushrooms in butter over high heat, until liquid is drawn out, 1 to 2 minutes. Reduce heat to medium and cook 5 minutes longer, until tender.

2. In a small bowl, beat eggs with a fork until blended. Pour over mushrooms. Cook, lifting and folding until eggs begin to set, about 2 minutes. Add cheeses and continue to stir and fold egg mixture until cheese barely melts, about 1 minute. Season with salt and pepper to taste.

3. Spoon eggs over toast. Top with picante sauce. Serve hot.

46 EGG-MUSHROOM SCRAMBLE

Prep: 5 minutes   Cook: 8 to 12 minutes   Serves: 3 or 4

2 tablespoons butter
8 to 10 white button
   mushrooms, sliced
6 eggs

3 tablespoons milk
½ teaspoon salt
¼ teaspoon pepper
Chopped parsley

1. In a large nonstick skillet, melt butter over high heat. When bubbly, add mushrooms. Sauté 2 minutes. Reduce heat to medium-high and sauté 5 to 8 minutes longer, until softened.

2. In a medium bowl, whisk eggs, milk, salt, and pepper. Pour over mushrooms. Slowly stir and fold eggs around skillet until curds of desired doneness form, 1 to 2 minutes.

3. Divide among 3 or 4 plates. Decorate each with parsley. Serve hot.

47 MUSHROOM-BRIE SCRAMBLE WITH HERBS

Prep: 5 minutes   Cook: 8 to 13 minutes   Serves: 4

2 tablespoons butter
8 to 10 mushrooms, sliced
⅓ cup small cubes of Brie cheese
½ teaspoon coarsely cracked black peppercorns

1 tablespoon chopped parsley
½ teaspoon dried thyme
1 tablespoon minced chives
6 eggs
3 tablespoons milk
½ teaspoon salt

1. In a large nonstick skillet, melt butter over high heat. When bubbly, add mushrooms. Sauté 2 minutes. Reduce heat to medium-high and sauté 5 to 8 minutes longer, until softened.

2. Meanwhile, mash Brie with peppercorns, parsley, thyme, and chives.

3. In a medium bowl, whisk eggs, milk, and salt. Pour over mushrooms. Slowly stir and fold eggs around skillet until curds begin to form, 1 to 2 minutes. Drop herbed Brie in pats into eggs. Lift and fold mixture until cheese softens, about 1 minute longer.

4. Spoon onto 4 plates. Serve hot.

48 EGGS 'N ONIONS

Prep: 5 minutes   Cook: 13 to 16 minutes   Serves: 2 to 3

2 tablespoons butter
1 large Bermuda or Spanish onion, halved and sliced
6 eggs

3 tablespoons milk *(cream)*
½ teaspoon salt
¼ teaspoon pepper
Chopped parsley

1. In a large nonstick skillet, melt butter over medium-high heat. When bubbly, add onions, reduce heat to medium, and cook, stirring occasionally, until browned, 12 to 14 minutes.

2. In a medium bowl, whisk eggs, milk, salt, and pepper until blended. Pour over onions. Cook, stirring and folding eggs with onions 1 to 2 minutes for soft curds, or until desired doneness.

3. Spoon onto plates. Decorate with parsley. Serve hot.

49   EGGS 'N ONIONS WITH MUSHROOMS
Prep: 5 minutes   Cook: 15 minutes   Serves: 4 to 6

2 tablespoons butter	6 eggs
1 large Bermuda or Spanish onion, halved and sliced	3 tablespoons milk
	1/4 teaspoon salt
8 to 10 white button mushrooms, sliced	1/8 teaspoon pepper
	Chopped parsley

1. In a large nonstick skillet, melt butter over high heat. When bubbly, add onions. Sauté 2 minutes and add mushrooms. Reduce heat to medium-high and sauté 8 to 10 minutes more. If mushroom liquid has not evaporated, drain off.

2. In a medium bowl, whisk eggs, milk, salt, and pepper. Pour over mushrooms and onions. Slowly stir and fold eggs until desired doneness.

3. Spoon onto plates. Or serve in center of table from large bowl. Decorate with parsley. Serve hot.

50   LOX 'N EGGS WITH ONIONS AND CREAM CHEESE
Prep: 10 minutes   Cook: 15 minutes   Serves: 3 to 4

Here the makings of a classic bagel are nestled in the warm, soft curds of scrambled eggs. Quick! Get me my Sunday paper!

2 tablespoons butter	1/2 cup lox ends and pieces (about 2 ounces)
1 large Bermuda or Spanish onion, sliced	1 (3-ounce) package cream cheese, cubed
5 eggs	Chopped parsley
3 tablespoons milk	
1/4 teaspoon pepper	

1. In a large nonstick skillet, melt butter over high heat. When bubbly, add onions. Sauté 2 minutes. Reduce heat to medium and sauté 8 to 10 minutes, until lightly browned.

2. In a medium bowl, whisk eggs, milk, and pepper.

3. Add lox to onions, stirring briefly. Pour eggs into skillet. With heat still on medium, sprinkle cheese over eggs. Slowly stir and fold eggs until desired doneness.

4. Spoon onto plates. Decorate each with parsley. Serve hot.

51 LOX 'N EGGS
Prep: 3 minutes   Cook: 2 minutes   Serves: 2

This dish is a favorite at hotels and delis where Jewish breakfasters and bruncher like the added treat of that which tops bagels scrambled into their eggs. You could replace the salty lox with a finer—but more expensive—smoked salmon, but lox is better here. And do yourself a favor: Buy ends and pieces; they're cheaper.

4 eggs	¼ cup lox ends and pieces
2 tablespoons milk	(about 1 ounce)
⅛ teaspoon white pepper	2 tablespoons butter

1. In a medium bowl, beat eggs, milk, and pepper with a fork. Stir in lox.

2. In a medium skillet, melt butter over high heat. When bubbly, pour in eggs. Reduce heat to medium. Cook, stirring and folding eggs gently until they set, about 2 minutes.

3. Remove from heat and serve at once.

52 LOX 'N EGGS WITH ONIONS
Prep: 5 minutes   Cook: 15 minutes   Serves: 3 or 4

The first time I ate this outside the home was when my parents took my brother and me to Miami Beach. You can imagine my surprise in the coffee shop at the Deauville Hotel when I saw this family food on the menu. I couldn't get enough of it.

2 tablespoons butter	Pinch of salt
1 large Bermuda or Spanish	¼ teaspoon pepper
onion, sliced	⅓ cup lox ends and pieces
6 eggs	(about 1½ ounces)
3 tablespoons milk	Chopped parsley

1. In a large nonstick skillet, melt butter over high heat. When bubbly, add onions. Sauté 2 minutes. Reduce heat to medium and sauté 10 to 12 minutes, until browned.

2. In a medium bowl, whisk eggs, milk, salt, and pepper.

3. Add lox to onions, stirring briefly. Pour eggs into skillet. Slowly stir and fold eggs until desired doneness.

4. Spoon onto plates. Sprinkle with parsley. Serve hot.

53 EGGS 'N ONIONS WITH TOMATOES
Prep: 5 minutes   Cook: 15 minutes   Serves: 4

2 tablespoons butter
1 large Bermuda or Spanish
  onion, halved and sliced
1 medium-size ripe tomato or
  2 plum tomatoes, seeded
  and chopped

6 eggs
3 tablespoons milk
¼ teaspoon salt
¼ teaspoon pepper
Chopped parsley

1. In a large nonstick skillet, melt butter over high heat. When bubbly, add onions. Sauté 2 minutes. Reduce heat to medium-high and sauté 8 to 10 minutes, until lightly browned. Add tomatoes and stir briefly.

2. In a medium bowl, whisk eggs, milk, salt, and pepper. Pour over tomatoes and onions. Slowly stir and fold eggs until desired doneness.

3. Spoon onto plates. Decorate each with parsley. Serve hot.

54 PASTRAMI 'N EGGS
Prep: 5 minutes   Cook: 4 to 6 minutes   Serves: 2

Pastrami is that once muscular breast plate that starts out as corned beef but gets dried, rubbed with tons of black pepper, spices, and salt (including saltpeter for its deep pink color), then smoked and steamed. The pastrami technique is intended to preserve the meat. You can find so-called turkey pastrami, but it is a meager imitation of beef pastrami. If your pastrami is extra lean and renders hardly any fat, you'll need a little oil or butter in the pan when you add the eggs. Add salt and pepper cautiously; pastrami has plenty of its own.

8 thin slices of kosher beef
  pastrami, fat trimmed,
  cut into large bite-size
  pieces or shredded
  (4 ounces)

4 eggs
Salt and pepper (optional)

1. In a medium nonstick skillet, fry pastrami over medium heat until lightly browned and some fat is rendered, 3 to 5 minutes.

2. In a medium bowl, whisk eggs, 1 tablespoon water, and salt and pepper, if using. Pour over pastrami. Gently and slowly stir eggs with a big spoon until soft curds form, about 45 seconds.

3. Spoon onto 2 plates.

55 [SALAMI 'N EGGS]
Prep: 5 minutes   Cook: 5 minutes   Serves: 2

This simple recipe is not without controversy. Should the salami be sliced in rounds and added to the eggs that way, or should the rounds be cut into strips or quarters? Whatever shape your salami takes, remember that the original salami used in this combination was kosher.

8 thin slices of kosher salami,
    or other salami, such as
    Genoa, cut into quarters
    (2 ounces)

4 eggs
    Pinch of salt
¼ teaspoon pepper

1. In a medium nonstick skillet, fry salami over medium heat until lightly browned and some fat is rendered, about 3 minutes.

2. In a medium bowl, beat eggs, 1 tablespoon water, salt, and pepper with a fork until blended. Pour over salami. Gently and slowly stir eggs with a large spoon until soft curds form.

3. Spoon onto 2 plates.

56 [EGGS PIPÉRADE] DÉLICE!
Prep: 15 minutes   Cook: 18 to 24 minutes   Serves: 4

This tasty way of pairing eggs with a zesty mélange of tomato, sweet peppers, and onion comes from the Basque country. Serve with crusty peasant bread or toast.

2 tablespoons olive oil
1 small onion, chopped
2 small bell peppers,
    preferably 1 red and
    1 green, cut into thin
    strips
2 garlic cloves, crushed
    through a press

2 medium tomatoes, peeled,
    seeded, and chopped
    Salt
6 eggs
¼ teaspoon pepper

1. In a medium nonstick skillet, heat olive oil over medium-high heat. Add onion and bell peppers, cover, reduce heat to medium-low, and cook, stirring several times, until vegetables are tender but not browned, 8 to 10 minutes.

2. Add garlic, tomatoes, and a pinch of salt. Cook, covered, until tomatoes soften and release their juices, about 5 minutes. Uncover, raise heat to high, and boil until most of liquid evaporates, 2 to 4 minutes.

3. In a medium bowl, whisk eggs with pepper and ½ teaspoon salt until blended. Pour over vegetables in skillet and immediately reduce heat to medium-low. Cook, stirring, until eggs thicken, but are still soft and moist, 3 to 5 minutes. Serve at once directly from skillet.

57 SCOTCH WOODCOCK
Prep: 5 minutes   Cook: 5 minutes   Serves: 4

Anchovies with bread is a long-held pairing in the British Isles. You can use your favorite whether it's oat bread, whole wheat, or plain white. This hearty breakfast or snack is easy to make.

3 tablespoons plus
    4 teaspoons butter
	1 cup half-and-half
	   Pinch of salt

4 teaspoons anchovy paste	¼ teaspoon pepper
4 slices of bread, toasted	4 anchovy fillets, drained
8 egg yolks	2 teaspoons minced chives

1. Spread 1 teaspoon butter, then 1 teaspoon anchovy paste on each slice of bread. Arrange on a platter or on 4 individual plates.

2. In a medium bowl, whisk yolks, half-and-half, salt, and pepper until blended. In a medium skillet, melt remaining 3 tablespoons butter over high heat. When foamy, pour in eggs and reduce to low. Cook, folding and stirring until creamy curds form, about 5 minutes.

3. Spoon eggs onto bread. Top each portion with an anchovy. Sprinkle with chives. Serve immediately.

58 BREAD CRUMB AND BACON BIT SCRAMBLE
Prep: 10 minutes   Cook: 11 to 13 minutes   Serves: 4

4 strips of bacon	6 eggs
1 cup fresh bread crumbs (see Note)	⅓ cup milk
	¼ teaspoon salt
2 teaspoons butter	¼ teaspoon pepper

1. In a medium skillet, fry bacon over medium heat until crispy, about 5 minutes. Drain on paper towels. Crumble.

2. Pour off all but 1 tablespoon bacon fat. Fry crumbs in fat on medium-high heat until golden brown, 2 minutes. Drain on paper towels.

3. With skillet on medium heat, add butter. In a medium bowl, whisk eggs, milk, salt, and pepper. Pour into skillet. Stir gently until nearly set, 3 to 4 minutes.

4. Add bacon and bread crumbs. Fold and stir until desired doneness, 1 to 2 minutes longer. Serve at once.

    NOTE: *To make fresh bread crumbs, tear 2 slices of bread—which may be stale or not —into large pieces. Place, crusts and all, in food processor. Process to fine crumbs. Store, tightly covered, in refrigerator.*

59 (AUSTIN SCRAMBLER) DELIEUX!

Prep: 15 minutes   Cook: 10 to 11 minutes   Serves: 6

Austin, Texas, was my home for twelve years, during a time when "designer" egg dishes were popular. This combination of scrambled eggs with mushrooms, avocado, and Monterey Jack cheese has remained in my breakfast and brunch repertoire.

3 tablespoons butter	2 ripe avocados, cubed
10 mushrooms, sliced	2 cups cubed Monterey Jack
¼ cup spicy red salsa	cheese (about 8 ounces)
8 eggs	1 tablespoon sliced black
¼ cup milk	olives
½ teaspoon salt	Alfalfa sprouts
¼ teaspoon pepper	Plain yogurt

1. In a large nonstick skillet, melt butter over high heat. When bubbly, add mushrooms. Sauté 3 minutes. Add salsa. Cook down to evaporate liquid a little, about 1 minute.

2. In a medium bowl, whisk eggs, milk, salt, and pepper. Pour into skillet. Reduce heat to medium. Drop avocado cubes over eggs. Stir and fold gently as eggs set. When eggs are nearly set but still somewhat runny, about 5 minutes, add cheese and olives. Stir and fold until desired doneness and cheese is stringy, 1 to 2 minutes longer.

3. Spoon onto plates. Top each serving with alfalfa sprouts and yogurt. Serve hot.

60 HOMINY SCRAMBLE

Prep: 5 minutes   Cook: 7 minutes   Serves: 2 to 3

Natives of the American Southwest like lots of hominy in scrambled eggs. This is not an unusual dish at the dinner table.

1 tablespoon bacon fat,	¼ teaspoon salt
vegetable shortening,	¼ teaspoon pepper
or oil	2 whole roasted green chiles,
1 (1-pound) can cooked	cut into thin strips (page
hominy, drained	53)
5 eggs	

1. In a cast-iron skillet or other heavy pan, heat fat over medium-high heat and fry hominy until well browned, about 5 minutes.

2. In a medium bowl, beat eggs, salt, and pepper with a fork. Pour over hominy. Cook, moving constantly with spatula, until eggs set, about 1 minute.

3. Serve generously topped with chile strips.

61 STRINGY EGG-CHEESE SCRAMBLE

Prep: 5 minutes   Cook: 1 to 1½ minutes   Serves: 3 to 4

Cheese cut into large cubes won't completely melt in the time it takes to finish the eggs, which means that a fork dragged through the cheese comes up with glorious strings.

5 eggs
2 teaspoons milk
¼ teaspoon salt
¼ teaspoon coarsely ground
    black pepper

1 tablespoon butter
¼ pound white cheese, such as
    Monterey Jack, Swiss,
    Edam, or Muenster, cut
    into ½-inch cubes

1. In a medium bowl, whisk eggs with milk, salt, and pepper.

2. In a medium skillet, melt butter over high heat. Pour in eggs and reduce heat to medium-high. Stir with a wooden spatula until eggs begin to set around edges but are still soft, about 30 to 60 seconds.

3. Add cheese. Stir and lift until cheese softens, about 30 seconds longer. Turn off heat. Stir 1 or 2 more turns. Serve immediately.

62 KHITCHERIE

Prep: 10 minutes   Cook: 5 to 6 minutes   Serves: 2

These Indian-style scrambled eggs with tomato, cilantro, and chile will brighten up any morning.

1 small onion, minced
2 tablespoons butter
1 tomato, seeded and
    chopped
1½ tablespoons coarsely
    chopped cilantro

1 fresh serrano, jalapeño, or
    other green chile, seeded
    and thinly sliced
5 eggs
¼ teaspoon salt
Pinch of pepper

1. In a medium skillet, cook onion in butter over medium-high heat until soft, about 2 minutes. Add tomato, cilantro, and chile.

2. Cook, stirring, just until tomato pieces begin to release juice, about 2 minutes.

3. In a medium bowl, beat eggs with salt and pepper with a fork. Pour over tomatoes. Move around with a spatula to form large soft curds, 1 to 2 minutes, or until desired doneness. Serve at once.

63   SHRIMP AND SCRAMBLED EGGS, CHINESE STYLE

Prep: 25 minutes   Cook: 6 minutes   Serves: 4

The shrimp marinates in an egg white while the extra yolk goes into the scrambled eggs. These eggs are best if cooked lightly rather than firm.

½ **pound medium shrimp,
  shelled and deveined**
6 **eggs—1 separated, 5 whole**
2 **teaspoons cornstarch**
3 **tablespoons vegetable oil**
¼ **teaspoon salt**

¼ **teaspoon white pepper**
1 **tablespoon oyster sauce**
2 **tablespoons chopped
  cilantro**
1 **scallion, chopped**

1. In a medium bowl, toss shrimp with egg white and cornstarch to coat.

2. In a wok or medium saucepan, heat 2 tablespoons of the oil. Add shrimp and cook, tossing, until golden, 1 to 2 minutes. Drain on paper towels and set aside.

3. In a medium bowl, beat egg yolk, whole eggs, salt, pepper, oyster sauce, and cilantro with a fork. In a nonstick wok or skillet, heat remaining 1 tablespoon oil over high heat. Pour in eggs. Slowly push eggs around pan with wide spatula. When partially set, add shrimp. Continue to lift and fold while cooking eggs to desired doneness.

4. Serve in bowls, with scallions sprinkled on top.

64   SCRAMBLED EGGS WITH TOMATOES

Prep: 5 minutes   Cook: 5 minutes   Serves: 2

2 **teaspoons sugar**
½ **teaspoon salt**
1 **tablespoon soy sauce**
1 **tablespoon rice wine or
  sherry**
  **Pinch of crushed hot red
  pepper**

2 **tablespoons oil**
5 **eggs, beaten**
1 **teaspoon minced garlic**
2 **medium tomatoes, cut into
  wedges**
1½ **teaspoons cornstarch mixed
  with 2 tablespoons water**

1. In a glass measuring cup, combine sugar, salt, soy sauce, wine, and red pepper for sauce. Set near stove.

2. In a medium skillet, heat 1 tablespoon of the oil over high heat. Pour in beaten eggs and cook, moving them slowly with a wide spatula, lifting and folding, until halfway set, about 1 minute. Transfer to a bowl; eggs will still be runny.

3. In same skillet, heat remaining 1 tablespoon oil. Stir in garlic and tomatoes. Return eggs to pan. Add sauce. Lift and fold once or twice. Add dissolved cornstarch and cook a few seconds until soft and glistening. Serve at once.

65 SCRAMBLED EGGS WITH BARBECUED PORK
Prep: 10 minutes   Cook: 1 to 2 minutes   Serves: 3

6 eggs
¾ cup frozen peas
1 cup shredded or finely
    sliced Chinese barbecued
    pork or ham

2 scallions, finely chopped
½ teaspoon salt
2 tablespoons vegetable oil

1. In a medium bowl with a fork, lightly beat eggs to blend. Stir in peas, barbecued pork, scallions, and salt.

2. In a medium skillet, heat oil over medium-high heat. Pour in eggs and cook, moving eggs around skillet slowly with spatula, lifting and folding them until scrambled, 1 to 2 minutes, or to desired doneness. Serve immediately.

66 CHINESE EGGS WITH RICE STICKS AND TWO PORKS
Prep: 10 minutes   Stand: 1 hour   Cook: 9 minutes   Serves: 4

This is a classic Chinese stir-fry, which uses eggs, ground pork, and Chinese barbecued pork (*cha siu*). If you don't have Chinese barbecued pork available, substitute shredded ham, leftover roast pork, or barbecued chicken. Dried rice stick noodles are sometimes labeled Chinese vermicelli or *mai fun*.

2 ounces Chinese rice stick
    noodles (*mai fun*)
¼ cup ground pork
1 teaspoon soy sauce
2 tablespoons plus 1 teaspoon
    vegetable oil
¼ teaspoon sugar
4 to 6 mushrooms, sliced

1 celery rib, chopped
2 scallions, chopped
¼ cup thinly sliced Chinese
    barbecued pork or ham
6 eggs
1 teaspoon salt
¼ teaspoon white pepper

1. Soak rice sticks in water 1 hour. Drain and cut into 1-inch lengths.

2. In a small bowl, mix *ground* pork, soy sauce, 1 teaspoon of the oil, and sugar. Set aside to marinate while you prepare remaining ingredients.

3. In a wok or large skillet, heat remaining 2 tablespoons oil over high heat. Add seasoned ground pork. Stir-fry 1 to 1½ minutes, until no longer pink. Add mushrooms, cover, and cook 2 minutes. Add celery and scallions and stir-fry 1 minute. Add *barbecued* pork and drained noodles. Cover and cook 2 minutes.

4. Whisk eggs with salt and pepper. Pour into wok. Cook over medium heat, lifting and folding over gently, just until eggs are cooked, 1 to 2 minutes. Serve immediately.

67 TRUFFLED SCRAMBLED EGGS

Prep: 2 minutes   Stand: 1 hour   Cook: 10 minutes   Serves: 2

Connoisseurs of rare fresh black or white truffles know their essence is so powerful that it can penetrate the shell of an unbroken egg. So allow at least a few hours and preferably a day to completely perfume these eggs.

4 **eggs, truffled if possible (see Note)**
4 **paper-thin slices of black or white truffle, cut into shreds**

Pinch of salt
2 **tablespoons heavy cream**
1 **tablespoon butter**

1. In a medium bowl, beat eggs lightly. Add truffles. If time allows, let stand 1 to 2 hours at room temperature covered with plastic wrap, or refrigerate up to 24 hours.

2. When ready to cook, mix salt and cream into eggs.

3. Melt butter in top of a double boiler over simmering water. Pour in egg-truffle mixture. Cook until softly set, stirring from time to time, about 10 minutes for large curds.

NOTE: *To truffle eggs without actually using up the truffle, enclose up to a dozen eggs and a 1-ounce piece of white or black truffle in a glass jar and screw the lid on tight; refrigerate. Next day, the eggs you crack for scrambled eggs will taste and smell strongly (and elegantly!) of truffles.*

68 TOAD ON THE HOT SEAT

Prep: 1 minute   Cook: 6 to 8 minutes   Serves: 1

Give the hole a manhole cover. Fry the circle of bread when you cook the egg. Take it out when it's done. Top the egg with the toasted cover at serving.

1 **slice of bread**
1 **tablespoon butter**
1 **egg**
3 **tablespoons shredded Monterey Jack, Cheddar, Swiss, or Longhorn cheese**

1 **to 2 tablespoons chile sauce or salsa or a few drops of Tabasco sauce**

1. Cut circle out of center of bread, using a juice glass or biscuit cutter. In a small skillet, melt butter over medium heat. Add bread and fry until underside is browned, 2 to 3 minutes.

2. Flip bread and crack egg into hole. Reduce heat to medium-low and cook 3 to 4 minutes, until white sets. Flip bread and egg. Cook second side 30 seconds.

3. Toss cheese with chile sauce and sprinkle over egg. Cover skillet and cook 30 seconds to melt cheese. Serve immediately.

69   TOAD IN THE HOLE
Prep: 1 minute   Cook: 5 to 6 minutes   Serves: 1

This is the favorite breakfast of my niece, Sara. She's made it for herself since she was five.

1 slice of bread, white or whole wheat	2 tablespoons butter
	1 egg

1. Cut circle out of center of bread, using a juice glass or biscuit cutter. In a small skillet, melt butter over medium heat. Add bread and fry until underside is browned, about 2 minutes.

2. Flip bread and crack egg into hole. Reduce heat to medium-low and cook 3 to 4 minutes, until white is set. If yolk is not set to your liking, cover skillet so egg steams until done.

---

70   SPAGHETTI ALLA CARBONARA
Prep: 10 minutes   Cook: 18 to 21 minutes   Serves: 4

While eggs aren't cooked in a skillet like scrambled eggs in this Italian classic, they are definitely scrambled before they're added to the spaghetti. Thus, one more random scrambler. This is an easy supper with ingredients usually on hand.

1 pound spaghetti	½ cup grated Parmesan or Romano cheese
6 slices of bacon, cut into 1-inch pieces	½ teaspoon coarsely ground pepper
3 garlic cloves, minced	Salt
1 tablespoon olive oil	
4 eggs, lightly beaten	

1. Bring a large pot of salted water to a boil. Add spaghetti and cook until tender but still firm, 10 to 12 minutes. Drain.

2. Meanwhile, in a large deep skillet or flameproof casserole, cook bacon over medium heat, turning, until lightly browned, about 5 minutes. Remove bacon with a slotted spoon and drain on paper towels. Pour off all but 2 tablespoons bacon fat from skillet.

3. Add garlic and olive oil to bacon drippings. Cook until garlic is soft and fragrant, about 2 minutes. Add spaghetti and bacon and toss to coat spaghetti with fat. Add eggs and toss over heat until they just begin to thicken but are not scrambled, 1 to 2 minutes.

4. Remove from heat, sprinkle on cheese and pepper, and toss to mix. Season with salt to taste. Serve at once.

71   EGGS RIDGEMONT

Prep: 2 minutes   Cook: 3 to 4½ minutes   Serves: 1

My sister-in-law Marilyn was so impressed that her husband—my brother Rob—knew about a recipe so elegant in phrase that she thought she'd surprise him by making it one weekend. She looked it up in all her cookbooks but could not find a dish he called Eggs Ridgemont. That's because only three people know how to make Eggs Ridgemont—Rob and his two college roommates. They all attended the University of Texas and lived in a house on Ridgemont Street in Austin. This is breakfast for the bleary-eyed.

**2   slices of bread, white, whole
      wheat, rye, or other
      Butter or margarine**

**2   eggs
      Salt and pepper**

1. Have bread ready in toaster slots.

2. In a medium skillet, melt 1 tablespoon butter over high heat. Swirl to evenly coat pan.

3. Start toaster, then crack eggs into skillet. Cover with lid, reduce heat to low, and fry until yolks are cooked to desired doneness, 3 to 3½ minutes for soft yolks, 4 to 4½ minutes for hard yolks.

4. When toast is ready, place slices side by side on plate. Butter toast.

5. Slide cooked eggs onto toast. Season with salt and pepper to taste.

72   ASSASSIN'S EGGS

Prep: 2 minutes   Cook: 1 to 2 minutes   Serves: 2

**2   tablespoons butter
4   eggs
      Salt and pepper**

**1   tablespoon white wine
      vinegar**

1. In a large nonstick skillet, melt butter over medium-high heat. When butter stops foaming, crack eggs into skillet. Season with salt and pepper to taste. Fry until whites set, about 1 minute. Gently flip eggs over with a wide spatula and fry until yolks are cooked to your liking, about 30 seconds longer for medium-firm yolks.

2. Transfer eggs to a warm serving plate. Immediately add vinegar to hot skillet. Boil, swirling, 3 seconds. Drizzle liquid in skillet over eggs and serve at once.

73   (FRIED EGGS)

Prep: 2 minutes   Cook: 2 to 3 minutes   Serves: 1

A fried egg is cooked in some sort of fat, usually butter but sometimes bacon fat or oil. The success of fried eggs is determined by how close you get them to be just as you'd order them at a great diner. Sunny-side up? Over easy?

1 tablespoon butter	**Salt and black pepper**
2 eggs	

1. In a small nonstick skillet, heat butter over high heat until foamy.

2. Crack each egg on side of skillet, hold low, open shell, and let fall gently into butter. Reduce heat to medium. Fry 2 to 3 minutes, until whites are set completely and yolks are done to stage you like. Sprinkle with salt and pepper.

3. Slide out of skillet or lift with spatula to serving plates. Serve immediately.

Variations:

(SUNNY-SIDE UP)

Remove from pan when whites are completely set and yolks are nearly set and still very yellow-orange.

OVER EASY

When whites are completely set and yolks are nearly set, flip eggs and cook about 30 seconds, just enough to film over yolk.

OVER WELL

After flipping, cook about 1 minute longer, until yolks are completely set.

WELL DONE

Actually a steamed-fried egg, for people who like their eggs sunny-side up but hate runny yolks. Cover skillet during last minute of frying.

74 QUICK TOMATO-EGG SUMMER DINNER
Prep: 10 minutes   Cook: 18 to 22 minutes   Serves: 1

This is a summer-only treat because ripe tomatoes are a must. This is a Tuscan favorite from my friend, Sacramento wine merchant Darrell Corti.

½ **red onion, sliced**
2 **tablespoons olive oil**
2 **absolutely ripe summer tomatoes, cored and cut into chunks**

2 **or 3 eggs**
Salt and pepper

1. In a medium skillet, cook red onion in olive oil over medium heat until soft, about 5 minutes.

2. Add tomato chunks. Cook 10 minutes over medium heat, stirring occasionally. If liquid remains, raise heat and boil it off.

3. Make 2 or 3 wells in tomatoes. Crack eggs into wells. Season with salt and pepper to taste. Return heat to medium, cover skillet, and cook until eggs set, 3 to 4 minutes.

75 NEW MEXICO-STYLE ENCHILADAS WITH EGG ON TOP
Prep: 10 minutes   Cook: 12 to 15 minutes   Serves: 8

1 **(10-ounce) can red enchilada sauce**
¾ **cup tomato puree**
2 **teaspoons pure chile powder**
½ **teaspoon ground cumin**
½ **teaspoon dried oregano**
½ **teaspoon garlic powder**
16 **corn tortillas**

1 **(16-ounce) can refried beans, warmed**
1 **cup minced white onion**
1½ **cups shredded Monterey Jack cheese**
8 **fried eggs (page 45)**
1 **cup shredded Longhorn, Colby, or Cheddar cheese**

1. Preheat oven to 350°F. In a nonreactive medium skillet, combine enchilada sauce, tomato puree, chile powder, cumin, oregano, and garlic powder. Mix well. Bring to a boil, reduce heat, and simmer 3 minutes.

2. With tongs, draw 8 tortillas through hot sauce and arrange on 2 lightly oiled baking sheets. Spread warm beans over each tortilla. Top evenly with onion and Jack cheese. Repeat with another layering of 8 sauce-dipped tortillas, beans, onion, and cheese.

3. Bake 8 to 10 minutes, until cheese melts. Meanwhile, prepare fried eggs, cooking 4 at a time in a skillet.

4. Top each stack of enchiladas with an egg. Sprinkle Longhorn cheese over top. Ladle any remaining sauce over stacks. Return to oven and bake 1 to 2 minutes, to soften Longhorn. Serve immediately.

Chapter 3

Omelets Galore

Omelets come in many shapes and sizes. And for speed and satisfaction, they can't be beat. Whether you like them flat, folded, fluffy, flipped, broiled, steamed, or baked, you are sure to find a selection to suit your fancy or to match whatever fixings happen to be on hand at the moment.

The richest omelets are those whipped at the last minute by hand. An electric mixer definitely does a good job in beating eggs, but for omelets it's too much beating and too many bubbles. The cooked result is tough.

The best cookware for omelets and frittatas is a heavy skillet made of good heat-conducting materials with a nonstick surface. A thick pan heats evenly, resists hot spots, and to my mind, keeps the eggs more comfortable as they cook. You don't need to blast an omelet with violently high heat, yet heat that is too low will take so long to cook the eggs that by the time they're done they've also toughened.

When is an omelet done? When you like it, even if the inside is a little juicy. Federal food safety guidelines frown on soft or runny centers in omelets because, they say, the egg didn't get hot enough to kill bacteria. Yet, if the yolk has coagulated, let alone cooked to firmness, it has reached a temperature of 160°F., which is 20 degrees more than the 140° needed to kill salmonella.

Here are some omelet myths dispelled:

Myth 1: Use your omelet pan only for omelets.

With today's nonstick surfaces on heavy-gauge pans, the pan isn't going to know what was last in it after it's washed.

Myth 2: Never wash your omelet pan.

A pan that has cooked eggs never finishes the job clean. Wash your pan in hot water with dishwashing soap.

Myth 3: Never whip the eggs with milk, only water.

Italians may like this advice, but Italy is not the only country to ever produce a cooked egg. A tablespoon of water whipped into a two-egg omelet batter, no question, turns out a silky omelet. So does the addition of Japanese dashi or chicken or vegetable stock. My roots are in Eastern

Europe. I find that a tablespoon or two of milk, half-and-half, cream, sour cream, yogurt, or buttermilk is familiar. Each gives an omelet a fine textural profile, and all are delicious.

Success with omelets comes from the following:

- Use the right size pan.
- Be sure the pan is hot and buttered or oiled before pouring in an egg mixture.
- When cooking the eggs, keep the heat about medium-high. If it's too hot, the omelet will scorch. If it's too low, you'll overcompensate by leaving it longer over heat, in which case it will overcook and toughen.
- Remove from heat when the omelet firms up on the outside, protecting an inside that is soft and moist. It will continue to cook on the plate from retained heat.

    Not to be overlooked is the frittata, an Italian-style thick, firm omelet cooked slowly in a skillet, often finished under the broiler, with ingredients mixed right in rather than folded in. These can be found in the following chapter. Baked omelets are to be found in Chapter 5 (pages 87–96).

76 CHEESE OMELET
Prep: 5 minutes   Cook: 1½ minutes   Serves: 2

    In the annals of egg cookery, few dishes satisfy as well as a perfectly prepared, simple cheese omelet. The beauty of making this at home is that you can choose your favorite cheese, though I've listed several of the most appropriate below.

4 eggs	1 tablespoon butter
1 tablespoon milk	1 cup shredded Cheddar,
¼ teaspoon salt	Monterey Jack, Colby, or
⅛ teaspoon pepper	Swiss cheese

1. Crack eggs into a medium bowl. Add milk, salt, and pepper and beat with a fork until just blended.

2. In a medium nonstick skillet or omelet pan, melt butter over high heat. When butter stops foaming, pour in eggs, swirling to distribute evenly. Reduce heat to medium-high and cook, lifting sides of omelet to let uncooked egg flow underneath, until eggs are nearly set but omelet is still moist on top, about 1 minute. Quickly sprinkle cheese over half of omelet.

3. Fold plain side over cheese and cook 30 seconds longer. Serve at once.

77 FRENCH OMELET AUX FINES HERBES
Prep: 5 minutes   Cook: 1½ minutes   Serves: 2

A French herb omelet traditionally includes fresh parsley, chives, chervil, and tarragon. Of course, you can make it with whatever fresh herbs you happen to have on hand. I like to use sage, chives, oregano, and thyme, which grow in my garden. To be truly French about the cooking, err on the side of underdone. Even if the omelet seems a little runny on top, pent-up heat inside will continue to set the eggs even after they are on the plate.

2 teaspoons chopped parsley	4 eggs
1 teaspoon minced fresh chives	Few shakes of salt and pepper
1 teaspoon chopped fresh tarragon	1 tablespoon butter

1. Combine parsley, chives, and tarragon in a medium bowl. Crack eggs into bowl. Add salt and pepper and beat with a fork just until blended.

2. In an 8-inch nonstick skillet or omelet pan, melt butter over high heat until foamy. Pour eggs into pan and cook, stirring rapidly in center and shaking pan to keep omelet loose, until nearly set but still moist on top, about 45 seconds. Cook without stirring just a few seconds to let underside firm up.

3. Remove from heat and with a wide spatula, fold in thirds (like a business letter) and slide onto a plate, seam side down. Serve immediately.

78 CURRIED OMELET WITH CHUTNEY AND SCALLIONS
Prep: 2 minutes   Cook: 2½ minutes   Serves: 2

5 eggs	1 tablespoon butter
¼ teaspoon salt	3 tablespoons chutney, such as Major Grey's
⅛ teaspoon white pepper	1 scallion, thinly sliced
½ teaspoon curry powder, preferably Madras	

1. In a medium bowl, beat eggs, salt, pepper, and curry with a fork until blended.

2. In a medium nonstick skillet or omelet pan, melt butter over high heat. When it stops foaming, pour in eggs. Let set about 20 seconds; reduce heat to medium-high. As edges set, lift them up to let uncooked egg flow under. When almost all egg is cooked but some in the middle remains runny, about 1½ minutes longer, spoon chutney and scallion down half of omelet.

3. Fold plain side over filling and cook 30 seconds. Ease out of skillet onto a serving platter. Serve immediately.

79 HERBED CREAM CHEESE OMELET

Prep: 5 minutes   Cook: 1½ minutes   Serves: 2

1 (3-ounce) package cream
   cheese, at room
   temperature
1 teaspoon chopped parsley
1 teaspoon minced fresh
   chives OR ONIONS

¼ teaspoon dried thyme
1 teaspoon chopped fresh
   basil (optional)
4 eggs
   Salt and pepper
1 tablespoon butter

1. In a small bowl, mash cream cheese with parsley, chives, thyme, and basil, if using.

2. Crack eggs into a medium bowl and add salt and pepper. Gently beat eggs with a fork.

3. In a medium nonstick skillet or omelet pan, melt butter over high heat until foamy. Pour eggs into pan. Reduce heat to medium. Cook, lifting edges to let uncooked egg flow underneath, until omelet is nearly set but still moist on top, 45 to 60 seconds. Spoon cream cheese–herb mixture down half of omelet in 6 or 8 dollops.

4. Fold plain side over cream cheese and cook 30 seconds longer. Slide onto a plate and serve at once.

80 ARTICHOKE OMELET

Prep: 5 minutes   Cook: 1 to 1½ minutes   Serves: 2

4 eggs
1 tablespoon milk
¼ teaspoon salt
⅛ teaspoon pepper
1 tablespoon butter
1 (7-ounce) jar marinated
   artichokes, drained and
   coarsely chopped

2 teaspoons drained capers
2 tablespoons grated
   Parmesan cheese

1. In a medium bowl, whisk eggs, milk, salt, and pepper with a fork until blended.

2. In a medium nonstick skillet or omelet pan, melt butter over high heat until foamy. Pour eggs into pan. Reduce heat to medium. Cook, lifting edges to let uncooked egg flow underneath, until omelet is nearly set but still moist on top, about 1 minute. Spoon artichokes over half of omelet. Sprinkle capers and cheese over artichokes.

3. Fold plain side of omelet over filling and cook 30 seconds longer. Slide onto a plate and serve immediately.

81 ASPARAGUS OMELET WITH POLONAISE SAUCE

Prep: 5 minutes   Cook: 5 to 8 minutes   Serves: 3

6 **large asparagus spears,**
   about ½ pound
4 **eggs, separated**
2 **tablespoons milk**
¼ **teaspoon salt**

⅛ **teaspoon pepper**
2 **tablespoons butter**
  Polonaise Sauce (recipe
   follows)

1. In a large skillet of boiling salted water, cook asparagus until just tender but still bright green, 2 to 3 minutes. Drain carefully and rinse briefly under cold running water. Set aside on a kitchen towel to drain thoroughly.

2. In a large bowl, beat egg yolks, milk, salt, and pepper until blended.

3. In another bowl, beat egg whites to firm, not stiff, peaks. Fold whites into yolks until no lumps remain.

4. In a medium nonstick skillet, melt butter over high heat. When butter foams, pour egg mixture into skillet, spreading evenly with spatula. Reduce heat to medium and cook until underside is light brown, about 2 minutes. Arrange asparagus with spears headed in both directions down center of eggs. Spoon about 3 tablespoons Polonaise Sauce over asparagus.

5. Carefully fold omelet in thirds (like a letter), encasing asparagus. Omelet will be very fluffy and airy. Cook 1 to 2 minutes longer, until omelet is set. If parts remain loose, invert omelet onto a dinner plate, then slide upturned omelet back into skillet for 30 to 60 seconds longer. Serve at once, with remaining Polonaise Sauce on the side.

82 POLONAISE SAUCE

Prep: 5 minutes   Cook: 2 to 3 minutes   Makes: ½ cup

4 **tablespoons butter**
2 **hard-boiled eggs, minced**
  (page 8)

3 **tablespoons chopped Italian**
  parsley

1. Place butter, eggs, and parsley in a small saucepan. Cook over low heat, stirring, until butter melts, 2 to 3 minutes.

2. Keep warm, if desired, for up to 1 hour by setting saucepan in a larger bowl of very hot water.

83 AVOCADO, SUN-DRIED TOMATO, AND LIME OMELET

Prep: 7 minutes   Cook: 4 to 5 minutes   Serves: 4

Always a favorite combination, tomatoes and avocados team up with lime juice, which adds its own zesty taste while keeping the avocado bright green. For even more flavor, use one tablespoon of the oil from the jar of tomatoes in place of half the olive oil.

2 ripe avocados, preferably
   Hass, pitted, peeled, and
   cut into ¾-inch dice
   Juice of 1 lime
8 oil-packed sun-dried tomato
   halves

8 eggs
2 tablespoons milk
¼ teaspoon salt
¼ teaspoon pepper
2 tablespoons olive oil

1. In a small bowl, gently toss avocado cubes with lime juice to coat. Cut tomato halves lengthwise into thick strips.

2. Crack eggs into a medium bowl. Add milk, salt, and pepper and whisk just until blended.

3. In a large nonstick skillet, heat olive oil over high heat. When hot but not smoking, pour eggs into skillet. Reduce heat to medium. Cook, lifting edges to let uncooked egg flow underneath, until omelet is nearly set but still moist in center, 3 to 4 minutes. Quickly spread tomatoes over half of omelet. Scoop avocado from lime juice with a slotted spoon and arrange over tomatoes.

4. Fold plain side over filling. Cook 1 minute longer. Slide onto a platter and serve at once.

84 CALIFORNIA OMELET WITH SUN-DRIED TOMATOES, GOAT CHEESE, AND FRESH BASIL

Prep: 5 minutes   Stand: 10 to 15 minutes   Cook: 3 minutes
Serves: 3

¼ cup sun-dried tomatoes
6 eggs
2 tablespoons milk (cream)
¼ teaspoon salt
⅛ teaspoon pepper

2 tablespoons olive oil
+ 3 ounces goat cheese (chèvre),
   mashed
1½ tablespoons chopped fresh
   basil

1. In a medium bowl, soak tomatoes in very hot tap water to cover until softened, 10 to 15 minutes. When plump, drain and cut lengthwise into fat strips.

2. In another medium bowl, whisk eggs, milk, salt, and pepper until blended.

3. In a large skillet, heat olive oil over high heat. When very hot but not smoking, pour in eggs. Reduce heat to medium. Cook, lifting edges to let uncooked egg flow underneath, until omelet is nearly set but still moist in center, about 2½ minutes. Quickly sprinkle dried tomato strips, goat cheese, and chopped basil over half of omelet.

4. Fold plain side of omelet over filling. Cook 30 seconds longer. Slide onto a platter and serve at once.

---

85   GREEN CHILE AND ONION OMELET WITH SMOKED CHEESE

Prep: 25 minutes   Cook: 8 minutes   Serves: 2 to 3

2 **poblano peppers, roasted (see Note), or 1 (4-ounce) can whole roasted chiles**	3 **garlic cloves, minced**
	1 **jalapeño pepper, seeded and minced**
6 **eggs**	4 **tablespoons butter**
2 **tablespoons milk**	5 **ounces shredded smoked Cheddar or Gouda cheese**
¼ **teaspoon salt**	**Sour cream**
¼ **teaspoon pepper**	
1 **medium onion, chopped**	

1. If using canned chiles, drain them well. Cut poblanos or chiles into strips. In a medium bowl, whisk eggs, milk, salt, and pepper until blended.

2. In a large skillet, cook onion, garlic, and jalapeño pepper in 2 tablespoons butter over medium-high heat until soft, about 5 minutes. Transfer to a plate and let cool slightly. Wipe out skillet.

3. In same skillet, melt remaining 2 tablespoons butter over high heat. When butter foams, pour in eggs; reduce heat to medium. Cook, lifting edges to let uncooked egg flow underneath, until omelet is nearly set but still moist in center, about 1½ minutes. Quickly scatter onion mixture over half of omelet. Top with chile strips and cheese.

4. Fold plain side over filling. Cook 30 seconds longer. Slide onto a serving plate. Top with a few dollops of sour cream and serve at once.

NOTE: *To roast peppers, broil whole peppers on a baking sheet as close to heat source as possible. Turn with tongs until blistered all over, 10 to 15 minutes. As peppers are done, drop into a plastic bag. They won't all blacken at the same rate. Steam inside bag until cool to touch, about 10 minutes. Peel off skin, split open, and discard stems, seeds, and ribs.*

86   GARDEN VEGETABLE OMELET
Prep: 10 minutes   Cook: 2 to 3 minutes   Serves: 4

This is a great way to use up leftovers. If you have some already cooked broccoli and cauliflower, proceed to step 2.

½ cup broccoli florets
½ cup cauliflower florets
   Salt
6 eggs
¼ teaspoon pepper
1 medium tomato, seeded and
      chopped

1 tablespoon butter
½ cup grated dry Jack cheese
1 ripe avocado, cubed
½ cup alfalfa, radish, or soy
      sprouts

1. Place broccoli and cauliflower in 2 small bowls with 1 tablespoon water in each. Season both with a light sprinkling of salt. Cover and microwave on High 1 minute, until just crisp-tender. Uncover, stir, and drain off liquid.

2. In a medium bowl, whisk eggs, ¼ teaspoon salt, and pepper until blended. Stir in tomato.

3. In a large nonstick skillet, melt butter over high heat. When foamy, pour in eggs. Reduce heat to medium. Cook, lifting edges to let uncooked egg flow underneath, until omelet is nearly set but still moist on top, 1 to 1½ minutes. Quickly distribute broccoli, cauliflower, cheese, avocado, and sprouts over half of omelet.

4. Fold plain side over filling. Cook 30 seconds longer. Slide out of skillet onto platter and serve at once.

87   RATATOUILLE OMELET
Prep: 5 minutes   Cook: 1 to 1½ minutes   Serves: 4 to 5

The ratatouille can be made several days in advance. If you've already used some of it in another recipe, this omelet will gladly accept the leftovers.

6 eggs
   Salt and pepper
2 tablespoons butter

½ recipe Oven Ratatouille
      (page 102)
¼ cup grated Parmesan cheese

1. In a medium bowl, whisk eggs with salt and pepper to taste until blended.

2. In a large nonstick skillet, melt butter over high heat. When foamy, pour in eggs; reduce heat to medium. Cook, lifting edges to let uncooked egg flow underneath, until omelet is nearly set but still moist on top, 45 to 60 seconds. Quickly spoon ratatouille over half of omelet. Sprinkle with cheese.

3. Fold plain side of omelet over filling. Cook 30 seconds longer. Slide out of skillet onto platter and serve at once.

88 GARLICKY MUSHROOM OMELET

Prep: 17 minutes   Cook: 7½ to 8 minutes   Serves: 2

2 tablespoons butter
4 ounces mushrooms, sliced
1 large garlic clove, minced
4 eggs

1 tablespoon milk *(cream)*
¼ teaspoon salt
⅛ teaspoon pepper
1 tablespoon chopped parsley

1. In a medium nonstick skillet, melt 1 tablespoon of the butter over medium heat. Add mushrooms and cook, tossing, until much of liquid evaporates, about 5 minutes. Add garlic and cook, stirring, 30 to 60 seconds longer. Transfer mushrooms to a small bowl. Wipe out skillet.

2. Crack eggs into a medium bowl. Add milk, salt, and pepper and beat with a fork just until blended.

3. Melt remaining 1 tablespoon butter in same skillet over high heat. When foamy, pour in eggs; reduce heat to medium. Cook, lifting edges to let uncooked egg flow underneath, until omelet is nearly set but still moist on top, about 1½ minutes. Quickly spoon mushroom-garlic mixture over half of omelet.

4. Fold plain side over mushrooms. Cook 30 seconds longer. Slide omelet onto a plate and divide in half. Serve at once, garnished with parsley.

89 OMELET WITH BELL PEPPER, TOMATO, AND RIPE OLIVES

Prep: 15 minutes   Cook: 8 to 10 minutes   Serves: 3 to 4

2 ripe medium tomatoes,
    seeded and chopped
2 garlic cloves, minced
1 medium white onion,
    chopped *red*
1 green bell *red* pepper, chopped
2 tablespoons olive oil

6 eggs
¼ teaspoon salt
¼ teaspoon pepper
2 tablespoons sliced black
    olives
1 tablespoon chopped parsley
    Sour cream

1. In a large nonstick skillet, cook tomatoes, garlic, onion, and bell pepper in 1 tablespoon of the olive oil over medium heat until thick and soft, 6 to 8 minutes. Scrape into a bowl and set aside. Wipe skillet clean.

2. In a medium bowl, whisk eggs, salt, and pepper until blended. Heat remaining 1 tablespoon olive oil in same skillet over high heat. Pour in eggs; reduce heat to medium. Cook, lifting edges to let uncooked egg flow underneath, until omelet is nearly set but still moist on top, 1 to 1½ minutes. Quickly spread tomato mixture and olives over half of omelet. Some of filling will leak into skillet.

3. Fold plain side of omelet over filling. Cook 15 to 30 seconds longer. Slide onto a serving plate. Sprinkle parsley on top. Spoon vegetable mixture left in skillet around omelet. Top with sour cream. Serve hot.

90   YUCATAN OMELET WITH GREEN CHILES AND PINEAPPLE

Prep: 10 minutes   Cook: 18 to 19 minutes   Serves: 3

4 fresh poblano or Anaheim
   chiles
1 medium onion, chopped
2 garlic cloves, minced
2 tablespoons butter
1 (8-ounce) can pineapple
   chunks, well drained,
   1 tablespoon syrup
   reserved

6 eggs
   Salt and pepper
   Cilantro sprigs and sour
   cream

1. Roast and peel chiles as described on page 53. Cut into thin strips.

2. In a large nonstick skillet or omelet pan, cook onion and garlic in 1 table-spoon of butter over medium-high heat until onion is soft and translucent, about 4 minutes. Add chiles and pineapple and toss to mix. Transfer to a bowl. Wipe out skillet.

3. Crack eggs into a medium bowl. Add reserved pineapple syrup and salt and pepper to taste. Whisk lightly to mix.

4. In same skillet, melt remaining 1 tablespoon butter over medium-high heat until foamy. Pour eggs into pan; reduce heat to medium. Cook, lifting edges to let uncooked egg flow underneath, until omelet is barely set but still moist on top, 3 to 4 minutes. Spoon reserved onion-chile-pineapple mixture on half of omelet.

5. Fold plain side over filling. Cook about 1 minute longer. Slide out of skillet onto a serving platter. Garnish with cilantro and sour cream and serve at once.

91   HANGTOWN FRY

Prep: 10 minutes   Cook: 7 to 8 minutes   Serves: 1

The eastern oysters traditionally called for means to use large oysters, such as Blue Points.

3 large eastern oysters,
   shucked
1 egg beaten with 1 teaspoon
   milk
   Cracker crumbs or bread
   crumbs

1 tablespoon vegetable oil
2 slices of bacon, cut in half
2 eggs

1. Dip oysters in egg wash; roll in crumbs. In a small skillet, panfry oysters in oil until pale gold, about 1 minute. Remove with a slotted spatula and set aside.

2. In another small skillet, fry bacon until cooked but not crisp, 4 to 5 minutes. Drain off fat.

3. Return skillet with bacon to stove. Beat eggs lightly with a fork. Pour a small amount of eggs over bacon. Place oysters on top and pour remaining eggs into skillet. Cook over medium-high heat until set, about 1 minute.

4. Fold omelet over oysters. Cover pan with lid and allow to steam about 1 minute longer, to blend flavors. Serve at once.

92 SPINACH AND FOUR-CHEESE OMELET WITH WALNUTS

Prep: 10 minutes   Cook: 4 minutes   Serves: 3 to 4

Made with an assortment of cheeses that happened to be left over at my friend Toni Allegra's house one spring night, this spinach omelet created an impromptu party at dinner. It would be pleasing at the breakfast hour, as well. Use whatever soft and hard cheeses you have on hand. For easier mixing, be sure the soft cheeses are at room temperature.

2 tablespoons Gorgonzola cheese	¼ teaspoon salt
1 tablespoon grated Parmesan cheese	⅛ teaspoon pepper
¼ cup cream cheese	2 tablespoons butter
½ cup chopped walnuts	1 (10-ounce) box frozen spinach, thawed and squeezed dry
5 whole eggs	Pinch of grated nutmeg
1 egg white	

1. In a food processor, combine Gorgonzola, Parmesan cheese, and cream cheese. Process until completely smooth and spreadable. Sprinkle nuts over cheese; set aside in processor bowl.

2. In a medium bowl, whisk whole eggs, egg white, 2 tablespoons water, salt, and pepper until blended and frothy.

3. In a large skillet, melt butter over high heat. When foamy, pour in eggs; reduce heat to medium. Cook, lifting edges to let uncooked egg flow underneath, until omelet is nearly set but still moist in center, about 2 minutes.

4. Quickly spread spinach down center of omelet. Scrape cheese-walnut mixture from food processor bowl over spinach. Sprinkle with nutmeg.

5. Fold in thirds like a letter. Slide out onto a platter, seam side down. Serve immediately.

93 SAM'S HANGTOWN FRY
Prep: 10 minutes   Cook: 13 minutes   Serves: 1

This Hangtown fry, as prepared at Sam's Grill in Placerville, California, is flat and calls for tiny Olympia oysters, no bigger than a thumbnail.

2 dozen Olympia oysters or
    6 regular oysters, cut into
    small pieces
About ¼ cup flour for
    dredging
1 egg beaten with 1 teaspoon
    milk

About ¼ cup bread crumbs,
    for dredging
Vegetable oil, for deep-
    frying
2 slices of bacon
2 tablespoons butter
3 eggs

1. Coat oysters in flour, dip in egg wash, then roll in bread crumbs. In a deep-fryer or deep saucepan, heat 1½ to 2 inches oil to 350°F. Deep-fry oysters until golden brown, about 2 minutes. Drain on paper towels.

2. In a skillet, fry bacon over medium heat, turning a couple of times, until crisp, 6 to 8 minutes. Drain on paper towels.

3. In a medium skillet, melt butter over medium-high heat. In a small bowl, beat eggs with a fork until well blended. Pour eggs into pan and stir. When eggs are half done, about 1 minute, place oysters on top. Let set about 30 seconds.

4. Flip entire omelet by inverting onto a plate, then sliding back into pan, cooked side up. Fry other side to lightly brown, about 1 minute. Slip omelet onto platter. Top with bacon and serve.

94 LOX AND CREAM CHEESE OMELET
Prep: 5 minutes   Cook: 2 minutes   Serves: 2

4 eggs
2 tablespoons milk *(creamy)*
⅛ teaspoon salt
⅛ teaspoon white pepper
1 tablespoon butter

1 (3-ounce) package cream
    cheese, cut into small
    cubes
2 ounces lox or Nova smoked
    salmon, coarsely chopped

1. Crack eggs into a medium bowl. Add milk, salt, and pepper and beat with a fork until just blended.

2. In a medium nonstick skillet or omelet pan, melt butter over high heat until foamy. Pour eggs into pan. Reduce heat to medium. Cook, lifting edges to let uncooked egg flow underneath, until omelet is nearly set but still moist on top, 45 to 60 seconds.

3. Spoon cream cheese down middle of omelet just off center. Sprinkle lox over cream cheese. Fold plain side of omelet over filling. Cook about 30 seconds longer. Slide out of pan onto a plate, divide in half, and serve.

95   SAUSAGE AND APPLE OMELET
Prep: 25 minutes   Cook: 24 to 26 minutes   Serves: 2

At Lynn's Paradise Cafe in Louisville, Kentucky, this dish is called "Lynn's Pigs 'n Pippins Omelette." Sausage is king at Lynn's Paradise Cafe, perhaps because the diner occupies a building that used to be a grocery store, complete with the original sausage-making machine.

6 ounces country pork
  sausage, spicy or mild,
  bulk or links
½ cup apple cider
1 medium cooking apple,
  such as Pippin or Granny
  Smith, cored and sliced
¼ teaspoon cinnamon
1 tablespoon brown sugar

1 medium red potato, cooked
  and cut into ¾-inch dice
Salt and pepper
3 eggs
1 tablespoon butter
½ cup shredded sharp
  Cheddar cheese
2 tablespoons sour cream

1. Crumble sausage into a cold medium skillet. Cook over medium heat, stirring, until meat is completely cooked and no pink remains, 12 to 15 minutes. Drain off fat.

2. In a medium saucepan, bring cider to a boil. Add sliced apple, cinnamon, and brown sugar. Cook over medium heat, stirring occasionally, until apples are softened and juice is reduced and thickened, about 10 minutes. Stir in cooked sausage and potato. Season with salt and pepper to taste.

3. In a small bowl, beat eggs with a fork until blended. Beat in a pinch of salt and pepper.

4. In a medium skillet or omelet pan, melt butter over medium-high heat. When foamy, pour in eggs. Let set briefly around edges, then lift sides to let runny egg flow underneath. When omelet is barely set in center, about 1 minute, sprinkle cheese over half. Spoon apple-sausage mixture over cheese. Top with sour cream. Fold plain half over filling. Slide onto a plate. Serve hot.

96   BOURBONED CHICKEN LIVER OMELET
Prep: 15 minutes   Cook: 16 minutes   Serves: 4 to 6

If you're having brunch before the Kentucky Derby, which is as traditional as betting the favorite, it's sure to have chicken livers in it somewhere.

½ pound chicken livers	8 eggs
3 tablespoons butter	Few shakes of salt and
3 tablespoons bourbon	pepper
1 medium onion, chopped	Sprigs of parsley

1. Pat chicken livers dry with a paper towel. In a large nonstick skillet, melt 1 tablespoon butter over medium-high heat. Add livers and cook, tossing, until lightly browned outside and no longer pink in center, 8 to 10 minutes. Drain livers to remove excess liquid.

2. Return livers to skillet over high heat. When sputtering hot, pour bourbon over livers and carefully ignite with a match. Remove from heat and let flames subside. Transfer livers to a bowl. Wipe out skillet.

3. In same skillet, melt remaining 2 tablespoons butter over medium heat. Add onion and cook until softened, about 3 minutes. Meanwhile, in a medium bowl, whisk eggs with salt and pepper until blended.

4. Pour eggs over onion. Cook, lifting edges so unset eggs can flow underneath, until center is barely set, 45 to 60 seconds.

5. Spoon reserved chicken livers down one side of omelet. Fold plain side over livers. Cook about 30 seconds longer. Slide out of skillet onto a platter. Serve at once, garnished with parsley.

---

97   TRUFFLE-PÂTÉ OMELET
Prep: 5 minutes   Cook: 2 minutes   Serves: 2

This is a true indulgence, which doesn't come along very often. Here's a good place to try truffled eggs (see Note, page 42). Prepare them the night before and use them to make this omelet.

1 small black truffle (1 ounce or less)	4 eggs
	¼ teaspoon salt
2 tablespoons mashed canned foie gras or other goose liver pâté	Pinch of pepper
	1½ tablespoons butter
	1 tablespoon chopped parsley

1. Shave truffle on slicing blade of a box grater or slice as thin as possible. Mash truffle into foie gras. In a medium bowl, lightly beat truffled eggs, salt, and pepper with a fork.

2. In a medium nonstick skillet or omelet pan, melt butter over high heat, until foamy. Pour eggs into pan. Reduce heat to medium. Cook, lifting edges to let uncooked egg flow underneath, until omelet is nearly set but still moist on top, 45 to 60 seconds.

3. Spoon pâté-truffle mixture over half of omelet. Fold plain side of omelet over filling. Cook 30 seconds longer. Slide onto a plate. Sprinkle with parsley and serve immediately.

98 WATERCRESS–CREAM CHEESE PUFF OMELET

Prep: 10 minutes   Cook: 6 to 8 minutes   Serves: 2

For more control over this omelet for a crowd, make many two-serving omelets in succession. Double or triple the filling as needed. Use a skillet with an ovenproof handle.

¼ cup packed watercress,
     tough stems removed
1 (3-ounce) package cream
     cheese, at room
     temperature
     Dash of Tabasco or other hot
     pepper sauce

3 eggs, separated
2 tablespoons milk
⅛ teaspoon salt
¼ teaspoon pepper
1 tablespoon butter

1. Preheat broiler. In a small bowl, blend watercress, cream cheese, and Tabasco until well mixed.

2. In a large bowl, beat egg yolks, milk, salt, and pepper until lemon colored.

3. In another large bowl, beat egg whites until firm, not stiff, peaks form. Fold whites into yolks until no lumps remain.

4. In a medium nonstick skillet or omelet pan with ovenproof handle, melt butter over medium-high heat. When butter foams, pour egg batter into skillet, spreading evenly with a spatula. Cook, reducing heat to medium when edges set, until underside is light brown, 3 to 4 minutes. Peek underneath by lifting edge with spatula.

5. Transfer skillet to broiler and broil about 6 inches from heat until brown on top, 2 to 3 minutes.

6. Spread watercress cream over half of omelet. Fold plain half of omelet over filling. Slide onto a plate, divide in half, and serve at once.

99   SOUFFLÉED OMELET WITH POACHED SALMON FILLING

Prep: 15 minutes   Cook: 17 minutes   Serves: 4

An omelet with the features of a soufflé deserves fresh poached salmon as the filling. With only six ounces of salmon needed, you might ask your fish retailer for trimmings at a good price.

6 **eggs, separated**
½ **teaspoon cream of tartar**
¼ **teaspoon salt**
¼ **teaspoon white pepper**
3 **tablespoons butter**
  Poached Salmon Filling
  (recipe follows)

Minced fresh dill and sour cream
1 **to 2 tablespoons salmon roe (optional)**

1. Set oven rack on lowest level and preheat to 350°F. In a large bowl with an electric mixer, beat egg whites until foamy. Add cream of tartar and beat to stiff peaks.

2. In another large bowl, beat egg yolks, salt, and white pepper until thick and pale, about 1 minute. Fold beaten whites into yolks. Do not overfold; it's okay if some white tufts show.

3. In a large heavy skillet with ovenproof handle, melt butter over high heat, swirling to coat sides and bottom. When butter foams, pour in egg mixture, spreading evenly. Reduce heat to medium and cook, undisturbed, until omelet is puffed and lightly browned on bottom, about 4 minutes.

4. Transfer to oven and bake about 8 minutes to brown top. Remove from oven and cut a gash down center of omelet without going through to bottom. Quickly spoon salmon filling over half of omelet. Fold plain side over filling. Slide omelet onto a serving plate. Garnish with dill, dollops of sour cream, and a dot or two of salmon roe, if using. Serve at once.

POACHED SALMON FILLING
Makes: about 1¼ cups

About 2 cups dry white wine or water
1 **bay leaf**
3 **or 4 sprigs of fresh dill plus 1½ teaspoons chopped dill**

6 **black peppercorns**
8 **ounces salmon fillet**
½ **cup sour cream**
2 **tablespoons mayonnaise**
  Pinch of salt

1. In a medium nonreactive saucepan, bring wine, bay leaf, dill sprigs, and peppercorns to a boil.

2. Add salmon. Reduce heat to a bare simmer and poach about 5 minutes, until flaky tender. Remove with a slotted spatula and let cool.

3. In a medium bowl, flake fish. Mix lightly with sour cream, mayonnaise, salt, and chopped dill just until smooth enough to spread.

100 CORN-OFF-THE-COB PUFF OMELET
Prep: 5 minutes   Cook: 5 to 6 minutes   Serves: 2 or 3

3 eggs, separated
1 teaspoon sugar
2 tablespoons milk
Few shakes of salt and
    pepper

1 cup corn kernels, fresh,
    frozen, or canned
2 tablespoons butter
Salsa and sour cream

1. Preheat broiler. In a large bowl, beat egg yolks, sugar, milk, salt, and pepper until lemon colored, about 2 minutes. Stir in corn.

2. In another large bowl, whip egg whites until firm, not stiff, peaks form. Fold whites into yolk-corn mixture until no lumps remain.

3. In a medium nonstick skillet or omelet pan with ovenproof handle, melt butter over medium-high heat until foamy. Pour egg batter into skillet, spreading evenly with a spatula. Cook, reducing heat to medium when edges set, until underside is light brown, 3 to 4 minutes. Peek underneath by lifting edge with spatula.

4. Transfer skillet to broiler and broil until pale gold on top, about 2 minutes. Fold in half and slide onto a platter. Serve hot, with salsa and sour cream on the side.

101 WESTERN OMELET
Prep: 10 minutes   Cook: 5 minutes   Serves: 3

4 tablespoons butter
½ cup diced ham
1 tomato, seeded and diced
½ cup minced onion

4 eggs
2 tablespoons cream
¼ teaspoon salt
⅛ teaspoon black pepper

1. In a medium nonstick skillet or omelet pan, melt 2 tablespoons of the butter over medium-high heat. Add ham, tomato, and onion and cook, stirring occasionally, until onion is softened, about 3 minutes. Transfer to a bowl.

2. Beat eggs, 2 tablespoons water, cream, salt, and pepper with a fork until just blended. In same skillet, melt remaining 2 tablespoons butter over high heat until foamy. Pour eggs into skillet; reduce heat to medium. Cook, lifting sides all around pan to let uncooked eggs flow underneath, until nearly set but still moist on top, about 1½ minutes.

3. Spoon ham mixture down one side of omelet. Fold plain side over filling and cook 30 seconds longer. Slide onto a plate. Serve immediately.

102 (DENVER OMELET)

Prep: 5 minutes   Cook: 5 minutes   Serves: 2

Why Denver is an adjective with diced onion and green bell pepper baffles even the people in its namesake city. Sam Arnold, a Western food historian and owner of the Fort restaurant outside Denver, says that during the early days of Route 66, eggs were considered the best-tasting and *safest* food to eat! He believes this is the only plausible explanation of how Denver got itself a dish.

While Denver is indeed part of the West, its omelet is not to be confused with the Western omelet. A Denver omelet has no filling, just specks of onion and green pepper cooked along with the eggs. A Western omelet contains ham, onion, and tomato that is cooked separately and tucked inside a folded omelet. Here are Sam Arnold's recipes for both.

2 **tablespoons butter**	4 **eggs**
½ **medium ~~green~~ bell pepper,** *red* **chopped**	2 **tablespoons cream**
	¼ **teaspoon salt**
¼ **cup finely diced onion**	⅛ **teaspoon white pepper**

1. In a medium skillet, melt butter over medium-high heat. Add bell pepper and onion and cook until softened, about 3 minutes.

2. In a medium bowl, beat eggs, 2 tablespoons water, cream, salt, and pepper with a fork until blended. Pour into skillet. Let set a moment, then lift edges to let uncooked egg flow under.

3. When underside is cooked and center is scarcely runny, about 1½ minutes, fold omelet in half. Slide out of pan and serve.

103 SHERRIED SHRIMP AND SCALLOP ? OMELET

Prep: 5 minutes   Cook: 10 minutes   Serves: 4

5 **tablespoons butter**	2 **tablespoons dry sherry**
3 **tablespoons flour**	2 **scallions, chopped**
1 **cup warm milk**	¼ **pound peeled shrimp**
1 **tablespoon tomato paste**	¼ **pound scallops**
Pinch of grated nutmeg	8 **eggs**
¼ **teaspoon salt**	2 **tablespoons grated**
⅛ **teaspoon pepper**	**Parmesan cheese**

1. In a medium saucepan, melt 2 tablespoons of the butter over medium-high heat. Add flour and cook, stirring, 1 minute. Gradually whisk in milk, tomato paste, nutmeg, salt, pepper, and sherry. Bring to a boil, whisking until sauce is thick and smooth, 1 to 2 minutes. Remove from heat.

2. In a medium skillet, melt 1 tablespoon butter over high heat. Add scallions, shrimp, and scallops. Sauté until shrimp are bright pink and curled, 1 to 2 minutes. Add to sauce.

3. In a large bowl, whisk eggs until blended. In a large skillet, melt remaining 2 tablespoons butter over high heat. When butter foams, pour eggs into pan. Reduce heat to medium and cook, undisturbed, 1 minute, until edges are set. Continue to cook, lifting edges to let uncooked egg flow underneath, until omelet is nearly set but still moist in center, 2 to 3 minutes longer. Quickly spoon two thirds of seafood sauce down half of omelet.

4. Fold plain side over filling. Cook 30 seconds longer. Slide omelet onto a platter. Spoon remaining sauce over omelet. Sprinkle Parmesan on top. Serve immediately.

---

104   TOFU OMELET INDONESIAN STYLE
Prep: 5 minutes   Cook: 4 minutes   Serves: 2

This is a flat omelet covered with a sweet peanut sauce. It makes an intriguing brunch or light supper dish. I like to serve it with pickled vegetables and rice.

2 (10¼-ounce) cakes soft tofu (bean curd)	3½ tablespoons crunchy-style peanut butter
3 tablespoons soy sauce	4 eggs
1 teaspoon brown sugar	1 tablespoon vegetable oil

1. Cut tofu into ½-inch cubes. Drain in a colander while you pull rest of dish together.

2. In a small bowl, mix soy sauce, brown sugar, and peanut butter, stirring to make sure sugar dissolves. Set sauce aside.

3. In a medium bowl, lightly whip eggs with a fork. Gently stir in tofu.

4. In a medium skillet, heat oil over high heat. When hot, carefully pour in egg mixture. Reduce heat to medium-high. Cook, lifting sides as they begin to set to let uncooked egg flow underneath, until bottom is golden and center remains slightly runny, about 2 minutes.

5. To flip, cover skillet with a flat lid or heavy dinner plate, invert, then slide omelet back into skillet, cooked side up. Cook second side about 1 minute longer to brown lightly.

6. Slide onto serving dish. Top with peanut-soy sauce. Serve hot, cut into wedges.

105   SOFT JAPANESE CHIVE OMELET
Prep: 15 minutes   Cook: 8 minutes   Serves: 4

This egg dish is prepared so the egg has no choice but to emerge from cooking soft, juicy, and rich. Serve the omelet hot, by itself or over steamed rice. If you can find Chinese chives, also called garlic chives, by all means use them.

2 ounces dried shiitake
   mushrooms or 2 large
   fresh
2 to 3 tablespoons vegetable
   oil
1½ tablespoons minced chives
1 cup Japanese dashi or
   vegetable or chicken
   stock

1 tablespoon sugar
   Pinch of salt
1 tablespoon soy sauce
6 eggs

1. If using dried shiitakes, cover with warm water and soak until softened, about 10 minutes. Remove from liquid and squeeze out excess moisture. Cut off and discard stems from shiitakes. Thinly slice caps.

2. In a medium nonstick skillet, heat oil over high heat. Add chives. A moment later, add mushrooms. Immediately pour in dashi, sugar, salt, and soy sauce. Simmer 3 minutes.

3. In a medium bowl, whisk eggs just to blend. Pour eggs into hot stock in skillet. Cook over medium-low heat without stirring until just set, about 4 minutes. Eggs should be extremely soft. Spoon into bowls and serve at once.

106   JAPANESE ROLLED OMELET WITH EEL
Prep: none   Cook: 3 to 4 minutes   Makes: 6 pieces

Unagi is Japanese freshwater eel. Pieces are packed in cans like sardines. Each long piece can be used inside a rolled-up omelet. Lacking eel, use canned sardine or mackerel. Look for unagi near the canned tuna fish shelf. This omelet rolls best while still hot.

2 tablespoons Japanese dashi
   or vegetable broth
1 teaspoon soy sauce

2 eggs
1 tablespoon vegetable oil
1 can eel (unagi)

1. In a medium bowl, mix dashi and soy sauce. Add eggs and beat well with a fork.

2. In a medium nonstick skillet or omelet pan, heat oil over medium-high heat. Pour in egg mixture. Cook over medium heat until very firm, 3 to 4 minutes.

3. Slide omelet onto a work surface or cutting board. Place eel pieces in a line across lower third of omelet. Roll up away from you.

4. Cut roll into 1- to 1½-inch pieces. Set on a platter, spirals up. Serve warm or cold.

---

107   DAVID'S EGG FOO YUNG
Prep: 10 minutes   Cook: 4 minutes   Serves: 3

Egg Foo Yung is a firm Chinese omelet, served in a rich brown sauce. My husband David SooHoo is a master Chinese chef from a long line of Chinese-American restaurant owners. The secret to making the egg foo yung stand tall in the skillet is to whip the eggs just moments before adding them to the pan. David knows. In his parents' restaurant, certain scolding awaited anyone who broke the yolks before the pan was ready. Here is the SooHoo family's recipe. Serve the dish with rice, garnished with Chinese parsley, which is another name for cilantro, or chopped chives.

4 **eggs**
½ **cup diced Chinese barbecued pork or shrimp**
½ **cup chopped onion**
½ **cup frozen peas**
1 **cup bean sprouts, cut into ½-inch pieces**

¼ **teaspoon salt**
⅛ **teaspoon white pepper**
About 2 tablespoons vegetable oil
Egg Foo Yung Sauce (recipe follows)

1. Crack eggs into a large mixing bowl, but don't break yolks yet. Add pork or shrimp, onion, peas, sprouts, salt, and pepper.

2. Coat a large nonstick skillet with oil and heat over high heat. While skillet heats up, use a large spoon to break eggs. Mix eggs and vegetables thoroughly.

3. Ladle egg mixture into hot skillet, making 6 pancakes. Reduce heat to medium. Cook until pancakes brown on bottom, about 1 minute. Flip cakes over. Brown second side, about 2 minutes longer.

4. Transfer hot egg foo yung to a serving platter. Cover with Egg Foo Yung Sauce and serve.

EGG FOO YUNG SAUCE
Makes: ¾ cup

¾ **cup chicken stock**
⅛ **teaspoon salt**
2 **teaspoons oyster sauce**

⅛ **teaspoon sugar**
⅛ **teaspoon sesame oil**
2 **teaspoons cornstarch**

1. In a small saucepan, combine all ingredients. Stir until cornstarch is completely dissolved.

2. Bring to a boil over high heat. Reduce heat to a simmer and cook, stirring, until sauce is thick and smooth, about 1 minute.

108   PERSIAN HERB OMELET

Prep: 20 minutes   Cook: 45 to 50 minutes   Serves: 4 to 6

This baked omelet is an herbal delight. Instead of using a cake pan, you can bake this in a casserole or in a 10-inch nonstick skillet with ovenproof handle.

3 tablespoons butter, melted	2 teaspoons chopped chives
½ pound fresh spinach, trimmed	3 scallions, coarsely chopped
1 cup parsley sprigs, tough stems removed	1 tablespoon flour
	½ teaspoon salt
½ cup fresh cilantro	¼ teaspoon pepper
1 tablespoon chopped fresh dill or 1½ teaspoons dried	8 eggs
	Yogurt

1. Set rack in center of oven and preheat to 350°F. Coat bottom and sides of a 9-inch cake pan with melted butter.

2. Rinse and dry well spinach, parsley, cilantro, dill, chives, and scallions and place in a food processor. Process until nearly a paste. Transfer to a large mixing bowl. Stir in flour, salt, and pepper.

3. In another large bowl, whisk eggs until blended. Pour into greens and stir to mix. Scrape into buttered cake pan.

4. Immediately set pan in oven and bake 45 to 50 minutes, until omelet is browned on top and no longer moist in center. Serve hot or cold directly from baking dish or slide onto a platter. Top with plain yogurt.

109   POTATO-TURMERIC OMELET

Prep: 10 minutes   Cook: 40 minutes   Serves: 4 to 5

To quicken the pace of mincing such a large amount of onion, use the fine-grating disk of a food processor. Even if you overprocess, the omelet will look and taste fine. Serve cut into wedges with pita bread and dollops of plain yogurt.

2 large baking potatoes, peeled and cut into ½-inch dice	1 teaspoon turmeric
	½ teaspoon salt
	¼ teaspoon pepper
1 large onion, finely minced or grated	3 tablespoons butter
	6 eggs

1. Place potatoes in a medium saucepan and cover by 1 inch with salted cold water. Set on high heat and bring to a boil. Cover, reduce heat to medium, and cook until knife glides easily into potatoes, 12 to 14 minutes. Drain.

2. In a large bowl, toss cooked potatoes with onion. Mix in turmeric, salt, and pepper. Let cool completely.

3. Set rack in center of oven and preheat to 350°F. Place butter in a 9-inch round cake pan and set in oven to melt. Coat bottom and sides of pan with melted butter. Return to oven until butter is very hot, at least 2 minutes.

4. In a medium bowl, whisk eggs until blended. Slowly stir eggs into potato-onion mixture, then immediately pour into buttered pan.

5. Bake 25 minutes, or until omelet is puffed and browned on top and center is firm. Serve hot or cold directly from pan, or flip onto a serving platter.

110 STRAWBERRY–SOUR CREAM OMELET

Prep: 10 minutes   Cook: 7 minutes   Serves: 3

1 pint strawberries
2 tablespoons sugar
4 eggs
2 tablespoons milk *(cream)*

Pinch of salt
2 tablespoons butter
¾ cup sour cream
2 tablespoons brown sugar

1. Wash and hull strawberries. Set aside the 8 prettiest ones for garnish and slice the rest.

2. Preheat broiler. In a medium bowl, combine sliced strawberries and sugar. In another bowl, beat eggs, milk, and salt with a fork until blended.

3. In an 8-inch nonstick skillet with ovenproof handle, melt butter over high heat. When hot and foamy, pour in eggs. Reduce heat to medium. Cook, lifting edges all around pan and tilting a little to let uncooked egg flow under until omelet is nearly set but still moist in center, about 4 minutes.

4. Transfer to broiler and broil until top is set, about 1 minute. Remove from broiler and slide out of pan onto an ovenproof serving plate.

5. Spread sweetened berry slices over omelet. Mix sour cream and brown sugar. Spread over berries. Return omelet to broiler to set cream, about 2 minutes. Garnish with whole strawberries and serve.

111   PINEAPPLE-RUM OMELET ?

Prep: 10 minutes   Cook: 5 minutes   Serves: 3

1 cup diced canned
    pineapple, drained
¼ cup apricot or peach jam
6 eggs

¼ cup plus 1 tablespoon sugar
2 tablespoons butter
½ cup light rum

1. In a small bowl, mix pineapple and jam. In a medium bowl, whisk eggs and 1 tablespoon sugar until blended but not frothy.

2. In a large heavy skillet, melt butter over medium-high heat until foamy. Pour in eggs and cook, lifting sides as they begin to set to let egg flow underneath, until omelet is barely set in center, 2 to 3 minutes.

3. Spoon pineapple-jam mixture down omelet off center. Fold plain half over pineapple. Sprinkle top with remaining ¼ cup sugar.

4. Increase heat to high. Pour in rum and carefully ignite with a match. Immediately bring to table while still alight. As soon as flames subside, cut into wedges and serve.

Chapter 4

Fabulous Frittatas

The first time I saw a frittata was the first time I
made one. I was cooking on a yacht sailing to Turkey from a
port in Greece, with passengers from Italy. One of the Italian
women asked if I would make a frittata for an afternoon snack.
She described the process, I followed her orders and in no
time produced a tantalizing sausage and pepper frittata.

The first thing you'll notice about a frittata is that
it's usually bigger than an omelet, but easier—a cheater's
omelet. It's like an egg-based pizza that's home to most any
leftover. And if you brown the top in the oven or broiler,
there's no flipping or folding.

Frittatas (actually *frittate* is the Italian plural) may
be soft and silky or lightly browned and crisped. There are
several ways to make them.

You start by pouring beaten eggs, sometimes
strengthened with bread crumbs, into a skillet of ingredients
sautéed in olive oil or butter. You can use onion, garlic,
tomato, artichoke hearts, green pepper, zucchini, bacon,
mushrooms—you name it. The eggs set on the bottom. Then
sometimes you flip the frittata to cook the other side. More
often you run the pan under the broiler just until the egg on
top is set and puffed and cheese, if used, is melted. If doing
this, you need to use a skillet with an ovenproof handle.
Another way to finish the frittata is to cover the skillet and
steam the frittata done. This produces a silky frittata.

The final texture depends in large part on the filling. Ricotta frittatas are very delicate while the Frittata with
Zucchini-Tomato Sauce is chunky with vegetables. Baked frittatas, often made with generous amounts of cheese, are rich
and custardy.

Eat frittatas hot, at room temperature, or cold.
They are good for short-notice get-togethers, or as my Italian
guests wanted it, a snack any time of day.

112 FRITTATA WITH ZUCCHINI-TOMATO SAUCE

Prep: 20 minutes   Cook: 9 to 11 minutes   Serves: 4 to 6

Crunchy pieces of zucchini in a hearty tomato sauce transform the plain frittata beneath. You'll have greater ease getting this frittata from skillet to plate if your skillet is nonstick.

6 eggs
2 tablespoons Italian-
    seasoned bread crumbs
¼ teaspoon salt

¼ teaspoon pepper
3 tablespoons olive oil
  Zucchini-Tomato Sauce
    (recipe follows)

1. In a medium bowl, whisk eggs, bread crumbs, salt, and pepper until well mixed.

2. In a 10-inch skillet, heat olive oil over high heat until very hot. Pour eggs into skillet. Immediately reduce heat to medium-low. Cook, lifting edges as they firm up to let uncooked egg flow under, until bottom is well set (lift with a spatula to check) but center is ever-so-slightly runny, 8 to 10 minutes.

3. Slide frittata out of skillet onto a plate. Invert back into skillet. Cook second side just long enough to set it, about 1 minute. Slide frittata back onto plate. Top with Zucchini-Tomato Sauce, cut into wedges, and serve.

113 ZUCCHINI-TOMATO SAUCE

Prep: 15 minutes   Cook: 7 minutes   Makes: about 2 cups

This zesty herbed fresh tomato sauce is great over eggs, but it makes a fine pasta sauce as well.

1 tablespoon olive oil
1 medium onion, finely
    chopped
2 teaspoons dried oregano
1½ teaspoons dried basil

1 zucchini, quartered
    lengthwise and sliced
2 ripe tomatoes, seeded and
    chopped
  Dash of salt

1. In a large skillet, heat olive oil over medium heat. Add onion, oregano, and basil. Cook until onion just begins to turn translucent, about 2 minutes.

2. Add zucchini, tomatoes, and salt. Continue to cook over medium heat until zucchini is tender and tomatoes form a slightly thickened sauce, about 5 minutes.

114 ARTICHOKE AND MUSHROOM FRITTATA
Prep: 15 minutes   Cook: 23 to 28 minutes   Serves: 4 to 6

With the exception of imported *bufala* mozzarella cheese, easy-to-find ingredients make this frittata an attractive option. Buffalo milk makes a very flavorful cheese, but if you can't find it use fresh mozzarella or packaged skim-milk mozzarella. Even Jack or Cheddar cheese will be fine, though lacking the when-in-Rome quality.

2 strips of bacon
6 to 8 fresh mushrooms, thinly sliced
3 tablespoons olive oil
½ large onion, finely chopped
6 brine-packed artichoke hearts, halved
½ red bell pepper, cut into strips

4 eggs
1 tablespoon Italian-seasoned bread crumbs
¼ teaspoon salt
¼ teaspoon pepper
6 ounces fresh mozzarella cheese, cut into 6 slices
2 teaspoons chopped parsley

1. In a small skillet, fry bacon over medium heat until crisp, 6 to 8 minutes. Or place bacon on a triple thickness of paper towels, cover with another paper towel, and microwave on High 1½ to 2 minutes. Let stand 3 minutes to make it crispy. Set aside.

2. In a small skillet, saufe mushrooms in 1 tablespoon olive oil over medium-high heat until barely softened, about 2 minutes. Set aside.

3. In a medium skillet with ovenproof handle, heat remaining 2 tablespoons oil over medium heat until very hot. Add onion, artichoke hearts, and pepper strips. Fry mixture so sides of artichokes lie flat and can brown. Brown vegetables well, about 7 minutes. Stir in cooked mushrooms.

4. Preheat broiler. In a medium bowl, whisk eggs, bread crumbs, salt, and pepper. Pour over vegetable mixture and cook until bottom sets and top is slightly runny, 8 to 10 minutes. Top frittata with crumbled bacon. Arrange cheese like spokes. Run frittata under broiler 50 seconds to 1 minute.

5. Slide out of pan onto serving dish. Sprinkle with parsley. Serve hot or cold, cut in wedges.

115 ASPARAGUS-ARTICHOKE FRITTATA

Prep: 10 minutes   Cook: 15 minutes   Serves: 4 to 6

½ **pound fresh asparagus,
   ends trimmed, then cut
   into 1-inch pieces**
1 **(7-ounce) jar marinated
   artichoke hearts**
2 **tablespoons diced pimiento**
8 **eggs**

¼ **cup milk**
½ **teaspoon salt**
¼ **teaspoon pepper**
¾ **cup shredded Gruyère or
   Swiss cheese**
1 **tablespoon butter**
2 **tablespoons olive oil**

1. In a medium saucepan of boiling salted water, cook asparagus until very bright but still crunchy, about 1 minute. Drain in a colander and rinse under cold running water. Drain well. Transfer to a small bowl.

2. Drain off most of marinade from artichoke hearts. Add artichokes and pimiento to asparagus.

3. In a large bowl, whisk eggs, milk, salt, and pepper until blended. Stir in cheese and asparagus-artichoke mixture.

4. Preheat broiler. In a large skillet with ovenpoof handle, melt butter in olive oil over medium-high heat. When foamy, pour in eggs. Reduce heat to medium and cook, lifting edges as they firm up to let uncooked egg flow under, until underside is light brown (lift with a spatula to check) but center is ever-so-slightly runny, about 12 minutes. Shake pan now and then, to make sure frittata is loose.

5. Transfer to broiler for 2 minutes, but check after 1 minute. Top should be light brown. Serve hot or cold, cut into wedges.

116 BROCCOLI AND DRIED TOMATO FRITTATA WITH JACK CHEESE

Prep: 5 minutes   Cook: 25 to 30 minutes   Serves: 6 to 8

 8 **to 10 dried tomatoes**
10 **eggs**
½ **cup chopped fresh cilantro**
1½ **cups chopped cooked
    broccoli**

¼ **teaspoon salt**
¼ **teaspoon pepper**
2 **tablespoons olive oil**
¾ **cup shredded Monterey
   Jack cheese (3 ounces)**

1. In a small bowl, soak tomatoes in very hot tap water to soften and plump them, at least 5 or up to 15 minutes.

2. Preheat oven to 350°F. In a large bowl, whisk eggs until blended. Drain and slice tomatoes thinly. Stir into eggs. Add cilantro, broccoli, salt, and pepper.

3. In a large nonstick skillet with ovenproof handle, heat oil over high heat. When hot, pour in egg mixture. Immediately reduce heat to medium. Cook about 5 minutes, until edges are set. Sprinkle cheese on top.

4. Immediately transfer to oven. Bake 20 to 25 minutes, until frittata is completely set and top is brown. Invert onto a dinner plate. Flip again onto a serving platter. Serve hot or cold, cut into wedges.

---

117 DINNER FRITTATA WITH SPAGHETTI AND SWISS CHARD

Prep: 15 minutes   Cook: 20 to 23 minutes   Serves: 4

1 **pound Swiss chard leaves,** washed, stems removed	2 **tablespoons chopped** parsley
6 **eggs**	2 **scallions, chopped**
2 **tablespoons milk**	2 **tablespoons olive oil**
½ **teaspoon salt**	1 **tablespoon minced garlic**
¼ **teaspoon pepper**	2 **cups cooked spaghetti or** other pasta
½ **cup grated Parmesan cheese**	

1. Toss chard (still wet from washing) in a very hot Dutch oven or wok over high heat. When three-fourths wilted (this may take less than 1 minute), pour into a colander and press out excess water.

2. Crack eggs into a medium bowl. Add milk, salt, pepper, cheese, and parsley, but don't whisk yet.

3. In a large nonstick skillet, cook scallions in olive oil over medium-high heat 1 minute. Increase heat to high; add chard and cook, stirring quickly, 30 seconds. Add garlic and spaghetti and cook, tossing, 1 minute. Remove pan from burner.

4. Quickly whisk eggs until just blended and pour over noodle-chard mixture. Return skillet to burner, cover, and reduce heat to low. Cook 12 to 15 minutes, until bottom is lightly browned.

5. Remove cover. Invert frittata onto a plate and slide back into skillet. Cook until second side is browned, about 5 minutes longer. Ease frittata onto a serving plate. Let cool 5 minutes before cutting into wedges. Serve hot, at room temperature, or cold.

118 GREEN BEAN, SMOKED CHICKEN, GARLIC, AND PARMESAN FRITTATA

Prep: 10 minutes   Cook: 9 to 10 minutes   Serves: 4

I got the idea for this when I saw a leftover chicken breast in the refrigerator after a weekend of zealous grilling with mesquite-flavored charcoal. A trip to a farmers' market produced dainty green beans. If you find such *haricots verts*, use them, otherwise use the thinnest, freshest beans the market offers.

4 ounces green beans, as thin
   as possible
6 eggs
2 tablespoons milk
¼ teaspoon salt
¼ teaspoon pepper

3 tablespoons olive oil
3 garlic cloves, minced
4 ounces smoked chicken, cut
   into thin strips
2 to 3 tablespoons grated
   Parmesan cheese

1. Break ends off beans. If beans are thick, cut into 1-inch lengths; if thin, leave whole.

2. Preheat broiler. Combine eggs, milk, salt, and pepper in a mixing bowl, but don't whisk yet.

3. In a medium nonstick skillet with ovenproof handle, heat olive oil over high heat. Add beans and cook, tossing, 2 minutes. Add garlic and chicken. Cook, tossing, until beans are crisp-tender and chicken is heated through, about 1 minute.

4. Whisk eggs just until blended. Pour into skillet over beans and chicken. Immediately reduce heat to medium. Cook, lifting edges as they firm up to let uncooked egg flow under, until center remains slightly runny but bottom is set (lift with a spatula to check), about 5 minutes.

5. Sprinkle Parmesan cheese over frittata and quickly set under broiler for 1 to 2 minutes, until frittata puffs up. Slide onto a serving platter. Serve hot or cold cut into wedges.

119 CARAMELIZED ONION FRITTATA WITH TURKEY SAUSAGE

*Prep: 5 minutes   Cook: 1 hour 10 minutes to 1 hour 20 minutes
Serves: 8 to 10*

¾ pound turkey sausage
10 eggs
1 teaspoon dried thyme
½ teaspoon salt
¼ teaspoon pepper

Caramelized Onions (recipe
   follows)
2 tablespoons olive oil
½ cup shredded Italian fontina
   or Gouda cheese

1. Preheat oven to 325°F. If turkey sausage is in links, remove from casings and crumble. In a medium skillet, brown sausage over medium heat until no pink remains, about 5 minutes. Drain off any accumulated fat.

2. In a large bowl, whisk eggs, thyme, salt, and pepper until blended. Add sausage and onions, mixing gently.

3. In a large skillet with ovenproof handle, heat olive oil over high heat. When very hot, add eggs. Immediately reduce heat to medium-low. Sprinkle cheese over eggs and cook until edges are set but middle has scarcely begun to cook, about 5 minutes.

4. Transfer skillet to oven and bake 20 minutes, until frittata is set and puffy. If a browner top is desired, run under broiler 1 minute. Invert or slide frittata onto serving dish. Serve hot or cold, cut into wedges.

CARAMELIZED ONIONS
Makes: about 1 cup

3 large onions, thinly sliced   3 garlic cloves, minced

1. In a large nonstick skillet, cook onions over low heat, stirring occasionally, 10 minutes, or until juices start to flow.

2. Add garlic and continue to cook over as low a heat as possible, 30 to 40 minutes longer, stirring now and then, until onions are caramelized to a rich brown. If you see them sticking, add a little water.

120 RICOTTA FRITTATA
Prep: 5 minutes   Cook: 7 to 10 minutes   Serves: 4

The rhythm and rhyme of "ricotta frittata," I confess, was the original inspiration for this egg-cheese combination. Of course, in Italian, ree-COE-tah does not rhyme with free-TAH-tah. For anyone who likes silken eggs, this delicate and smooth dish is just about perfect.

1 cup ricotta cheese   ¼ teaspoon pepper
8 eggs   3 tablespoons butter
3 tablespoons milk (creamy)   2 to 3 tablespoons grated
½ teaspoon salt   Parmesan cheese

1. Preheat broiler. Empty ricotta into a strainer set over a bowl to drain while you pull rest of frittata together.

2. In a medium bowl, whisk eggs, milk, salt, and pepper until blended.

3. In a large nonstick skillet with ovenproof handle, melt butter over high heat. When bubbly, pour in eggs. Wait 5 seconds, then reduce heat to medium-low. Cook, lifting edges as they firm up to let uncooked egg flow under, until center remains slightly runny but bottom is well set (lift with a spatula to check), 6 to 8 minutes.

4. Spread ricotta evenly over surface of eggs. Sprinkle Parmesan cheese on top. Quickly transfer skillet to broiler and broil 1 to 2 minutes, or until frittata puffs and middle is lightly set. Slide onto a serving platter. Serve hot or cold, cut into wedges.

121 THREE-PEPPER FRITTATA

Prep: 10 minutes   Cook: 40 to 45 minutes   *Serves: 6 to 8*

Cindy Indorf didn't know how much she enjoyed cooking eggs until she helped me out as a recipe tester for this book. This is her creation.

2 green bell peppers
1 yellow bell pepper
2 red bell pepper
1 small onion, chopped
2 tablespoons olive oil
10 eggs
1 tablespoon roasted garlic, mashed (page 170)

¼ cup shredded basil leaves
⅓ cup grated Parmesan cheese
¼ teaspoon salt
½ teaspoon freshly ground pepper
1 cup grated mozzarella cheese *Gruyère or Jack*

1. Broil whole bell peppers on a baking sheet as close to heat as possible, turning with tongs, until black and blistered all over, 10 to 15 minutes. As peppers blacken, drop into a bag. Steam peppers inside bag until cool to touch. Peel off charred skin, cut open, and discard stems and seeds. Cut roasted peppers into strips.

2. Preheat oven to 325°F. In a large skillet with ovenproof handle, cook onion in 1 tablespoon oil over medium heat until soft, about 4 minutes. In a medium bowl, whisk eggs until blended. Add pepper strips, garlic, basil, Parmesan cheese, salt, and pepper. Scrape cooked onion from skillet into eggs. Mix well.

3. Wipe out skillet and return to high heat with remaining 1 tablespoon oil. When oil is hot, pour in egg mixture. Immediately reduce heat to low. Sprinkle mozzarella cheese over eggs. Cook just until edges set, about 5 minutes.

4. Transfer skillet to oven and bake about 20 minutes, until top is completely set and lightly browned. Loosen edges. Place dinner plate over frittata and invert to unmold. Place serving plate on top. Flip again to turn out frittata or serve directly from skillet.

122 RICOTTA FRITTATA WITH TARRAGON AND PEAS

Prep: 12 minutes   Cook: 10 to 13 minutes   *Serves: 4*

1 cup ricotta cheese
8 eggs
3 tablespoons milk
½ teaspoon salt
¼ teaspoon pepper
2 teaspoons chopped parsley

½ teaspoon dried tarragon
3 tablespoons butter
1 cup frozen peas
2 to 3 tablespoons grated Parmesan cheese

1. Preheat broiler. Empty ricotta into a strainer over a bowl to drain while you pull rest of frittata together.

2. In a medium bowl, combine eggs, milk, salt, and pepper, but don't whisk yet. Place ricotta in a small bowl. Mix in parsley and tarragon.

3. In a large nonstick skillet with ovenproof handle, melt butter over high heat. Add peas and cook, tossing, until bright green, about 1 minute.

4. Lightly whisk eggs just to blend. Pour over peas and immediately reduce heat to medium-low. Cook, lifting edges as they firm up to let uncooked egg flow under, until center remains slightly runny but bottom is well set (lift with a spatula to check), 8 to 10 minutes.

5. Cover frittata evenly with ricotta. Sprinkle Parmesan cheese on top. Transfer to broiler and broil 1 to 2 minutes, until frittata puffs up and middle is lightly set. Slide onto a serving platter. Serve hot or cold, cut into wedges.

---

123 LEEK, POTATO, AND RED PEPPER FRITTATA

Prep: 10 minutes   Cook: 24 to 30 minutes   Serves: 6 to 8

3 leeks, white parts only	4 tablespoons butter
1 red bell pepper, roasted, or	8 eggs
½ cup jarred roasted peppers	⅓ cup plain yogurt or sour cream
1 large baking potato, peeled and cut into ½-inch dice	½ teaspoon salt
	¼ teaspoon pepper

1. Hold cut leeks upright under running water to rinse out sand. Slice into thin rounds. Cut roasted pepper into strips.

2. In a large nonstick skillet with ovenproof handle, cook potato in 2 tablespoons butter over high heat, stirring, 2 minutes. Add leeks; reduce heat to low. Cover and cook 12 to 15 minutes, until potato can easily be pierced with a knife.

3. Preheat broiler. In a large bowl, whisk eggs, yogurt, salt, and pepper until blended.

4. Stir red pepper strips into potato. Add remaining 2 tablespoons butter and raise heat to high, stirring. When sizzling, pour eggs over vegetable mixture.

5. Immediately reduce heat to medium-low. Cook, lifting edges as they firm up to let uncooked egg flow under, until center remains slightly runny but bottom is well set (lift with a spatula to check), 8 to 10 minutes.

6. Transfer skillet to broiler for 1 to 2 minutes, until edges puff and frittata is golden, with middle lightly set. Flip onto a serving platter. Serve hot or cold, cut into wedges.

124 SPANISH POTATO OMELET

Prep: 10 minutes   Cook: 18 to 24 minutes   Serves: 2 to 3

Here's a confusing nomenclature. In English, this Castilian egg classic is called an omelet. In Spanish, it is a *tortilla de patata*, yet in reality, the dish is, in fact, a frittata, which is why I have placed it in this chapter. The traditional tortilla, given here, is made with potato and onion, though, of course, Spanish tortillas are good with cured meats and other vegetables, especially red bell pepper.

3 tablespoons olive oil	5 eggs
1 large baking potato, peeled and sliced paper thin	½ teaspoon salt
1 medium onion, chopped	¼ teaspoon pepper
2 garlic cloves, minced	2 teaspoons chopped parsley

1. In a heavy 10-inch skillet, heat 2 tablespoons olive oil over medium-high heat. Add potatoes, onion, and garlic. Stir briefly to coat with oil. Cover, reduce heat to medium-low, and cook, stirring occasionally, until potatoes are tender, 15 to 20 minutes. Pour into a strainer to remove any excess oil.

2. In a large bowl, beat eggs, salt, pepper, and parsley with a fork until blended. Stir in drained potato-onion mixture. Return skillet to medium-high heat and add remaining 1 tablespoon olive oil. When oil is hot, pour eggs into skillet. Reduce heat to medium. As edges begin to set, push sides toward center, so uncooked egg can flow to edge. When nearly set but still moist on top, about 2 minutes, turn over by covering skillet with a flat lid or heavy dinner plate, invert, then slide tortilla back into skillet, cooked side up.

3. Cook 1 to 2 minutes longer to lightly brown bottom. Slide onto a serving plate. Serve hot or cold, cut into wedges.

125 PLUM TOMATO–BASIL FRITTATA WITH CREAM CHEESE

Prep: 10 minutes   Cook: 23 minutes   Serves: 6 to 8

This frittata cooks like a steamed custard, rising and expanding, then flips out of the skillet like a cake. The secret is to keep the heat very, very low so the frittata cooks slowly.

¾ cup (packed) fresh basil leaves	3 tablespoons butter
12 eggs	4 to 5 plum tomatoes, sliced into rounds
½ teaspoon salt	1 (8-ounce) package cream cheese, cubed
½ teaspoon pepper	

1. Stack basil leaves in batches, roll each stack cigarette-style, and slice across finely into thin ribbons.

2. In a large bowl, whisk eggs, ¼ cup water, salt, and pepper with a fork until frothy, or just until combined with an electric hand mixer.

3. In a large nonstick skillet, melt butter over high heat. When bubbly, add tomatoes and cook until juices begin to dry up, 1 to 2 minutes. Reduce heat to medium. Sprinkle basil on top and cook about 1 minute longer.

4. Pour in eggs. Top with cream cheese.

5. Immediately cover skillet, reduce heat to very low, and cook about 20 minutes, or until sides are completely set but top remains slightly jiggly.

6. Invert onto serving plate. Let stand 5 to 10 minutes to firm up. This frittata is good warm and delicious cold. Cut into wedges to serve.

---

126 TOMATO-POTATO FRITTATA WITH BASIL AND PARMESAN CHEESE
Prep: 15 minutes   Cook: 22 to 27 minutes   Serves: 4

1 **medium baking potato,**	8 **eggs**
peeled and cut into	2 **tablespoons milk**
½-inch dice	½ **teaspoon salt**
8 **thick slices ripe summer**	¼ **teaspoon pepper**
tomatoes (about 2 large)	¾ **cup grated Parmesan cheese**
2 **tablespoons butter**	2 **tablespoons chopped fresh**
1 **tablespoon olive oil**	**basil**
1 **large onion, thinly sliced**	

1. Cook potato in a large saucepan of boiling salted water until tender, 10 to 12 minutes; drain. Or microwave potato in a 1-quart bowl with 1 cup salted water, covered tightly with a plate or microwave-safe plastic wrap, on High 8 minutes. Remove covering, stir, drain, and let cool.

2. Meanwhile, arrange tomato slices on a large plate.

3. In a large nonstick skillet with ovenproof handle, melt butter and oil over high heat. When bubbly-hot, add onion. Reduce heat to medium and cook until onion is lightly browned, about 5 minutes.

4. Preheat broiler. Whisk eggs, milk, salt, pepper, and ¼ cup of the Parmesan cheese until blended. Add potato to skillet, tossing with onion. Pour eggs into skillet. Immediately reduce heat to medium-low. Cook, lifting edges as they firm up to let uncooked egg flow under, until center remains slightly runny but bottom is set well (lift with a spatula to check), about 6 to 8 minutes. Sprinkle with remaining Parmesan.

5. Transfer skillet to broiler for 1 to 2 minutes, until frittata puffs and middle is lightly set. Slide out of pan onto a serving platter. Sprinkle basil over top. Serve hot or at room temperature, cut into wedges.

127   HERBED FRITTATA WITH DRIED TOMATOES AND BLUE CHEESE

Prep: 10 minutes   Cook: 8 to 11 minutes   Serves: 4 to 6

¼ cup dried tomatoes
6 eggs
2 tablespoons milk *(cream)*
¼ teaspoon salt
¼ teaspoon pepper
2 tablespoons butter

3 ounces blue cheese, such as Saga, Roquefort, Oregon blue, or Maytag blue, crumbled
1 tablespoon chopped fresh basil or parsley

1. In a medium bowl, soak tomatoes in very hot tap water to cover, at least 5 minutes or up to 15 minutes, until plump. Drain and cut into fat, lengthwise strips.

2. Preheat broiler. In a medium bowl, whisk eggs, milk, salt, and pepper until blended.

3. Melt butter in a 10-inch skillet with an ovenproof handle over high heat. When butter foams, pour in eggs. Immediately reduce heat to medium. As edges of eggs begin to set, after about 1 minute, lift edges to let uncooked eggs flow under. Continue to cook until firm but still moist, 6 to 8 minutes.

4. Sprinkle tomato strips, crumbled blue cheese, and chopped basil all over frittata. Transfer to broiler and broil 1 to 2 minutes, until frittata is puffed and cheese is barely melted. Serve hot or cold, cut into wedges.

128   SUN-DRIED TOMATO AND BASIL FRITTATA WITH GOAT CHEESE

Prep: 10 minutes   Cook: 22 minutes   Serves: 4 to 6

OK, so dried tomatoes and goat cheese are a California cliché. Know why? Because they're truly delicious together.

5 or 6 dried tomatoes (see Note)
½ cup (packed) fresh basil leaves
6 eggs
¼ teaspoon salt
¼ teaspoon pepper

2 scallions, sliced, white parts and most of the green
2 tablespoons olive oil
4 ounces fresh white goat cheese (chèvre), crumbled

1. In a medium bowl, soak tomatoes in very hot tap water to cover to soften and plump them, at least 5 minutes or up to 15 minutes. Drain and thinly slice tomatoes.

2. Stack basil leaves in batches, roll the stacks cigarette-style, and slice across into thin ribbons.

3. In a large bowl, whisk eggs, 3 tablespoons water, salt, and pepper until frothy. Stir in scallions.

4. In a nonstick 10-inch skillet, heat olive oil over high heat. Add dried tomatoes. Cook 1 minute. Reduce heat to medium. Add basil and cook 1 minute longer, until heated but still bright in color.

5. Pour eggs into skillet. Cook until edges set slightly, about 1 minute. Top with goat cheese. Cover, reduce heat to very low, and cook about 20 minutes, or until center of frittata is set but still moist.

6. Turn out frittata onto a dinner plate, then invert to a second plate, cheese side up. Serve hot or at room temperature, cut into wedges.

NOTE: *Oil-packed dried tomatoes may also be used. Drain them briefly before using. Use 1 tablespoon of the tomatoes' oil in place of 1 tablespoon of olive oil called for in the recipe.*

---

129 ZUCCHINI AND TOMATO FRITTATA
Prep: 10 minutes   Cook: 12 to 16 minutes   Serves: 4 to 6

6 **eggs**	3 **tablespoons bread crumbs**
3 **tablespoons milk**	½ **teaspoon dried oregano**
¼ **teaspoon salt**	1 **medium-large tomato, cut**
¼ **teaspoon pepper**	**into 5 slices or 2 or 3 plum**
2 **medium zucchini**	**tomatoes, thickly sliced**
2 **tablespoons olive oil**	2 **to 3 tablespoons grated**
2 **garlic cloves, minced**	**Parmesan cheese**

1. In a large bowl, combine eggs, milk, salt, and pepper, but don't whisk yet. Quarter zucchini lengthwise, then cut crosswise into ¼-inch-thick wedges.

2. Preheat broiler. In a nonstick 10-inch skillet with an ovenproof handle, heat olive oil over high heat. Add zucchini and cook 1 minute. Add garlic, reduce heat to medium, and cook 1 to 2 minutes longer, until zucchini is softened. Toss with bread crumbs and oregano.

3. Whisk eggs just until blended and pour over zucchini. Immediately reduce heat to medium-low. Cook, lifting edges as they firm up to let uncooked egg flow under, until bottom is well set (lift with a spatula to check), but center is slightly runny, 8 to 10 minutes.

4. Top with tomatoes, 1 in center and 4 around, overlapping if necessary. Or cover at random with smaller tomato slices. Sprinkle Parmesan cheese on top.

5. Run under broiler 2 to 3 minutes, until frittata is lightly browned and puffed. Slide onto a serving platter. Or turn over onto a plate, then invert again onto a serving plate, tomato side up. Serve hot or cold, cut into wedges.

130   SICILIAN UNCLE'S OVEN FRITTATA
Prep: 10 minutes   Cook: 28 to 38 minutes   Serves: 6

Not everyone has a Sicilian uncle, but my friend Kathleen Abraham does. His unique frittata, which is stirred while in the oven, is the family's died-and-gone-to-heaven dish.

1   pound Italian sausage
    (about 4 links), mild or
    medium-hot
4   scallions, sliced
½   pound fresh asparagus, cut
    into 1-inch diagonal
    pieces

¾   pound mozzarella cheese,
    shredded
6   eggs

1. Preheat oven to 350°F. Remove sausage from casings. In a 10-inch cast-iron skillet with ovenproof handle, cook sausage over medium heat, stirring to break up lumps, until meat is well done, 8 to 10 minutes. With a slotted spoon, transfer sausage to a bowl. Drain off all but 1 tablespoon fat.

2. In same skillet, cook scallions and asparagus in remaining fat over medium-high heat, stirring frequently, until asparagus is lightly browned, 3 to 5 minutes.

3. Scatter sausage over vegetables. Sprinkle cheese over sausage. Whisk eggs lightly, just enough to break yolks. Pour over ingredients in skillet. Transfer skillet to oven.

4. Bake 15 to 20 minutes, stirring several times during first 5 minutes to mix sides toward center, until frittata is set around edges but still moist in center. During last 5 minutes, preheat broiler. Brown top under broiler, 2 to 3 minutes. Serve hot, warm, or cold, cut into wedges.

131   COMPANY FRITTATA SQUARES
Prep: 15 minutes   Cook: 30 minutes   Makes: 24 (2-inch) squares

This is not a true frittata, but the effect is similar. Because it keeps well, it is marvelous for entertaining. The recipe can be doubled.

4   tablespoons butter
2   medium onions, chopped
3   (7-ounce) jars marinated
    artichoke hearts, drained
12   soda crackers, crumbled
8   to 10 drops of Tabasco or
    other hot pepper sauce

1½   cups shredded Swiss cheese
1½   cups shredded Cheddar
    cheese
12   eggs
¼   teaspoon salt
¼   teaspoon pepper

1. Set rack in center of oven and preheat to 350°F. Butter a 9 x 13-inch glass baking dish.

2. In a large skillet, melt butter over medium-high heat. Add onions. Cook, stirring occasionally, until tender, about 5 minutes.

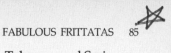

3. In a medium bowl, mix artichoke hearts, crackers, Tabasco, and Swiss and Cheddar cheeses. Stir in onions.

4. In a large bowl, whisk eggs, salt, and pepper until blended. Pour over artichoke mixture in bowl and stir gently to mix. Pour entire mixture into buttered baking dish.

5. Bake 25 minutes, until lightly browned on top. Remove to a rack and let cool 10 minutes before cutting into squares. Serve hot, at room temperature, or cold.

---

132 BAKED VEGETABLE FRITTATA WITH WINE AND HERBS

Prep: 20 minutes   Cook: 40 to 45 minutes   Serves: 6

5 tablespoons olive oil
1 onion, chopped
3 garlic cloves, minced
¼ cup dry white wine
1 red bell pepper, chopped
2 celery ribs, chopped
½ pound fresh mushrooms, sliced
1 zucchini, quartered lengthwise and sliced
1 medium tomato, seeded and chopped

1 tablespoon chopped fresh thyme, basil, oregano, parsley, and/or chives
½ teaspoon salt
¼ teaspoon pepper
6 eggs
3 tablespoons milk *(cream)*
1 cup shredded mozzarella or provolone cheese

1. Set rack in center of oven and preheat to 350°F. Butter a 9 x 13-inch glass baking dish.

2. In a medium skillet, heat 3 tablespoons of the olive oil over medium-high heat. Add onion and cook, stirring occasionally, until softened, about 3 minutes. Add garlic and stir a moment. Pour in wine and boil over high heat until evaporated to about 1 tablespoon, about 2 minutes. Transfer to a large mixing bowl. Wipe out skillet.

3. In same skillet, heat remaining 2 tablespoons oil over medium-high heat. Add bell pepper and celery and cook, stirring, until softened, about 3 minutes. Add mushrooms and zucchini and cook 3 minutes longer. Add tomato and herbs. Cook until mixture is dry, about 4 minutes. Season with half of salt and pepper.

4. Add vegetables to onion and mix well. Spread vegetables in buttered baking dish. In a medium bowl, whisk eggs, milk, and remaining salt and pepper until blended. Pour evenly over vegetables.

5. Bake 15 minutes. Remove from oven and sprinkle cheese over top. Return to oven. Bake 10 to 15 minutes, until frittata is almost set but jiggly in center. Let cool 5 minutes on a wire rack before cutting into squares.

133 EAST SACRAMENTO FRITTATA RUSTICA
Prep: 20 minutes   Cook: 31 to 43 minutes   Serves: 8

Chef Steve Campanelli of the restaurant Andiamo! in Sacramento won a prize for this recipe. Long before the prize, this frittata was so popular it hit the papers and was snipped out and magnetized to thousands of refrigerators citywide.

6 eggs
2 cups small or large curd
   cottage cheese
½ cup plus 2 tablespoons
   grated Asiago, Parmesan,
   or Romano cheese
2 to 3 tablespoons minced
   fresh basil
¼ teaspoon salt
⅛ to ¼ teaspoon cayenne
   Pinch of black pepper
2 cups cooked pasta, such as
   penne, spaghetti, or
   linguine

5 tablespoons olive oil
2 cups sliced fresh
   mushrooms (about
   10 ounces)
1 small onion, chopped
½ red bell pepper, diced
1 garlic clove, minced
6 ounces thinly sliced
   prosciutto, cut into thin
   strips, or bacon
1 cup shredded fresh spinach
1 tablespoon chopped parsley

1. Preheat oven to 400°F. In a large bowl, whisk together eggs, cottage cheese, ½ cup of Asiago, basil, salt, cayenne, and black pepper. Add pasta and toss to mix.

2. In a large nonstick skillet with ovenproof handle, heat 3 tablespoons of olive oil over high heat. When hot, add mushrooms, onion, bell pepper, garlic, and prosciutto. Cook, stirring often, until mushrooms give up their liquid and it evaporates, 7 to 8 minutes.

3. Add spinach and continue to cook until spinach wilts, about 1 minute longer. Add cooked vegetables to egg mixture. Stir gently to combine. Wipe out skillet.

4. Coat same skillet with remaining 2 tablespoons olive oil and set over medium heat. When hot, add egg mixture. Let cook without stirring, shaking pan now and then, until edges firm up but center is still moist and slightly runny, 3 to 4 minutes.

5. Transfer skillet to oven. Bake 20 to 30 minutes, until frittata is firm around edges and center is completely set. Loosen edges with a spatula. Place a round platter over frittata and carefully invert frittata onto plate. Garnish with remaining 2 tablespoons Asiago and chopped parsley. Serve hot or at room temperature, cut into wedges.

NOTE: *The frittata can also be baked. Prepare egg mixture through step 3. Pour into a buttered 9 x 13-inch glass baking dish and bake in a 350°F. oven about 30 minutes, until set. Serve cut into squares.*

Chapter 5

Shirred to Please (and Other Baked Eggs)

The easiest eggs of all are baked in their own little cups or plopped on top of other ingredients and all baked together. Even baked sweet and savory omelets emerge from the oven puffed and browned, ready to eat.

This is the sure (shirr) way to please anyone looking for easy recipes for eggs. The classic shirred egg starts out as a hot dish with hot butter on top of the stove. Once the egg goes in the dish, it is transferred immediately to a waiting hot oven to finish setting the yolk and white. The modern take on this classic egg dish is to microwave the butter until it's melted and piping hot, crack in the egg, and finish the shirring process in the oven.

The looser translation of the shirring method, and by far the easiest, is to bypass the hot-butter step and proceed directly to the oven. Raw eggs bake in the oven unwatched and untouched until time's up. Eggs cook slowly by this method, but also very evenly. It usually takes 10 to 15 minutes before the whites set, and sometimes 20 to 25 minutes to cook a yolk to medium doneness.

The traditional cookware for shirred eggs is a small gratin dish. Ramekins or custard cups work well, too, but usually take only one egg at a time. If you don't have ramekins (I don't), use oven-safe coffee cups or dessert bowls. The advantage to making shirred eggs in coffee cups is that you can serve the hot cups on their saucers for easy handling and a great presentation.

134 BASIC SHIRRED-TO-PLEASE-ANYTIME EGGS

Prep: 2 minutes   Cook: 20 minutes   Serves: 4

4 teaspoons butter
4 tablespoons heavy cream
4 eggs

Salt and pepper
Tabasco or other hot pepper
  sauce (optional)

1. Place rack in center of oven and preheat to 325°F.

2. Place 1 teaspoon butter in each of four 6-ounce ramekins. Set all in microwave. Cook on High 30 seconds to melt butter.

3. Set ramekins on baking sheet. Pour 1 tablespoon cream into each ramekin. Crack egg into cream. Season lightly with salt and pepper. Bake 20 minutes, or until set. Butter and cream will float to top. Serve with Tabasco, if you like 'em hot.

135 SHIRRED TO PLEASE FLORENTINE

Prep: 5 minutes   Cook: 27 minutes   Serves: 6

These little servings are beautiful baked in clear glass cups.

1 pound fresh spinach,
  stemmed and washed, or
  1 (10-ounce) package
  frozen chopped spinach,
  thawed and squeezed dry

6 teaspoons butter
6 eggs
6 tablespoons heavy cream
Salt and pepper
Pinch of grated nutmeg

1. Preheat oven to 325°F. Cook fresh spinach in a big pot over high heat, stirring, until wilted, about 1 minute. Rinse with cold water, squeeze well to remove as much liquid as possible, and chop. You should have about 1 cup.

2. Place 1 teaspoon butter in each of six 8-ounce ramekins or custard cups. Set all in microwave. Cook on High 45 seconds to melt butter.

3. Set ramekins on a baking sheet. Spoon spinach over butter, dividing evenly. Make a well in spinach and add an egg. Spoon 1 tablespoon cream over each egg. Season with salt and pepper. Dust with nutmeg.

4. Bake 25 minutes, or until eggs set around edges.

NOTE: *To microwave spinach, place 1 pound wet washed spinach leaves in bowl without extra water. Microwave on High for 3 minutes. Drain on paper towels.*

136 FREE-FORM SHIRRED EGGS FOR COMPANY

Prep: 15 minutes   Cook: 20 to 25 minutes   Serves: 6

2 tablespoons butter
½ cup heavy cream
12 eggs

Salt and pepper
¼ cup chopped parsley

1. Preheat oven to 350°F. Place butter in a 9x13-inch glass baking dish. Either melt butter in microwave on High for 20 seconds or set dish in preheating oven until butter melts. Swirl to coat bottom.

2. Pour cream into dish. Crack eggs into dish. Season with salt and pepper. Set baking dish in larger pan filled with 1 inch hot water. Cover all loosely with foil. Bake 20 to 25 minutes, or until eggs are set.

3. If eggs are not set enough to your liking, run under broiler 30 seconds to 1 minute to finish cooking. Sprinkle parsley on top and serve at once.

137 EGGS BAKED IN CHILI CUPS

Prep: 5 minutes   Cook: 25 minutes   Serves: 4

Spooned into ramekins in minutes, this combo turns a can of chili into an eggs-ceptional supper.

1 (15-ounce) can beef chili,
    with or without beans
4 eggs
    Salt and pepper
½ cup grated Longhorn or
    Cheddar cheese

1½ tablespoons finely minced
    red onion or scallion
1 tablespoon finely minced
    cilantro

1. Preheat oven to 350°F. Fill four 6-ounce ramekins or custard cups evenly with chili. Set cups on a baking sheet.

2. Make a depression in center of each with back of spoon. Crack an egg into each depression. Season lightly with salt and pepper.

3. Bake 20 minutes. Sprinkle cheese on top, dividing evenly. Bake 5 minutes longer. Eggs will jiggle but will set under the hot melted cheese. Let stand 1 minute to set up. Serve hot, garnished with red onion and cilantro.

Variation:

138 CASSEROLE EGGS BAKED IN CHILI

Use same ingredients as in recipe 137, but spread chili in a lightly greased 8-inch square baking dish. Make 4 depressions in chili with back of spoon. Crack eggs into depressions. Sprinkle with salt and pepper. Bake 25 minutes. Top with cheese. Bake 8 minutes longer. Serve each portion sprinkled with onion and cilantro.

139   EGGS BAKED ON ITALIAN SAUSAGE ?
Prep: 5 minutes   Cook: 33 minutes   Serves: 4

¾ pound Italian sausage, bulk
or links with casing
removed
1 teaspoon minced fresh sage
or ½ teaspoon dried

¼ cup heavy cream
4 eggs
4 slices of mozzarella,
fontina, or provolone
cheese

1. Preheat oven to 350°F. Shape sausage into 4 patties about 3 inches in diameter. In a large skillet, cook sausage patties over medium heat, turning once, until golden brown on both sides, about 8 minutes total. Drain on paper towels.

2. While patties fry, mix sage with cream.

3. Set each patty in a 6-ounce ramekin, individual baking dish, or heatproof coffee cup. Crack egg over sausage. Pour sage cream over eggs.

4. Set ramekins in a baking pan. Pour very hot tap water halfway up sides of pan. Bake 20 minutes. Set a slice of cheese on top of each ramekin and bake 5 minutes longer, or until eggs are set. Serve hot.

140   LEEK, SPINACH, AND PARMESAN EGGS TOPPED WITH MORE EGGS
Prep: 10 minutes   Cook: 25 to 30 minutes   Serves: 4

If this seems like it's gilding the egg, it is. Whole eggs bake beneath a foam of leek-spinach soufflé.

8 eggs
2 leeks (white parts only),
well rinsed and coarsely
chopped
1 tablespoon plus 4 teaspoons
butter

1 (10-ounce) package frozen
chopped spinach, thawed
and squeezed dry
Salt and pepper
3 tablespoons grated
Parmesan cheese

1. Preheat oven to 375°F. Separate 4 eggs; leave others whole.

2. In a medium skillet, cook leeks in 1 tablespoon butter over medium heat until wilted, about 5 minutes. Transfer leeks to a food processor. Add 4 egg yolks and puree until smooth. Chop spinach; add to yolk base with salt and pepper to taste.

3. Beat whites to stiff peaks. Fold into yolk mixture. Fold in Parmesan cheese.

4. Place 1 teaspoon butter in each of four 12-ounce ramekins or individual gratin dishes and set in preheating oven to melt. Crack whole eggs into cups. Cover with leek-spinach mixture. Bake until tops brown and mixture is set, 20 to 25 minutes. Serve hot.

141 EGGS BAKED IN TOMATO CUPS

Prep: 5 minutes   Cook: 20 minutes   Serves: 4

4 medium tomatoes
4 tablespoons Brie cheese, at
 room temperature
4 (1-inch) pieces of anchovy
 fillet

4 eggs
 Salt and pepper
½ teaspoon dried basil

1. Preheat oven to 350°F. Slice off upper fourth of tomatoes. Seed tomatoes but don't scrape out flesh. Slice sliver off bottom so tomatoes stand upright.

2. Set tomatoes in an 8-inch square baking dish. Fill each with 1 tablespoon Brie, 1 piece of anchovy, and 1 raw egg.

3. Sprinkle with salt, pepper, and basil. Bake until eggs set, about 20 minutes. Serve hot. (CHEESE)?

142 ANDALUSIAN EGGS WITH SPRING VEGETABLES AND HAM

Prep: 15 minutes   Cook: 32 to 37 minutes   Serves: 4

1 medium onion, finely
 chopped
1 garlic clove, minced
1 tablespoon chopped parsley
2 tablespoons olive oil
2 medium tomatoes, seeded
 and chopped, or 1 cup
 drained canned diced
 tomatoes
6 ounces ham, cut into ½-inch
 dice

6 ounces firm Spanish
 chorizo, sliced (see Note)
1 cup fresh or frozen peas
¼ teaspoon salt
¼ teaspoon pepper
8 eggs
8 fresh asparagus spears,
 trimmed
8 (1-inch) pieces roasted red
 bell pepper, fresh or
 jarred

1. Preheat oven to 350°F. In a heavy skillet, cook onion, garlic, and parsley in olive oil over medium-high heat until onion softens, about 2 minutes.

2. Add tomatoes and cook until liquid evaporates somewhat, about 8 minutes. Add ham, chorizo, peas, salt, and pepper and cover. Reduce heat to low and simmer 2 minutes, until peas are bright green.

3. Spoon vegetable mixture into four 12-ounce ramekins or small soufflé dishes. Crack 2 eggs over each. Top each ramekin with 2 asparagus spears and 2 pieces red pepper.

4. Bake 20 to 25 minutes, or until yolks are set to desired doneness. Serve hot.

NOTE: *Spanish chorizo is made exclusively with pork, is heavily flavored with paprika, and is dry cured. When used, it is generally cut into small pieces. Mexican chorizo is soft and crumbly and is not a substitute for Spanish chorizo. If Spanish chorizo is unavailable, double the amount of ham.*

143 MIDDLE EASTERN EGGS IN YOGURT-GARLIC SAUCE

Prep: 15 minutes   Cook: 32 to 38 minutes   Serves: 4 to 6

This dish calls for dried mint. If you have mint growing in your yard or simply prefer the taste of it freshly cut, use twice as much as the dried amount.

3 cups plain regular or lowfat yogurt	⅛ teaspoon white pepper
2 tablespoons cornstarch	2 to 3 large garlic cloves, crushed through a press
2 teaspoons dried mint	2 tablespoons butter
1 teaspoon salt	6 eggs

1. Preheat oven to 375°F. Place yogurt in a medium saucepan. Dissolve cornstarch in ¼ cup cold water. Whisk cornstarch mixture into yogurt. Bring to a boil over medium heat, stirring constantly. Simmer, stirring occasionally, 10 minutes.

2. In a small bowl, mash mint, salt, pepper, and garlic to a paste with a fork.

3. In a small skillet, melt butter over medium-high heat. Add mint-garlic paste and cook, stirring, until very fragrant, 2 to 3 minutes. Remove from heat.

4. Pour hot yogurt into an 8-inch square baking dish. Crack eggs into yogurt, spacing evenly. Spoon garlic-mint paste over eggs.

5. Bake 20 to 25 minutes, until eggs set hard. Serve hot, scooping up egg and sauce for each person.

144 POTATO-EGG CASSEROLE

Prep: 15 minutes   Cook: 1 hour and 10 to 15 minutes   Serves: 4

3 to 4 large baking potatoes, peeled and thinly sliced (about 2¼ pounds)	2 garlic cloves, peeled and gently crushed
½ teaspoon salt	½ teaspoon paprika
1 bay leaf	3 tablespoons olive oil
	4 eggs

1. Preheat oven to 350°F. In a large bowl, toss potatoes with salt, bay leaf, garlic, paprika, and olive oil. Pour into a 6-cup casserole or 8-inch square baking dish.

2. Cover with foil and bake 1 hour, or until potatoes are tender.

3. Crack eggs on top of hot potatoes. Cover and return to oven. Bake until eggs are set to your liking, 10 to 15 minutes for medium-firm yolks.

145   LATE NIGHT SHIRR THING
Prep: 15 minutes   Cook: 30 minutes   Serves: 3 to 6

1½ cups prepared tomato soup
1½ cups bread crumbs
1½ cups chopped vegetables,
    such as carrots, peas,
    potatoes, green beans,
    zucchini, broccoli

2 shallots, minced
¼ teaspoon salt
⅛ teaspoon cayenne
6 eggs
1½ cups shredded Cheddar
    cheese

1. Place rack in center of oven and preheat to 350°F. Butter an 8-inch square baking dish.

2. In a medium bowl, combine soup, crumbs, vegetables, shallots, salt, and pepper. Spread in baking dish.

3. Make 6 indentations to hold eggs. Crack 1 egg into each indentation. Sprinkle top with cheese.

4. Bake 30 minutes, or until eggs are set and cheese is completely melted. Serve hot.

146   BAKED CHEESE OMELET
Prep: 5 minutes   Cook: 25 to 28 minutes   Serves: 4

This comes out very large and fluffy. Because it bakes, you won't have to pay much attention to it as it cooks.

2 tablespoons butter
2 tablespoons flour
1 cup hot milk
¼ teaspoon salt
⅛ teaspoon cayenne

½ cup shredded Cheddar or
    Longhorn cheese
4 whole eggs, separated
1 egg yolk
    Chopped parsley

1. Set rack in lower third of oven and preheat to 350°F.

2. Generously butter a large nonstick skillet with an ovenproof handle. In a medium saucepan, melt butter over medium-high heat. When bubbly, sprinkle in flour. Cook, stirring, 1 minute. Gradually whisk in milk. Bring to a boil, whisking until smooth and thick, 1 to 2 minutes. Season with salt and cayenne. Stir in cheese.

3. In a medium bowl, beat 5 egg yolks well. Whisk into cheese sauce. In a large bowl, beat 4 egg whites to stiff peaks. Fold into yolk mixture.

4. Pour batter into buttered skillet, spreading evenly. Cover and bake 20 minutes. Uncover and bake 3 to 5 minutes longer, until top is firm. Slide out of pan onto a platter. Cut into wedges and serve, garnished with chopped parsley.

147   SAUSAGE-POTATO DINNER CASSEROLE WITH PEPPERS AND CHEESE

Prep: 10 minutes   Cook: 1 hour 22 minutes   Serves: 4

1 large baking potato, peeled and cut lengthwise into ½-inch-wide strips	1 medium tomato, seeded and chopped
¼ teaspoon salt	2 tablespoons coarsely chopped flat-leaf parsley
¾ pound bulk Italian sausage	4 eggs
½ medium red bell pepper, cut into thin strips	¾ cup grated Swiss cheese

1. Preheat oven to 400°F. Spread out potato strips on a lightly oiled baking sheet. Bake 35 minutes, turning occasionally. Lightly salt potatoes after 20 minutes. Remove from oven. Reduce oven temperature to 350°.

2. Meanwhile, in a medium skillet, cook sausage over medium heat, breaking into large crumbles, until no longer pink, about 15 minutes. Strain in a colander. Return empty pan, which will be coated with a thin film of fat, to medium heat. Add pepper strips and cook 3 to 4 minutes, until slightly softened but still bright red.

3. In an 8-inch square baking dish, toss sausage with potatoes, pepper strips, tomato, and parsley. Spread to fill dish evenly. Make 4 shallow depressions in mixture and crack eggs into wells.

4. Bake 25 minutes, until yolks are just set. Sprinkle with cheese. Bake 3 minutes longer. Serve immediately.

Variation:

148   SAUSAGE-POTATO-EGG DINNER IN RAMEKINS

Preheat oven to 350°F. Prepare potato and sausage mixture as in recipe 147. Divide sausage mixture among four 12-ounce ramekins. Crack 1 egg on top of each. Set ramekins on baking sheet, then place in oven. Bake 20 minutes, until yolks are set. Sprinkle with cheese and bake 3 minutes longer.

149 SHERRIED EGGS

Prep: 5 minutes   Cook: 16 to 18 minutes   Serves: 4

4 slices of cooked ham
8 eggs
¼ cup half-and-half
2 tablespoons dry sherry (wine)
½ teaspoon Worcestershire
   sauce

⅛ teaspoon cayenne
1 cup shredded Swiss or
   Gruyère cheese

1. Preheat oven to 375°F. Butter four 8-ounce ramekins or custard cups and set all on a baking sheet.

2. Place 1 ham slice in bottom of each ramekin. Break 2 eggs over ham. Stir together half-and-half, sherry, Worcestershire, and cayenne. Spoon sauce over each pair of eggs.

3. Bake 8 minutes. Remove from oven and sprinkle with cheese. Return to oven and bake 8 to 10 minutes longer, or until yolks are set to desired doneness. Serve at once.

---

150 BAKED BLUE CORNMEAL OMELET

Prep: 5 minutes   Cook: 16 minutes   Serves: 4

This recipe follows a Hopi tradition of mixing eggs with blue cornmeal before cooking. While the color of the meal is blue, the taste is very similar to yellow cornmeal, which can be substituted.

8 eggs
¼ cup blue cornmeal
½ teaspoon salt
¼ teaspoon pepper

3 tablespoons bacon
   drippings or solid
   vegetable shortening

1. Set rack in center of oven and preheat to 400°F. In a large bowl, whisk eggs well until foamy. Gradually whisk in cornmeal, salt, and pepper.

2. In a large cast-iron skillet, heat bacon drippings over high heat, swirling to coat bottom and sides. When hot, pour in eggs. Immediately put skillet in oven.

3. Bake 8 minutes. Reduce oven temperature to 350° and bake 8 minutes longer, or until omelet puffs, turns light brown, and is just set in center. Serve hot, cut into wedges.

151 GERMAN PANCAKE

Prep: 5 minutes   Cook: 15 minutes   Serves: 2

Really a cross between a soufflé and an omelet, this baked pouf of eggs fortified with flour makes a dramatic presentation for brunch or a light supper.

1 tablespoon butter	¼ teaspoon salt
3 eggs	About ⅓ cup raspberry,
½ cup milk	blackberry, or strawberry
¼ cup flour	preserves
1 tablespoon sugar	Powdered sugar

1. Preheat oven to 425°F. Place butter in a 9-inch round cake pan or 10-inch round pie plate and put in oven to heat pan and melt butter, 3 to 5 minutes.

2. Meanwhile, in a mixing bowl, whisk eggs, milk, flour, sugar, and salt until well blended. Swirl melted butter to coat bottom and sides of pan. Pour batter into pan.

3. Bake 15 minutes, or until pancake is puffed and golden brown. Serve right away, slathered with preserves and sprinkled with powdered sugar.

Variation:

152 DUTCH BABIES

Prepare recipe 151 for German Pancake as described, but melt 2 teaspoons butter in each of four 8-ounce custard cups. Pour batter into hot cups, dividing evenly. Bake 12 minutes. Remove from oven, spoon 1 heaping tablespoon preserves into center of each, and sprinkle all over with powdered sugar. Serve and eat directly from cups.

Chapter 6

Real People Eat Quiche

Quiche took America's fancy in the 1960s and 1970s, during the height of the French food craze in America. While some foods fell by the wayside, quiche, with its simple baked custard filling adorned with any variety of enhancements—from bacon and onions to crab, broccoli, and cheese—never left the culinary repertoire for a good, simple reason: Quiche is comfort food incarnate. And it can be served hot, warm, or cold.

In its various forms, the contemporary quiche is really just a baked egg-and-cream custard contained in a crust but augmented by cheeses, vegetables, meats, or seafood. The custard may contain heavy cream, milk, sour cream, or yogurt. Quiche Lorraine is the world's most famous quiche. Classically it contains lots of onions and a bit of bacon. Originally, cheese was just an option, but these days it's hard to find a Quiche Lorraine without Swiss or Gruyère.

The pastry for quiche began as an ordinary bread dough. This was replaced by a short pastry sturdy enough to hold the liquid custard. That kind of crust can be found following the recipe for Quiche Lorraine. Another crust in this chapter is a durable butter pastry, and yet a third is a fine thin crust. I think you'll find my Rice Crust unique—and simple as A, B, C. Several quiches are made without a crust.

You may choose from a variety of quiche baking dishes. Metal ones with fluted sides and a removable bottom, sometimes called tart pans, allow you to remove the pan and expose the entire quiche. The sides of these pans are usually somewhat flared and can go up to three inches high. The quiches in this chapter are substantial and fit nicely in 9-inch quiche pans with 1½- to 2-inch sides. (Remember, the diameter measurement is taken across the bottom, not the sides.) Ceramic quiche dishes with scalloped sides and often decorated work the same way as a pie plate. You can serve directly from these baking dishes as you would from a pie plate.

Although nothing matches the quality of a homemade crust, you can use a store-bought frozen crust. Depending on the amount of filling—you can judge from the size crust recommended—use either a 9-inch pie crust or a 9-inch deep-dish pie crust. Thaw before filling.

If I may part with one important baking secret, it's this: Place your quiche on a baking sheet, preferably rimmed, in the oven. If the filling overflows—and it often does—you're spared a nasty cleanup. It's also much easier to get a quiche in and out of the oven if it's on a baking sheet.

153   QUICHE LORRAINE
Prep: 5 minutes   Cook: 36 to 43 minutes   Serves: 4

Originally from the Lorraine region of eastern France, Quiche Lorraine is a pastry crust simply filled with fried bacon, eggs, and cream, though Gruyère cheese is often added. In France, Quiche Lorraine isn't a high riser like the chunky wedges Americans enjoy for lunch or dinner, but a flat savory pie, rather thin and cataloged in French cooking as an appetizer.

8 slices of bacon	1¾ cups heavy cream
1 (8-inch) Lorraine Crust,	¼ teaspoon salt
partially baked (recipe	2 tablespoons butter, in small
follows)	pieces
4 eggs	

1. Place rack in center of oven and preheat to 350°F. In a large skillet, cook bacon over medium heat, turning with tongs a few times, until crisp, 6 to 8 minutes. Or place on a triple thickness of paper towels, covered with another paper towel, and microwave on High 1½ to 2 minutes. Let stand 3 minutes to make it crispy. Coarsely crumble bacon over bottom of a partially baked Lorraine Crust.

2. In a medium bowl, beat eggs, cream, and salt. Pour over bacon. Dot top with butter.

3. Bake 30 to 35 minutes, or until a knife inserted 1 inch from edge comes out clean. Let stand 10 minutes before cutting into wedges. Serve warm, at room temperature, or cold.

154   LORRAINE CRUST
Prep: 5 minutes   Chill: 1 hour   Cook: 12 minutes
Makes: an 8- or 9-inch quiche shell

Yes, the butter is held at room temperature. This is not a flaky crust, but one made to be a sturdy holder for the quiche filling.

1 cup plus 2 tablespoons flour	3½ tablespoons cold water
Pinch of salt	
5 tablespoons butter, at room	
temperature, in small	
pieces	

1. Place rack in center of oven and preheat to 425°F. Measure flour and salt into a food processor. Top with bits of butter. Turn on machine and immediately pour in water. When dough forms a ball, less than 20 seconds, stop machine. Flatten dough into a disk, wrap in plastic, and refrigerate at least 1 hour.

2. Roll out pastry to fit an 8-inch quiche pan, pie plate, or cake pan. Set pastry in pie plate, building up sides slightly higher than plate's rim. Prick all over with a fork. Line pastry with aluminum foil or wax paper with a slight overhang; fill foil with raw rice, dry beans, or pie weights to keep pastry flat as it bakes.

3. Bake 12 minutes. Pastry will be only partially baked, with edges a yellow-beige. Pull up on edges of foil and lift up to remove weights. (Save weights to use another time.) Let cool on rack for at least 10 minutes before filling.

155 QUICHE LORRAINE WITH BROWNED ONIONS

Prep: 10 minutes   Cook: 49 to 61 minutes   Stand: 10 minutes
Serves: 4 to 6

While the classic Quiche Lorraine contains only bacon, onions are an excellent, and not uncommon, addition. Here the onion is cooked until golden brown to bring out its sweetness and accentuate the flavor.

6 slices of bacon	⅛ teaspoon sugar
Buttery Quiche Crust (page 101), partially baked	5 eggs
3 tablespoons butter	2 cups heavy cream
1 tablespoon vegetable oil	¼ teaspoon salt
1 large Vidalia or other sweet onion or 2 medium yellow onions, thinly sliced	⅛ teaspoon grated nutmeg
	Dash of cayenne
	¼ cup shredded Gruyère or Swiss cheese (optional)

1. In a large skillet, cook bacon over medium heat, turning with tongs a few times, until crisp, 6 to 8 minutes. Or place on a triple thickness of paper towels, cover with another paper towel, and microwave on High 1½ to 2 minutes. Let stand 3 minutes, or until crispy. Coarsely crumble bacon into bottom of crust.

2. Place rack in center of oven and preheat to 350°F. In a large skillet, melt 1 tablespoon of the butter in the oil over medium-high heat. Add the onion and cook 3 minutes. Reduce the heat to medium, sprinkle on the sugar, and cook, stirring occasionally, until the onion is golden brown, 10 to 15 minutes longer. Drain onion on paper towels. Scatter over bacon.

3. In a medium bowl, whisk eggs, cream, salt, nutmeg, and cayenne until blended. Pour into crust. If using cheese, sprinkle over custard. Dot with remaining butter.

4. Bake 30 to 35 minutes, or until a knife inserted 1 inch from edge comes out clean. Let stand 10 minutes before cutting into wedges. Serve warm, at room temperature, or cold.

156 LEEK AND POTATO QUICHE WITH CHIVES

Prep: 40 minutes   Cook: 78 to 80 minutes   Serves: 6 to 8

1 large baking potato, peeled
   and cut into ½-inch dice
2 tablespoons butter
4 leeks (white parts only),
   well rinsed and sliced
   Buttery Quiche Crust,
   partially baked (page 101)
1 cup shredded Swiss or
   Gruyère cheese

4 whole eggs
2 egg yolks
1½ cups half-and-half, light
   cream, or whole milk
¼ teaspoon salt
   Pinch of grated nutmeg
   Pinch of cayenne
½ cup grated Parmesan cheese
¼ cup minced fresh chives

1. Place rack in center of oven and preheat to 325°F. In a medium saucepan of boiling salted water, cook potato until tender, 8 to 10 minutes. Drain and let cool.

2. In a large skillet, melt butter over medium heat. Add leeks and cook until softened, about 5 minutes. Add potato. Cook, turning with a wide spatula, until potatoes are lightly browned, about 5 minutes. Remove from heat.

3. Spread Swiss cheese over bottom of crust. Spread leek-potato mixture over cheese. In a medium bowl, whisk whole eggs, egg yolks, half-and-half, salt, nutmeg, and cayenne until blended. Mix in Parmesan cheese and chives. Pour slowly into crust.

4. Place quiche on a baking sheet and place in oven. Bake 1 hour, until lightly browned. A knife inserted 1 inch from edge should come out clean. Let stand 5 to 10 minutes before serving.

157   BUTTERY QUICHE CRUST

Prep: 5 minutes   Chill: 1 to 1½ hours   Cook: 10 to 12 minutes
Makes: a 9-inch quiche shell

This is an all-purpose quiche crust, partially baked so that it is all ready to accept the filling. The pastry for this crust will fit across the bottom and up the sides of a 9-inch springform pan with no overhang. It will also line a 9-inch pie plate with enough trim for building up a ridge for crimping. You may also choose from a variety of quiche baking dishes.

1¾ **cups flour**
½ **teaspoon salt**
1 **stick plus 2 tablespoons cold**
    unsalted butter

2 **tablespoons solid vegetable**
    shortening
¼ **cup ice-cold water**

1. Measure flour and salt into a food processor. Top with pieces of cold butter and shortening. Pulse a couple of times, then run machine until no solid lumps of butter remain, stopping once or twice to check.

2. With machine on, pour ice water through feed tube. Stop immediately when dough compresses, pulls away from sides, and begins to form a ball, less than 30 seconds. Shape dough into a disk. Wrap in plastic wrap and refrigerate at least 1 hour.

3. Place rack in center of oven and preheat to 425°F. Line a 9-inch quiche pan or pie plate with pastry. If pan is fluted, lightly press dough into sides and trim edge even with rim. If using a pie plate, turn edges under and crimp a decorative pattern around rim. Prick bottom and sides all over with a fork. If pastry is soft, refrigerate in pie plate 30 minutes.

4. Place a piece of foil larger than pie plate in the bottom, so you have an overhang to grab onto. Fill with raw rice, dried beans, or pie weights. Bake 10 to 12 minutes, until edges turn pale. Pull up on edges of foil and lift to remove. Pour off dry weights, which you can save for repeated use. Let the crust cool at least 10 minutes before filling.

158 RATATOUILLE QUICHE *DELICE!*
Prep: 10 minutes   Cook: 1 to 1¼ hours   Serves: 6 to 8

You'll need a deep-dish quiche or tart pan for this, with sides 1½ to 2 inches high.

1½ cups Oven Ratatouille
    (recipe follows)
Buttery Quiche Crust,
    formed in a 9-inch deep-
    dish pie or springform
    pan, partially baked
    (page 101)
½ cup shredded Parmesan
    cheese

4 whole eggs
2 egg yolks
¾ cup heavy cream
¾ cup milk
¼ teaspoon salt
¼ teaspoon pepper
1½ cups shredded Jarlsberg or
    Swiss cheese

1. Preheat oven to 300°F. Spread ratatouille over bottom of quiche shell. Sprinkle Parmesan cheese over ratatouille.

2. In a medium bowl, whisk whole eggs, egg yolks, cream, milk, salt, and pepper until blended. Stir in Jarlsberg cheese. Slowly pour into crust. Set quiche on a baking sheet.

3. Bake 1 to 1¼ hours, until a knife inserted halfway between edge and center comes out clean. Let cool 10 minutes on a wire rack before cutting into wedges.

159 OVEN RATATOUILLE
Prep: 20 minutes   Cook: 45 minutes   Makes: 3 cups

This recipe is from an idea by Janet Fletcher, author of *More Vegetables, Please,* published by Harlow & Ratner. The technique—to bake, rather than to stand and stir ratatouille—is in the "why-didn't-I-think-of-this-before?" department.

1 onion, cut into 8 wedges
1 small eggplant (about
    ¾ pound), peeled and cut
    into 1-inch pieces
½ green bell pepper, seeded
    and cut into 1-inch pieces
½ red bell pepper, seeded and
    cut into ½-inch pieces
1 zucchini, halved lengthwise
    and cut crosswise into
    ½-inch pieces
2 ripe tomatoes, cored,
    seeded, and cut into
    8 wedges

2 large garlic cloves, minced
¼ cup olive oil
1½ tablespoons chopped
    parsley
1½ tablespoons chopped fresh
    oregano or marjoram or
    1½ teaspoons dried
½ teaspoon dried thyme
1 teaspoon salt
½ teaspoon pepper

1. Preheat oven to 375°F. In a large bowl, combine onion, eggplant, bell peppers, zucchini, tomatoes, and garlic. Add olive oil, parsley, oregano, thyme, salt, and pepper and stir vegetables gently. Transfer mixture to a 9x13-inch baking dish; cover with foil.

2. Bake 25 minutes. Uncover and bake 20 minutes longer, stirring now and then, until vegetables are very soft and thickened. Let cool. The ratatouille keeps well, covered, for up to 4 days in refrigerator.

---

160 GREEN CHILE QUICHE

Prep: 20 minutes   Cook: 40 minutes   Serves: 6 to 8

Serve this south-of-the-border quiche with your favorite salsa.

4 eggs
1 egg yolk
¾ cup heavy cream
½ cup sour cream
1 tablespoon pure chile powder
¼ teaspoon salt
3 fresh poblano or Anaheim chiles, roasted, peeled, seeded, and chopped (page 53), or 1 can diced mild green chiles, drained

2 fresh jalapeño peppers, seeded and minced
1 scallion, sliced
1 tablespoon chopped cilantro
¾ cup shredded Monterey Jack cheese
Buttery Quiche Crust, partially baked (page 101)

1. Place rack in center of oven and preheat to 350°F. In a medium bowl, whisk eggs, egg yolk, cream, sour cream, chile powder, and salt until smooth.

2. In a large bowl, combine roasted chiles, jalapeño, scallion, cilantro, and cheese. Spread over crust. Pour egg mixture slowly into crust. Set quiche on a baking sheet.

3. Bake 40 minutes, until custard is puffed in center and a knife inserted halfway between the center and edge comes out clean. Let cool 10 minutes before cutting into wedges.

Variation:

161 GREEN CHILE QUICHE WITH BEANY BOTTOM

Spread contents of a 15-ounce can refried beans over Buttery Quiche Crust (page 101). Top with chile-cheese mixture, pour custard over, and bake and cool as directed in recipe 160.

162 GREENBRIER QUICHE

Prep: 15 minutes   Cook: 48 minutes   Serves: 6 to 8

Courtesy of the Greenbrier resort in White Sulphur Springs, West Virginia, comes a quiche ordered so often that it has a place in *The Greenbrier Cookbook*, a collection of the resort's favorite recipes. It's true that the inside of the Greenbrier feels like a cruise ship without the rocking action. So it's fitting that this pastry and silken filling are served beneath the strands of crystal chandeliers.

Greenbrier Quiche Crust, partially baked (recipe follows)
¼ cup diced Virginia ham or other baked ham
½ cup minced onion
1 tablespoon butter
½ cup grated Asiago cheese
½ cup grated Gruyère or Swiss cheese
3 eggs

1½ cups milk (CREAM)
1 tablespoon chopped fresh dill TARRAGON
Pinch of grated nutmeg
¼ teaspoon salt
¼ teaspoon freshly ground black pepper
8 slices of Oven-Roasted (page 165) Tomatoes (page 106)
8 sprigs of dill

1. Place rack in center of oven and preheat to 350°F. In a small skillet, cook ham and onion in butter over medium heat until onion is soft but not brown, about 3 minutes.

2. Sprinkle Asiago and Gruyère cheeses evenly over bottom of crust. Scatter cooked ham and onion over cheese.

3. Whisk together eggs, milk, chopped dill, nutmeg, salt, and pepper until blended. Pour into shell. Arrange roasted tomato slices around rim and dill sprigs in center. Set quiche on a baking sheet.

4. Bake 45 minutes, or until center is just set. Let cool slightly before serving.

163 GREENBRIER QUICHE CRUST

Prep: 5 minutes   Chill: 20 minutes   Cook: 10 minutes
Makes: a 9-inch quiche shell

1 cup flour
4 tablespoons cold butter, cut into small pieces

½ teaspoon salt
1 egg yolk
1 to 2 tablespoons cold water

1. Measure flour into a food processor. Top with butter pieces. Pulse, then run machine until mixture has texture of coarse meal.

2. With machine on, drop salt and egg yolk down feed tube, followed immediately by cold water. Process just until dough forms a loose mass. Stop immediately. Shape dough into a disk. Wrap in plastic wrap and refrigerate at least 20 minutes.

3. Place rack in center of oven and preheat to 375°F. Butter a 9-inch pie plate. Roll out pastry very thin and line plate. Trim and crimp. Prick pastry all over with fork. If pastry is soft, refrigerate 30 minutes.

4. Line pastry shell with aluminum foil. Fill with raw rice, dried beans, or pie weights. Bake 10 minutes. Remove foil and rice. Let crust cool before filling.

164 THREE-MUSHROOM QUICHE

Prep: 16 minutes   Stand: 30 minutes   Cook: 69 to 72 minutes
Serves: 6 to 8

Fungi fanatics will appreciate the mushroom hunt before preparing this quiche. You should be able to find all these mushrooms at a supermarket. If the cremini are not available, simply double the white mushrooms and call it Two-Mushroom Quiche.

2 ounces dried *FRESH* shiitake mushrooms	4 whole eggs
1 medium onion, chopped	2 egg yolks
2 tablespoons butter	1 cup heavy cream
5 medium white button mushrooms, sliced	1 cup milk
5 medium brown cremini mushrooms, sliced	½ teaspoon salt
1 teaspoon Chinese oyster sauce *OR CREAM*	¼ teaspoon white pepper
	Buttery Quiche Crust, partially baked (page 101)
	½ cup grated Parmesan cheese

1. In a medium bowl, soak shiitakes in hot tap water to cover until softened, about 30 minutes, while you prepare rest of quiche. Pat shiitakes very dry with paper towel. Discard stems and slice caps.

2. Preheat oven to 300°F. In a large skillet, cook onion in butter over medium-high heat 1 or 2 minutes, just to soften. Add white and brown mushrooms. Cook, stirring often, until liquid cooks away, 8 to 10 minutes. Remove from heat and stir in oyster sauce.

3. In a medium bowl, whisk whole eggs, egg yolks, cream, milk, salt, and pepper until custard is blended. With a slotted spoon, transfer mushrooms to bottom of quiche shell. Top with Parmesan cheese. Pour custard slowly over cheese. Set quiche on a baking sheet.

4. Bake 1 hour, or until a knife inserted halfway between edge and center comes out clean. Let stand 10 minutes before cutting into wedges.

165 OVEN-ROASTED TOMATOES

Prep: 15 minutes   Cook: 2 hours   Makes: about 18 slices

6 large plum tomatoes, cored
　　and cut lengthwise in
　　³⁄₈-inch slices
2 tablespoons extra virgin
　　olive oil
1 garlic clove, minced
2 teaspoons minced shallot
2 teaspoons chopped fresh
　　basil or ½ teaspoon dried

1 teaspoon chopped fresh
　　oregano or ¼ teaspoon
　　dried
½ teaspoon chopped fresh
　　thyme or ⅛ teaspoon
　　dried
*½ teaspoon freshly ground
　　black pepper
⅛ teaspoon salt

1. Preheat oven to 250°F. In a large bowl, gently toss tomato slices with all remaining ingredients.

2. Spread out tomato slices in a single layer on a wire rack over a baking sheet. Roast about 2 hours, until tomatoes are leathery and most moisture has evaporated.

3. Remove from oven. Let cool on rack.

166 PROVOLONE QUICHE WITH SUN-DRIED TOMATOES

Prep: 10 minutes   Cook: 35 to 40 minutes   Serves: 4 to 6

This is a shallow quiche that actually looks like a tart. It's as good straight from the oven as it is eaten cold outdoors at a picnic.

⅔ cup diced oil-packed sun-
　　dried tomatoes
1 tablespoon finely minced
　　garlic
½ pound provolone cheese,
　　cut into ¼-inch dice
1 scallion, sliced
2 teaspoons chopped fresh
　　oregano or ¾ teaspoon
　　dried

Buttery Quiche Crust,
　　partially baked
　　(page 101)
4 eggs
1½ cups half-and-half
Pinch of cayenne
¼ teaspoon salt
⅛ teaspoon pepper

1. Place rack in center of oven and preheat to 350°F. Sprinkle tomatoes, garlic, cheese, scallion, and oregano over crust.

2. In a large bowl, whisk eggs, half-and-half, cayenne, salt, and pepper until blended. Pour slowly over filling. Set quiche on a baking sheet and place in oven.

3. Bake 35 to 40 minutes, until top is golden and center is just set. It is done when a knife inserted near the center comes out clean. Let cool on a wire rack 10 minutes before slicing into wedges.

167 QUICHE WITH GARLIC, SPINACH, AND LEEKS

Prep: 15 minutes   Cook: 67 to 82 minutes   Serves: 6 to 8

3 large or 4 medium leeks, white parts only, well rinsed and sliced
1 tablespoon butter
1 pound fresh spinach or 1 (10-ounce) package frozen spinach, thawed and squeezed dry
2 tablespoons olive oil
1 tablespoon minced garlic
¾ cup shredded Parmesan cheese

Buttery Quiche Crust, partially baked (page 101)
4 whole eggs
3 egg yolks
2 cups half-and-half
¼ teaspoon salt
½ teaspoon pepper
Pinch of grated nutmeg

1. Place rack in center of oven and preheat to 300°F. In a large skillet, cook leeks in butter over medium heat until soft, about 5 minutes. Remove from heat.

2. If using fresh spinach, rinse well, shake a little, and add wet spinach to a very hot wok or Dutch oven. Stir quickly until partially wilted, less than 1 minute. Immediately pour into a colander and rinse with cold water. When cool enough to touch, press out excess water. If using thawed frozen, simply squeeze dry.

3. In a medium skillet, sauté spinach in olive oil over high heat 30 seconds. Add garlic and toss. Stir quickly a few more times. Spinach should retain some form and not be completely limp. Remove from heat.

4. Sprinkle Parmesan cheese over bottom of quiche shell. Top with cooked leeks and spinach. In a medium bowl, whisk eggs, egg yolks, half-and-half, salt, pepper, and nutmeg until blended. Slowly pour into crust. Set quiche on a baking sheet and place in oven.

5. Bake 1 to 1¼ hours, or until a knife inserted halfway between the edge and center comes out clean. Let cool 10 minutes before cutting into wedges.

168 SMOKED SALMON QUICHE WITH DILL AND SOUR CREAM

Prep: 5 minutes   Cook: 40 to 50 minutes   Serves: 6 to 8

1 cup sour cream
2 whole eggs
4 egg yolks
2 teaspoons fresh minced dill
  or 1 teaspoon dried
¼ teaspoon powdered ?
  mustard

¼ teaspoon salt
¼ teaspoon white pepper
Buttery Quiche Crust,
  partially baked
  (page 101)
¼ pound sliced smoked
  salmon

1. Preheat oven to 350°F. In a medium bowl, whisk sour cream, eggs, egg yolks, dill, mustard, salt, and pepper until blended. Pour into quiche shell.

2. Top with smoked salmon pieces, pushing down a little so they're submerged. Set quiche on a baking sheet and place in oven.

3. Bake 40 to 50 minutes, or until a knife inserted halfway between the edge and center comes out clean. Let cool 10 minutes before cutting into wedges.

169 SMOKED SALMON QUICHE WITH CREAM CHEESE AND RIPE OLIVES

Prep: 10 minutes   Cook: 50 to 60 minutes   Serves: 6

¼ pound smoked salmon,
  sliced or in pieces
1 (8-ounce) package cream
  cheese, cut into ½-inch
  cubes
Buttery Quiche Crust,
  partially baked
  (page 101)

4 whole eggs
2 egg yolks
1 cup heavy cream
¼ teaspoon salt
¼ teaspoon white pepper
¼ cup sliced black olives

1. Place rack in center of oven and preheat to 325°F. Cut smoked salmon into strips. Arrange cream cheese cubes over bottom of quiche shell.

2. In a medium bowl, whisk eggs, egg yolks, cream, salt, and pepper until blended. Pour over cream cheese. Arrange salmon over custard to resemble spokes of a wheel, pushing down to submerge. Scatter black olives on top. Set quiche on a baking sheet and place in oven.

3. Bake 50 to 60 minutes, until golden on top and a knife inserted between the center and edge comes out clean. Let cool on a rack 10 minutes before slicing.

170 FRESH SALMON QUICHE IN RICE CRUST
Prep: 10 minutes   Cook: 1 hour   Serves: 6

This is a beautiful quiche with a hint of pink. It makes use of leftover salmon and rice, always a good combination.

1 cup shredded Swiss cheese	1 egg yolk
1 cup grated Parmesan cheese	1 tablespoon tomato paste
Rice Crust, partially baked (recipe follows)	1½ cups half-and-half
	2 teaspoons chopped fresh
1½ cups cooked fresh salmon, coarsely flaked	dill or 1 teaspoon dried
	¼ teaspoon salt
3 whole eggs	¼ teaspoon pepper

1. Preheat oven to 300°F. Sprinkle Swiss and Parmesan cheeses evenly over crust. Top with salmon.

2. In a medium bowl, whisk eggs, egg yolk, tomato paste, half-and-half, dill, salt, and pepper until blended. Pour into crust. Set quiche on a baking sheet and place in oven.

3. Bake 1 hour, or until a knife inserted halfway between edge and center comes out clean. Let stand 10 minutes on a wire rack before cutting into wedges.

---

171 RICE CRUST
Prep: 5 minutes   Cook: 8 to 10 minutes   Makes: a 9-inch quiche shell

1 egg white	1 teaspoon salt
1½ cups cooked rice	¼ teaspoon pepper
1 tablespoon minced fresh chives	

1. Preheat oven to 350°F. In a medium bowl, whisk egg white until frothy. Stir in rice, chives, salt, and pepper.

2. With a rubber spatula or wet hands, press rice mixture over bottom and up sides of a 9-inch pie plate. Bake 8 to 10 minutes, until very pale. Let cool on rack for at least 10 minutes before filling.

172   CRAB QUICHE
Prep: 10 minutes   Cook: 50 to 60 minutes   Serves: 6

For rich, smooth texture, there's nothing like a Maryland blue crab. As a recent resident of the West Coast, I can't say the same for the stringy meat in Dungeness crab—although its meat is sweet. Atlantic crab is preferred in this quiche.

4 whole eggs	12 ounces lump crabmeat,
2 egg yolks	picked over for shell and
1½ cups half-and-half	cartilage
1 tablespoon sherry	1½ cups shredded Swiss cheese
⅛ teaspoon cayenne	Buttery Quiche Crust,
¼ teaspoon dried thyme	partially baked
¼ teaspoon salt	(page 101)
1 scallion, sliced	

1. Place rack in center of oven and preheat to 300°F. In a large bowl, whisk whole eggs, egg yolks, half-and-half, sherry, cayenne, thyme, and salt until smooth.

2. Arrange scallion, crabmeat, and cheese in bottom of crust. Pour custard slowly over filling. Set quiche on a baking sheet and place in oven.

3. Bake 50 to 60 minutes, until golden on top and a knife inserted halfway between the edge and center comes out clean. Let cool 10 minutes on a wire rack before cutting into wedges.

173   OYSTER QUICHE DELUXE
Prep: 15 minutes   Cook: 1½ hours   Serves: 6 to 8

This rich quiche is so plump with oysters, it's extra high. Bake it in a springform or deep-dish pie pan that is at least three inches high.

½ cup shredded Parmesan	1 teaspoon Chinese oyster
cheese	sauce
Buttery Quiche Crust,	⅛ teaspoon white pepper
partially baked	1½ cups shredded Swiss cheese
(page 101)	1 tablespoon minced fresh
4 whole eggs	chives
3 egg yolks	1½ to 1¾ cups shucked oysters,
2 teaspoons cornstarch	well drained
2½ cups heavy cream	

1. Place rack in center of oven and preheat to 300°F. Sprinkle Parmesan cheese over bottom of crust.

2. In a medium bowl, whisk whole eggs, egg yolks, cornstarch, and cream until very smooth. Whisk in oyster sauce and white pepper. Stir in Swiss cheese and chives.

3. Pat oysters dry with paper towels. Gently stir into custard. Pour custard into crust. Set quiche on a baking sheet and place in oven.

4. Bake about 1½ hours, or until a knife inserted halfway between the edge and center comes out clean. Let stand 10 minutes on a wire rack before cutting into wedges.

174   CRUSTLESS QUICHE WITH SHRIMP, SOUR CREAM, AND LEMON

Prep: 15 minutes   Cook: 53 to 63 minutes   Serves: 6 to 8

2 scallions, thinly sliced
1 tablespoon butter
1½ teaspoons finely grated
    lemon zest
¾ pound peeled medium
    shrimp (about 2 cups)
6 eggs
¼ teaspoon salt
¼ teaspoon pepper

Pinch of grated nutmeg
Pinch of cayenne
1¼ cups milk
½ cup sour cream or thick
    plain yogurt
¾ cup shredded Parmesan
    cheese
½ cup shredded Jarlsberg
    cheese

1. Place rack in center of oven and preheat to 300°F. Generously butter a 9-inch pie plate.

2. In a medium skillet, cook scallions in butter over medium-high heat until wilted, about 1 minute. Add lemon zest and shrimp. Toss until shrimp are bright pink, about 1½ minutes.

3. In a medium bowl, whisk eggs, salt, pepper, nutmeg, cayenne, milk, and sour cream until blended. Do not allow mixture to foam.

4. Spread shrimp mixture in pie plate. Top with Parmesan and Jarlsberg cheeses. Slowly pour in egg mixture. Set quiche on a baking sheet and place in oven.

5. Bake 50 to 60 minutes, or until a knife inserted halfway between the center and edge comes out clean. Let cool 10 minutes on a wire rack before cutting into wedges.

175 SHRIMP AND SCALLOP QUICHE IN RICE CRUST

Prep: 15 minutes   Cook: 45 to 60 minutes   Serves: 6

½ cup shredded Swiss cheese
½ cup shredded Parmesan
   cheese
Rice Crust, partially baked
   (page 109)
1 cup coarsely chopped
   cooked shrimp
1 cup cooked bay scallops
3 whole eggs

2 egg yolks
1 tablespoon tomato paste
2 teaspoons brandy
1½ cups half-and-half
2 teaspoons chopped fresh
   dill or 1 teaspoon dried
¼ teaspoon salt
¼ teaspoon pepper

1. Preheat oven to 300°F. Sprinkle Swiss and Parmesan cheeses evenly over quiche shell. Top with shrimp and scallops.

2. In a medium bowl, whisk eggs, egg yolk, tomato paste, brandy, half-and-half, dill, salt, and pepper until blended. Pour into crust. Set quiche on a baking sheet and place in oven.

3. Bake 45 to 60 minutes, or until a knife inserted halfway between the edge and center comes out clean. Let cool 10 minutes on a wire rack before cutting into wedges.

176 NO-CRUST QUICHE WITH BACON, POTATOES, AND CHEDDAR CHEESE

Prep: 15 minutes   Cook: 55 to 70 minutes   Serves: 6 to 8

1 large or 2 medium baking
   potatoes, peeled and cut
   into ½-inch dice
8 strips of bacon, coarsely (HAM)
   chopped
1 medium onion, sliced

2 cups shredded sharp
   Cheddar cheese
6 eggs
¾ cup heavy cream
¼ teaspoon salt
¼ teaspoon pepper

1. Preheat oven to 350°F. In a 4-cup measure or large microwave-safe bowl, microwave potato pieces in 1 cup salted water, tightly covered, on High for 8 minutes. Stir and drain.

2. Meanwhile, in a large skillet, fry bacon and onion over medium-high heat, stirring, until bacon bits are browned but not yet crisp and onion is softened, about 5 minutes.

4. Drain off most of fat. Add drained potatoes. Reduce heat to medium and cook 5 minutes longer. Scrape contents of skillet onto a plate lined with a triple thickness of paper towels. Spoon into a buttered 9-inch pie plate. Top with Cheddar cheese.

5. In a medium bowl, whisk eggs, cream, salt, and pepper until blended. Pour over cheese. Set pan on a baking sheet and place in oven.

6. Bake 45 to 60 minutes, or until a knife inserted halfway between the edge and center comes out clean. Let cool 10 minutes on a wire rack before cutting into wedges.

---

177 CRUSTLESS QUICHE WITH GARLICKY SWISS CHARD

Prep: 10 minutes   Cook: 56 minutes   Serves: 6 to 8

1 pound Swiss chard, washed, stems removed	⅛ teaspoon pepper
2 scallions, thinly sliced	Pinch of grated nutmeg
1 tablespoon butter	Pinch of cayenne
1 tablespoon olive oil	2 cups milk
4 garlic cloves, minced	1 tablespoon melted butter
6 eggs	1½ cups shredded Parmesan cheese
¼ teaspoon salt	

1. Place rack in center of oven and preheat to 300°F. Generously butter a 9-inch pie plate.

2. In a hot wok or large pot, toss wet chard over high heat, stirring and turning often, until very limp, about 3 minutes. Scrape into a colander and press out excess water. Chop chard coarsely.

3. In same pot, cook scallions in butter and oil over high heat about 1 minute, until fragrant. Return chard to pot and cook, stirring, 1 minute. Add garlic and stir about 1 minute longer, until fragrant but not browned. Pour chard onto a large plate and spread out to cool.

4. In a large bowl, whisk eggs, salt, pepper, nutmeg, cayenne, milk, and melted butter without allowing mixture to foam.

5. Spread chard in pie plate. Top with Parmesan cheese. Pour in egg mixture. Set quiche on a baking sheet and place in oven.

6. Bake 50 minutes, or until a knife inserted between center and edge comes out clean. Let cool 10 minutes on a rack before cutting into wedges.

Chapter 7

Poached and Posh

It's a common myth that poaching eggs is a difficult procedure. In truth, poaching eggs is easy, and the technique has the added bonus that the eggs cook in water instead
of butter or oil. The term comes from the French *pocher*, which
means to place in a pocket. When an egg is poached properly,
the yolk is pocketed smoothly in the white.

To make poached eggs, raw eggs are cracked out
of their shells into a skillet or saucepan full of water or other
liquid, such as stock, milk, or even yogurt. They cook in this
liquid held at barely a simmer. Simmering water registers only
180°F., so the eggs poach at a cooler temperature than the
212°F. of a full boil.

Even this technique, while hailed as the usual way
to poach eggs, is not as failproof as poaching eggs in water
even cooler than a simmer. For this method, a skillet is used
instead of a saucepan. About 3 inches of water is brought to a
full boil in the skillet. The eggs are slipped into the water from
a cup or caucer, so they can glide into the water at the water's
level, rather than being dropped in. Once the eggs are in, the
heat is turned off, a cover goes on, and in three minutes these
eggs will be poached. Eggs poached this way won't develop
strings and sinews that flail about in moving water. You can
poach up to six eggs at a time, and you don't need any fancy
equipment.

Poached eggs have always held on to their special
allure, especially on menus that serve breakfast and brunch.
I've always suspected that it's because even out of the shell
they still look like whole eggs, and there's that mystery about
what's inside. Will the yolk be runny or bounce? It's always a
gamble. But the ideal poached egg is cooked to the same stage
of doneness all the way through.

Once you poach a perfect batch of eggs, their ver-
satility will quickly become apparent. While beautiful under a
blanket of Hollandaise, they taste and look great on top of
things, as well—a thick slick of polenta toast, a slab of fried
summer tomato, a crisp potato pancake. On the upper scale,
you'll find poached eggs in artichoke bottoms and acting as
the melting agent when it rests on top of a wedge of creamy
Brie cheese.

178 ELAINE'S PERFECT POACHED EGGS

Prep: 5 minutes   Cook: 3 minutes   Serves: 2 or 4

As long as it's white, the type of vinegar you use here doesn't matter; you won't taste it. Distilled white, white wine, cider vinegar, or even rice vinegar are all fine. Serve poached eggs plain, topped with a sauce or salsa, or as part of another recipe.

4 eggs
1 tablespoon vinegar

1 teaspoon salt

1. In a large deep skillet, bring at least 2 inches of water to a boil.

2. Meanwhile, crack each egg into its own small cup (such as a tea cup) or small bowl.

3. When water boils, add vinegar and salt. Lower lip of each egg cup ½ inch below surface of water; tip to let eggs flow out. Immediately cover skillet and turn off heat. (If you have an electric stove, remove pan from heat.) Time exactly 3 minutes for medium-firm yolks.

4. Remove eggs from water with a slotted spoon, briefly letting excess water drain back into skillet.

Variation:

179 DO-AHEAD POACHED EGGS

Poach batches of eggs, as many as you like, as described in recipe 178. Poach to firmness you prefer. As they become done, transfer poached eggs to a large bowl of cold water. Make sure water covers eggs. Refrigerate, uncovered, up to 3 days. To rewarm, bring a large pot of water to a boil for 30 seconds. Gently lower about 4 poached eggs at a time into the water and warm through. Carefully remove them, one by one, with a slotted spoon. If there is time, drain warmed eggs on a clean cloth towel. Proceed with serving idea.

180   POACHED EGGS ON TOMATO WITH BERMUDA ONION AND BRIE

Prep: 5 minutes   Cook: 3 minutes   Serves: 1

This dish began one evening when some leftovers took the following form. The dish is so rich that one egg per serving ought to do it. For ease of serving, present each portion in a ramekin or bowl.

1 poached egg (page 116)
1 thick slice of Bermuda or
    other sweet white or
    yellow onion

1 thick slice of tomato
2 ounces Brie, cut into pieces
    Salt and pepper
    Dash of Tabasco sauce

1. Prepare poached egg.

2. In a 12-ounce ramekin, stack onion and tomato slices. Top with Brie.

3. With a slotted spoon, slip hot poached egg into center of cheese. Season with salt and pepper to taste. Sprinkle with Tabasco. Serve immediately.

181   POACHED EGGS ON TOP OF SAUTÉED TOMATOES

Prep: 10 minutes   Cook: 7 minutes   Serves: 4

2 medium tomatoes
2 tablespoons butter
4 large fresh basil leaves
4 poached eggs (page 116)

Salt and pepper
1 tablespoon finely grated
    Parmesan cheese

1. Preheat broiler. Thinly slice off both poles of tomatoes so they stand upright. Halve tomatoes at equator. If desired, squeeze and flick out seeds.

2. In a medium skillet, melt butter over high heat. When bubbly, sauté tomatoes, upside down, until browned, about 3 minutes.

3. Place tomatoes right side up on ovenproof plates. Make depression in center if tomato hasn't softened enough on its own. Layer cavity of tomato with basil, poached eggs, a sprinkling of salt and pepper, and Parmesan cheese.

4. Broil 30 seconds to 1 minute to brown tops. Serve immediately.

182   MICROWAVE HOLLANDAISE SAUCE
Prep: 5 minutes   Cook: 1 minute   Makes: ⅔ cup

1   stick (4 ounces) butter, at
     room temperature
3   egg yolks

1   tablespoon fresh lemon
     juice
⅛   teaspoon cayenne

1. In a 4-cup microwave-safe bowl, soften butter in microwave on High about 5 to 10 seconds.

2. Add egg yolks, whisking vigorously until smooth.

3. Return to microwave for four 15-second intervals on High, stirring sauce after each heating.

4. Whisk in lemon juice and cayenne. Use immediately or keep warm with the bowl set in a larger bowl of hot water.

183   POACHED EGGS ON POTATO PANCAKES
Prep: 5 minutes   Cook: 3 minutes   Serves: 4

Potato Pancakes (recipe
  follows)
8 poached eggs (page 116)

Salt and pepper
⅔ cup sour cream

1. Set 3 potato pancakes on each of 4 plates. Top each pancake with a poached egg. Sprinkle with salt and pepper.

2. Place a large dollop of sour cream to side. Serve right away.

184   POTATO PANCAKES
Prep: 10 minutes   Cook: 30 minutes   Makes: 8 to 12

2 medium baking potatoes,
     peeled and cubed
1 egg
½ medium onion, in rough
     pieces

¼ cup matzo meal
½ teaspoon baking powder
½ teaspoon salt
    Pinch of white pepper
    Vegetable oil

1. In a blender, puree potatoes, egg, onion, matzo meal, baking powder, salt, and white pepper until smooth. Pour into a pitcher or spouted mixing bowl.

2. In a large heavy skillet, heat 1 inch vegetable oil. Drop batter into hot oil by ¼-cup portions without crowding pan. Fry over medium-high heat until golden brown, 2 to 3 minutes per side. Drain on paper towels.

3. If making ahead, set cooked pancakes on a wire rack over a baking sheet in 150°F. oven. Pancakes will stay crisp about 45 minutes.

185   POTATOES EGGS BENEDICT
Prep: 10 minutes   Cook: 1 hour   Serves: 4 or 8

4 **small baking potatoes,**
   scrubbed
8 **poached eggs (page 116)**
   Salt and pepper
2 **medium tomatoes, seeded**
   and chopped (about
   1½ cups)

2 **cups shredded ham (about**
   ½ pound)
   Blender Hollandaise Sauce
   (page 117)

1. Preheat oven to 450°F. Prick potatoes with a fork. Bake 1 hour; let cool slightly. Or arrange like spokes of a wheel on double thickness of microwave-safe paper towels and microwave on High 12 minutes.

2. Meanwhile, poach eggs; keep warm.

3. Halve each potato. Season pulp with salt and pepper to taste; fluff with fork. Make a shallow trough in each half. Spoon about 3 tablespoons chopped tomatoes into each potato.

4. Top with 2 tablespoons shredded ham. Set poached egg on top of ham. Spoon 2 to 3 tablespoons hollandaise sauce over each. Serve immediately.

186   POACHED EGGS ON BUTTERED SWEET CORN AND RED CHILE
Prep: 6 minutes   Cook: 6 to 6½ minutes   Serves: 4

2 **to 3 ears of fresh sweet corn**
   or 2 cups frozen corn
   kernels
2 **tablespoons butter**
½ **teaspoon crushed hot red**
   pepper

   Salt and black pepper
¼ **cup yogurt, sour cream, or**
   crème fraîche
4 **poached eggs (page 116)**
3 **tablespoons bread crumbs**
   or cracker crumbs

1. Preheat broiler. If using fresh corn, cut kernels from cobs. In a medium skillet, cook corn in butter over medium-high heat until tender but not mushy, 2 to 2½ minutes. Add hot pepper and season with salt and black pepper to taste.

2. Transfer corn to a small baking dish or pie plate. Stir in yogurt. Arrange poached eggs on corn. Sprinkle crumbs on top.

3. Run under broiler about 1 minute to lightly brown tops of eggs. Serve immediately.

187   BEST EGGS BENEDICT MADE AT HOME

Prep: 10 minutes   Cook: 10 minutes   Serves: 2 or 4

The best known poached and posh egg is the one we call Benedict. It's an American improvisation often mistaken as French. Open to variation, the basic dish is a stacking of the best of breakfast ingredients. The bottom layer is a toasted English muffin. Next comes a grilled or fried slice of ham. Then a poached egg. The top and final layer, the French part, is a thick gilding of Hollandaise sauce.

Eggs Benedict is a launching pad for personal flair. The eggs may nestle in a bed of spinach or artichoke bottoms may replace the ham. I like to garnish the dish with tomato slices and watercress for color.

You don't need a professional chef in the house to enjoy Eggs Benedict. What you *do* need is the easiest technique for poached eggs ever and some savvy with Hollandaise sauce, whether classic, blender, or microwave.

4 slices of ham, country or
    baked ham or Canadian
    bacon
2 English muffins, split
    Butter
	4 poached eggs (page 116)
	¾ cup Hollandaise sauce
	    (pages 117–118)
	    Cayenne or paprika

1. In a large skillet, fry ham over medium heat 4 to 6 minutes per side, until lightly browned. Drain on paper towels.

2. Toast English muffin halves. Place 2 halves side-by-side on each plate. Spread with as much butter as you like. Top each muffin half with a slice of ham.

3. Prepare poached eggs to desired doneness. Scoop eggs from water with a slotted spoon, let drain a moment, then set on top of ham.

4. Spoon 2 to 3 tablespoons Hollandaise sauce over eggs. Sprinkle with a light dusting of cayenne or paprika. Serve immediately.

188 CLASSIC HOLLANDAISE SAUCE

Prep: 5 minutes   Cook: 2 to 4 minutes   Makes: 1½ cups

Hollandaise sauce is intended to be served warm, not hot. If it thickens too much after you've made it in any of the following ways, whisk in a few drops of cold water.

4 egg yolks
2 sticks (8 ounces) butter, cut
    into small bits
2 to 3 tablespoons fresh lemon
    juice

⅛ teaspoon cayenne
Salt

1. In a double boiler over simmering water, whisk egg yolks until thick, about 1 minute.

2. Whisk in butter bit by bit until it is blended and sauce begins to thicken, 1 to 3 minutes. Pay close attention.

3. Whisk in lemon juice and cayenne. Whisk briskly until sauce is thick and cooked but not curdled. It may "catch" in 15 seconds or less. Immediately remove from heat. Season with salt to taste.

4. Transfer sauce to a heatproof bowl. Set in a larger pan of hot water until ready to serve.

    NOTE: *If sauce should break or curdle, try whisking very hard while adding a couple of droplets of ice-cold water.*

189 BLENDER HOLLANDAISE SAUCE *(with blender.)*

Prep: 5 minutes   Cook: ½ minutes   Makes: 1 cup plus 2 tablespoons

Here the heat from melted butter thickens the egg yolks instantly. This is probably the easiest Hollandaise sauce in the world.

4 egg yolks
2 sticks (8 ounces) butter
2 tablespoons fresh lemon
    juice

⅛ teaspoon cayenne
Salt

1. Place egg yolks in a blender.

2. In 2-cup glass measure, combine butter with lemon juice and cayenne. Microwave, uncovered, on High about 1½ minutes, or until melted and very hot.

3. Whirl yolks in blender. With machine on, slowly pour in hot lemon butter. Blend until thick and fluffy. Season with salt to taste.

4. Keep warm in a heatproof bowl set in a larger pan of hot water, or refrigerate up to 24 hours in a covered container (a jar is best). To reheat, uncover jar and set in pan of simmering water about 8 minutes, until warmed.

190   POACHED EGGS DIAVOLO ON POLENTA TOAST

Prep: 10 minutes   Cook: 8 to 9 minutes   Serves: 6

1 shallot, minced
5 tablespoons butter
1 tablespoon Dijon mustard
1 tablespoon chopped parsley
1 tablespoon minced fresh chives
1 teaspoon dried oregano
½ teaspoon crushed hot red pepper
2 tablespoons balsamic vinegar

3 tablespoons flour
1½ cups hot milk
½ teaspoon salt
¼ teaspoon pepper
1 egg yolk beaten with 1 tablespoon milk or cream
1 tablespoon tomato paste
6 poached eggs (page 116)
6 slices of Polenta Toast (recipe follows)

1. In a small skillet, saute shallot in 2 tablespoons of butter over medium-high heat until light gold, 2 to 3 minutes. Remove from heat. Add mustard, parsley, chives, oregano, hot pepper, and vinegar. Mix well.

2. In a medium saucepan, melt remaining 3 tablespoons butter over medium-high heat. When foaming, add flour all at once. Cook, stirring, 1 full minute, until very pasty. Gradually add hot milk, which will sputter, and keep stirring. Bring to a boil. Reduce heat to medium-low and cook, whisking, 2 minutes.

3. Whisk in salt, pepper, and beaten egg yolk. Add shallot-mustard mixture. Whisk in tomato paste.

4. Arrange Polenta Toast on plates. Top toasts with poached eggs. Cover with sauce. Serve immediately.

191   POLENTA TOAST

Prep: 5 minutes   Chill: 3 hours   Cook: 12 minutes
Makes: 8 to 12 slices

1 cup yellow cornmeal or specially ground polenta meal

½ teaspoon salt
¼ teaspoon pepper
3 tablespoons butter

1. In a medium microwave-safe bowl, stir together 3 cups water, cornmeal, salt, and pepper, mixing well. Microwave on High, uncovered, 5 minutes, stirring twice. At end of time, stir very well. Return to microwave and cook on High 5 minutes longer. Stir in butter.

2. Pour polenta into a buttered 9x5x3-inch loaf pan and cover with plastic wrap. Refrigerate at least 3 hours or overnight, until firm.

3. Preheat broiler. Unmold and cut polenta into ¾- to 1-inch-thick slices. Place on a buttered cookie sheet. Toast under broiler.

192 EGGS SARDOU WITH CREAMED SPINACH

Prep: 15 minutes   Cook: 4 to 4½ minutes   Serves: 6

Creamed Spinach (recipe
  follows)
6 canned artichoke hearts
6 anchovy fillets
6 poached eggs (page 116)

1 to 1¼ cups Hollandaise
  sauce (pages 117–118)
¾ cup finely chopped baked
  ham
¼ cup finely chopped scallions

1. Spread creamed spinach in a pie plate, ceramic tart pan, or 9-inch shallow round casserole dish. Arrange artichoke bottoms on spinach. Cover with microwave-safe plastic; microwave on High 1 to 1½ minutes, to warm artichoke bottoms.

2. Top each artichoke with 1 anchovy fillet, then 1 poached egg. Pour warm hollandaise sauce over all.

3. Sprinkle ham and scallions over top. Serve immediately.

193 CREAMED SPINACH

*Prep: 15 minutes   Cook: 4 to 5½ minutes   Makes: about 3 cups,
6 servings*

2 pounds fresh spinach
  (see Note)
4 tablespoons butter
2 tablespoons flour
1 cup warm milk

¼ teaspoon salt
⅛ teaspoon pepper
  Pinch of grated nutmeg
2 scallions, chopped

1. Rinse spinach well, remove stems, and coarsely chop leaves. Keep slightly wet spinach in a colander until ready to use.

2. Heat a large pot or wok over high heat. Add wet spinach; let sizzle. Stir until wilted, but still bright green, 1 to 1½ minutes. Return to colander and drain, mashing to remove as much water as possible.

3. In a medium saucepan, melt 2 tablespoons of the butter over high heat. When butter foams, add flour all at once. Cook, stirring, 1 full minute, until very pasty. Slowly whisk in warm milk, which will sputter. Cook, stirring, until sauce boils and is thickened and smooth, 1 to 2 minutes. Remove from heat. Season sauce with salt, pepper, and nutmeg.

4. In same pot used to wilt spinach, melt remaining 2 tablespoons butter over high heat. Add drained spinach and scallions. Cook, tossing, 1 minute. Pour sauce over spinach, stirring to blend very well. Mixture should be smooth and thick, but a bit soupy.

NOTE: *Frozen chopped spinach may be substituted. Thaw 2 (10-ounce) packages, drain, and cook in 2 tablespoons butter 2 to 3 minutes. Add to white sauce.*

194 EGGS SARDOU
Prep: 15 minutes   Cook: 4 minutes   Serves: 4 to 8

During one of many visits to New Orleans I pondered: "Which came first, New Orleans or the egg?" No other city in America is so in love with eggs. My theory is that the city is obsessed with brunch. This is because no one gets up before noon after dragging in late from a night of music.

At a New Orleans brunch, eggs star. Antoine's, as I understand it, is the city's oldest restaurant and has made eggs a passion. As this dish was put together and served, it took the name of Victorien Sardou, a visiting French playwright. Here is a home cook's adaptation, easily assembled by preparing poached eggs ahead and keeping them in warm water.

8 **canned artichoke hearts**
8 **anchovy fillets**
8 **poached eggs (page 116)**
    Classic Hollandaise Sauce
    (page 117)

1 **cup chopped baked ham**
½ **cup finely chopped scallions**

1. Arrange artichoke bottoms on a round microwave-safe plate, platter, or pie dish. Cover tightly with microwave-safe plastic. Microwave on High 30 to 45 seconds, to warm.

2. Top each artichoke with 1 anchovy fillet, then 1 poached egg. Spoon warm Hollandaise sauce over all.

3. Sprinkle ham and scallions over top. Serve at once.

195 EGGS POACHED WITH SPINACH AND LOBSTER
Prep: 10 minutes   Cook: 12 to 15 minutes   Serves: 8

There's no point in making this impressive recipe in small quantities. To make the cost and effort worth it, show these eggs off to friends. The ramekins may be filled ahead of time, covered with plastic, and kept refrigerated overnight. By morning, they'll need only a stove-top poaching before being served.

1 **pound fresh spinach,**
    cooked and squeezed
    (page 123), or 1 (10-ounce)
    package frozen chopped
    spinach, thawed
½ **cup bread crumbs**

Salt
4 **tablespoons butter**
1 **cup rock lobster tail meat or**
    shrimp
8 **eggs**

1. In a food processor, puree spinach with bread crumbs and salt to taste. Use mixture to line 8 (1-cup) ramekins or custard cups.

2. Drop ½ tablespoon butter into each dish. Top with lobster. Crack 1 egg over lobster in each ramekin.

3. Set ramekins in a large skillet of boiling water to reach halfway up sides of ramekins. Cover and steam 12 to 15 minutes, until whites are completely set and yolks are medium-firm. (Eggs will continue to cook in the ramekins.) Serve hot or warm.

---

196 EGGS BLACKSTONE WITH SAUTERNE ? HOLLANDAISE

Prep: 5 minutes   Cook: 10 minutes   Serves: 2

This dish is a favorite among the townsfolk of Mill Valley, California. The sauterne called for is the inexpensive dry kind that is sold by the jug, not the precious sweet French variety.

4 slices of tomato	4 poached eggs (page 116)
3 strips of bacon	Sauterne Hollandaise
2 English muffins	(recipe follows)

1. On an ungreased griddle or in a cast-iron skillet, grill tomato slices over medium-high heat until lightly charred, about 5 minutes per side, scraping with a metal spatula to turn.

2. Meanwhile, in another skillet, fry bacon over medium heat until crisp, 6 to 8 minutes, turning now and then. Drain on paper towels. Crumble.

3. Split muffins. Toast until medium-brown.

4. Place 2 muffin halves on each of 2 dinner plates. Top each with a tomato slice, a sprinkling of crumbled bacon, and a poached egg. Spoon warm hollandaise over all. Serve immediately.

---

197 SAUTERNE HOLLANDAISE ?

Prep: 5 minutes   Cook: 7 to 9 minutes   Makes: 1 cup

½ cup California Sauterne or	6 egg yolks
any dry white wine	6 tablespoons butter, cut into
⅓ cup fresh lemon juice (from	small bits
2 or 3 lemons)	⅛ teaspoon cayenne

1. In a small nonreactive saucepan, combine sauterne and lemon juice. Boil until mixture reduces by half, about 5 minutes.

2. In a double boiler over simmering water, whisk egg yolks until thick, about 1 minute. Whisk in butter bit by bit until sauce thickens, 1 to 3 minutes.

3. Whisk in wine-lemon mixture and cayenne. Whisk hard until sauce is thick. Remove from heat. Transfer sauce to a heatproof bowl. Set in a larger pan of hot water until ready to serve.

198   EGGS IN PURGATORY
Prep: 5 minutes   Cook: 7 minutes   Serves: 2

This is a skillet breakfast. With your favorite prepared tomato sauce, you can throw it together in a flash.

2 cups tomato sauce
1 teaspoon dried oregano
1 teaspoon dried basil
¼ teaspoon pepper
  Salt
4 eggs
⅓ cup shredded Swiss,
  Parmesan, or Cheddar
  cheese

4 slices of Italian bread
  Butter
1 tablespoon chopped parsley
  Hot pepper sauce

1. In a medium nonreactive skillet, combine tomato sauce with oregano, basil, and pepper. Season with salt to taste. Cover and bring to a boil over medium-high heat.

2. Crack each egg into a small cup or ramekin. When sauce boils, uncover and gently lower eggs into sauce, submerging rim of cup so egg flows out. Sprinkle with cheese.

3. Cover skillet and reduce heat to no more than a simmer. Cook 5 minutes for yolks of medium doneness.

4. Meanwhile, toast bread and spread with desired amount of butter. Place 2 slices of buttered toast on each of 2 dinner plates.

5. Uncover skillet. Sprinkle parsley over cheese. With a large spoon, scoop out eggs, including some sauce and cheese, onto slices of bread. Serve immediately. Pass hot sauce at table.

199   DANA'S L'EGGUMES
Prep: 10 minutes   Cook: 35 minutes   Serves: 4

New York food writer Dana Jacobi indulges in eggs when she needs comfort and familiarity. When she does, the egg is on top—a soft-to-medium poached egg on top of steaming savory lentils. The yolk must be runny so it becomes a sauce.

½ medium carrot, finely
  chopped
½ medium onion, finely
  chopped
1 celery rib, finely chopped
3 garlic cloves, minced

1 tablespoon olive oil
1 cup chicken stock
1 cup dried lentils
¼ teaspoon salt
  Pinch of pepper
4 poached eggs (page 116)

1. In a medium saucepan, cook carrot, onion, celery, and garlic in olive oil over medium-high heat until slightly softened, 2 to 3 minutes.

2. Add chicken stock, 1 cup water, lentils, salt, and pepper. Bring to a boil. Reduce heat to medium-low, cover, and cook until lentils are soft but not mushy, about 30 minutes.

3. To serve, spoon about ¾ cup hot lentils onto each of 4 plates. Nestle a poached egg on top. Serve immediately.

---

200   POACHED EGGS ON FRIED GREEN TOMATOES WITH BACON MILK GRAVY
Prep: 10 minutes   Cook: 20 minutes   Serves: 4

A great fall pleaser! The taste of green tomatoes is strong and comes through in a mouthful of eggs, gravy, and bacon.

4 **strips of bacon**	1 **egg, beaten**
8 **slices of large green**	2 **tablespoons flour**
tomatoes, cut ½ inch thick	1½ **cups warm milk**
2 **tablespoons brown sugar**	**Salt and pepper**
1¼ **cups quick corn muffin mix**	8 **poached eggs (page 116)**

1. In a medium skillet, fry bacon over medium heat until crisp, about 8 minutes, turning now and then. Drain bacon on paper towels. Crumble and set aside. Drain off all but 2 tablespoons fat from skillet.

2. Meanwhile, sprinkle tomato slices with brown sugar. Dip slices in muffin mix, egg, and again in muffin mix.

3. Fry in bacon grease over medium heat until golden brown, about 3 to 4 minutes per side. Drain on paper towels.

4. Quickly add flour to skillet, stirring until a thick paste forms, about 1 full minute. Gradually whisk in warm milk, which will sputter. Bring to a boil. Reduce heat to medium-low and cook, stirring, until thickened, 2 minutes. Season with salt to taste and lots of pepper.

5. Place 2 fried tomato slices on each of 4 plates. Top with poached eggs and generous spoonfuls of gravy. Sprinkle crumbled bacon on top. Serve immediately.

201 FRIED GREEN TOMATOES IN POLENTA BATTER WITH POACHED EGGS

Prep: 10 minutes   Cook: 11 minutes   Serves: 4

A frothy batter made with the rough-milled cornmeal used in from-scratch polenta fries to a golden brown. Polenta meal is ground slightly grittier than regular cornmeal, which means that you get double the crunch.

2 large green tomatoes cut into
    8 slices ½ inch thick
2 tablespoons brown sugar
2 eggs, separated
⅓ cup polenta or regular
    yellow or white cornmeal
½ cup flour

½ teaspoon salt
¼ teaspoon pepper
   Vegetable oil, for frying
8 poached eggs (page 116)
   Tabasco or other hot pepper
   sauce

1. Arrange tomatoes in a single layer on a platter or tray. Sprinkle with brown sugar.

2. In a medium bowl, beat egg yolks and ¼ cup water with a fork until blended. Add cornmeal, ¼ cup of the flour, salt, and pepper. If very thick, thin with a little more water.

3. In another medium bowl, beat egg whites to medium-stiff peaks. Fold whites gently into yolk-cornmeal base.

4. Pile remaining ¼ cup flour on a small plate. In a large skillet, heat about 1 inch oil over medium heat until hot.

5. Press both sides of each tomato slice into flour. Dip deeply in polenta batter to completely encase slice. Immediately fry tomatoes in oil until golden brown, about 4 minutes per side. Drain on paper towels.

6. Place 2 tomato slices on each of 4 plates. Top each with a poached egg. Serve right away. Pass Tabasco at table.

Chapter 8

Border Crossings

The best edible gift Mexico has given its bordering American neighbors is breakfast. Mexican breakfast is something of a legend in my hometown of El Paso, Texas. It's a priority in Austin and San Antonio and out in Las Cruces, New Mexico. People think nothing of specifying this special category when deciding on a breakfast destination, as in "Let's go out for a Mexican breakfast."

Mexican breakfast is exceptionally savory with soft and pliant flour tortillas, fresh nubby corn tortillas, green chiles, spicy red sauce, various salsas, avocados, sour cream, and lots of cheese. Sometimes the coffee is plain, American style. If you're lucky, it's *café con leche*, with hot steaming milk poured into the dark brewed coffee.

Always, of course, there are eggs: scrambled, fried, or poached. And with the right heat of salsa, Mexican breakfast can be a real awakener! It is with abiding homesickness for Texas that the following recipes salute eggs the way we do them on the border.

202   BREAKFAST BURROS
Prep: 10 minutes   Cook: 5 minutes   Makes: 6

Dating to about 1968 in Tucson, my friend Peter Quinlan was forced to make himself breakfast as a teenager when he woke up late and everyone had already gone to work. He experimented with lots of egg dishes. Today, Peter's burros are famous wherever he and his family have traveled and worked, from Arizona to Oman.

7 eggs
¼ teaspoon dried oregano
¼ teaspoon salt
⅛ teaspoon pepper
1 tablespoon olive oil
2 tablespoons canned diced roasted green chiles
8 strips of bacon, cooked and crumbled

½ cup grated sharp Cheddar cheese
6 (7-inch) flour tortillas
Ground cumin (optional)
Tomato salsa and green chile salsa

1. In a large bowl, whisk eggs, oregano, salt, and pepper until blended.

2. In a large skillet, heat olive oil over high heat. When hot, pour in eggs; reduce heat to medium. Add chiles and push eggs around pan with a spatula until half-set, about 2 minutes.

3. Add bacon and cook, stirring. When almost set, about 2 minutes longer, add cheese and cook 1 minute or to desired doneness.

4. Fill each tortilla with egg and roll up burro style (see Note). Upon request, sprinkle individual fillings with a shake or two of cumin. Serve hot with a selection of salsas.

NOTE: *To roll burro style, lay eggs in a line off center on a tortilla, leaving about a 1½-inch border on bottom. Fold short flap over eggs, then fold bottom flap up. Complete the roll so eggs are tucked in and won't leak out.*

203   BREAKFAST QUESADILLAS
Prep: 5 minutes   Cook: 5 minutes   Serves: 2

½ cup shredded Monterey Jack cheese
2 (7-inch) flour tortillas
3 eggs
1 tablespoon milk
Salt and pepper

1 tablespoon butter
2 to 3 tablespoons canned green chiles, diced or strips
Red or green salsa
Sour cream

1. Pile cheese onto 1 tortilla. In a small bowl, beat eggs with milk and a pinch of salt and pepper until blended.

2. In a medium nonstick skillet, melt butter over high heat. When butter foams, pour in eggs. Reduce heat to medium. Move eggs slowly around pan with a wide spatula until soft curds form, about 2 minutes. Stir in chiles.

3. Quickly spoon eggs over cheese to within 1 inch of tortilla's edge. Top with second tortilla and press lightly. Slide quesadilla into skillet over medium heat. Fry 1 minute on each side, until cheese is nearly melted.

4. Slide onto a serving plate. Cut in half. Serve with salsa and sour cream.

---

204   CORN AND GREEN CHILE EGG BURRITO
Prep: 10 minutes   Cook: 5 minutes   Makes: 6

Nothing graces eggs like fresh corn straight from the cob. If you've got the urge but it isn't the season, it's all right to use frozen corn. And for sheer energy, nothing kicks like fresh green chiles. If you must use canned, add a tablespoon or so of fresh jalapeño pepper in the tiniest mince you can get.

½ **medium onion, minced**
1½ **cups fresh or thawed frozen**
    corn kernels
1 **tablespoon butter**
2 **minced garlic cloves**
4 **eggs**
2 **poblano or Anaheim chiles,**
    roasted, peeled, seeded,
    and diced (page 53), or
    2 canned whole green
    chiles

¼ **teaspoon salt**
⅛ **teaspoon pepper**
6 **(7-inch) flour tortillas**
2 **tablespoons coarsely**
    chopped cilantro
Green salsa

1. In a medium nonstick skillet, cook onions and corn in butter over medium-high heat, about 2 minutes, just to soften. Add garlic. Reduce heat to medium.

2. In a medium bowl, whisk eggs well. Stir in chiles, salt, and pepper and pour into skillet. Reduce heat to medium. Cook, stirring gently and pushing with a spatula, until eggs form soft curds, about 2 minutes.

3. Meanwhile, heat tortillas in a stack in a microwave, with a double layer of microwave-safe paper towels bottom and top, 20 to 25 seconds on High.

4. Spoon eggs into warm tortillas, sprinkle with cilantro, and roll up. Serve with green salsa at table.

205 HUEVOS RANCHEROS WITH SCRAMBLED EGGS

Prep: 10 minutes   Cook: 17 minutes   Serves: 4

Traditionally huevos rancheros are made with fried eggs, but scrambled are delicious too. The scrambled eggs can be plain or spiced. One bite of these is a guaranteed wake-up call.

½ large white onion, chopped
2 garlic cloves, minced
1 teaspoon minced fresh seeded jalapeño pepper
1 tablespoon vegetable oil
1 (10-ounce) can red chile sauce, such as red enchilada sauce
1 (8-ounce) can tomato sauce
1 teaspoon dried oregano

1 (15-ounce) can refried beans
8 eggs
¼ cup milk
¼ teaspoon salt
⅛ teaspoon pepper
¼ cup red salsa
2 tablespoons butter
4 corn tortillas
1 cup shredded Monterey Jack or Longhorn cheese

1. In a medium saucepan, cook onion, garlic, and jalapeño in oil over medium-high heat until soft, about 5 minutes. Add chile sauce, tomato sauce, and oregano. Bring to a boil. Reduce heat to medium-low and simmer, uncovered, about 8 minutes.

2. Meanwhile, empty refried beans into a microwave-safe bowl and stir in 1 tablespoon water. Cover with microwave-safe plastic and microwave on High 1 minute. Stir and microwave, covered, 1 to 1½ minutes longer, to heat through. Stir well. Set aside.

3. In a large bowl, whisk eggs, milk, salt, pepper, and salsa until blended. In a large skillet, melt butter over high heat. When foamy, pour in eggs. Let set a moment, reduce heat to medium-low, then move eggs slowly with a spatula until large curds form, about 4 minutes. Eggs should be very moist. Remove from heat.

4. Spoon some refried beans onto 1 side of each of 4 dinner plates. Drag a tortilla through sauce and place next to beans. Top each tortilla with a spoonful of eggs. Sprinkle cheese over everything on each plate, then spoon more sauce over all, so cheese melts. Serve immediately.

206   HUEVOS RANCHEROS

Prep: 10 minutes   Cook: 13 minutes   Serves: 4

Huevos Rancheros, or ranch eggs, are part of the breakfast tradition in Mexico and in most any self-respecting Mexican restaurant in the United States. Along the border and in a sweep through Texas, New Mexico, Arizona, and California, the basic elements of eggs, tortillas, beans, cheese, and some sort of sauce—usually a really spicy red one—converge on one plate. Old-timers would dip corn tortillas in hot shortening before topping them with eggs. New-timers may prefer to dip tortillas in sauce or steam-heat them in a microwave, thus avoiding excess oil.

½ **large white onion, chopped**
2 **garlic cloves, minced**
1 **teaspoon minced fresh**
   seeded jalapeño pepper
1 **tablespoon vegetable oil**
1 **(10-ounce) can red chile**
   sauce, such as red
   enchilada sauce
1 **(8-ounce) can tomato sauce**
1 **teaspoon dried oregano**

4 **fried eggs, sunny-side up or**
   over easy (page 45)
1 **(15-ounce) can refried beans**
4 **corn tortillas**
   Salt and pepper
1 **cup shredded Monterey**
   Jack or Longhorn cheese
   Avocado slices
   Green chile salsa

1. In a medium saucepan, cook onion, garlic, and jalapeño in oil over medium-high heat until soft, about 5 minutes. Add chile sauce, tomato sauce, and oregano. Bring to a boil. Reduce heat to medium-low and simmer, uncovered, about 8 minutes.

2. Meanwhile, prepare fried eggs in a large skillet so you'll be able to fry all 4 in same pan. Empty refried beans into a microwave-safe bowl and stir in 1 tablespoon water. Cover with microwave-safe plastic wrap and microwave on High 1 minute. Stir and microwave, covered, 1 to 1½ minutes longer to heat through. Stir well.

3. Spoon some beans onto 1 side of each of 4 plates. Drag tortilla through sauce and place alongside beans. Top each tortilla with a fried egg. Season with salt and pepper to taste. Top everything on each dish with cheese, then spoon sauce over all, so cheese melts.

4. Garnish with avocado slices and/or green salsa. Serve immediately.

207 POTATO-AND-EGG BURRITO

Prep: 4 minutes   Cook: 20 minutes   Makes: 4

A classic among breakfasts in Texas and Mexico, it's not a true potato-and-egg burrito unless it's got sliced jalapeño peppers. A nonstick pan will speed the cleanup, but you'll get better browning in a black cast-iron skillet.

1 tablespoon vegetable oil	Salt and pepper
1 medium white onion, halved and sliced	4 eggs
1 medium baking potato, peeled and cut into small dice	1 small fresh jalapeño pepper, seeded and sliced into rings
1 or 2 garlic cloves, minced	4 (7-inch) flour tortillas

1. In a heavy medium skillet, heat oil over high heat. When hot, add onion. Stir and fry about 2 minutes. Add potato and garlic. Stir and fry about 3 minutes longer, until skillet looks dry.

2. Cover and reduce heat to low. Cook 12 to 14 minutes longer, stirring occasionally, until potatoes are cooked through. Remove cover and turn heat to high. Sprinkle with salt and pepper. Fry potatoes until well browned, about 1 minute longer.

3. Beat eggs with salt and pepper to taste. Pour over potatoes. Push gently around skillet until large curds form around potatoes, about 1 minute. Remove from heat. Fold in jalapeño pepper.

4. Spoon into flour tortillas. Roll up burrito style and eat.

208 MIGAS CON CHILI

Prep: 10 minutes   Cook: 12 minutes   Serves: 3 to 4

Migas is a scramble of eggs with torn-up tortillas. It's a great way to use leftover—even stale—corn tortillas. Dotty Griffith, food editor of the *Dallas Morning News* for nearly 17 years, knows her beans about chili. This recipe is one of her all-time greats.

5 corn tortillas	½ cup chili con carne
About ¾ cup vegetable oil	½ cup grated Cheddar cheese
1 small onion, chopped	Chopped tomato (optional)
6 eggs	Warm flour tortillas, warmed (see Note)
¼ teaspoon salt	
⅛ teaspoon pepper	

1. Cut corn tortillas into bite-size pieces. In a large skillet, heat ¼ inch of oil until almost smoking. Add tortilla pieces and fry, stirring, over medium heat until crisp, about 2 minutes. Drain on paper towels.

2. Pour all but 2 tablespoons oil from skillet, reserving discarded oil for another use. Add onion, and cook over medium-high heat until soft, about 3 minutes.

3. Whisk eggs. Reduce heat to medium-low and pour eggs, tortilla chips, salt, and pepper into skillet. Cook, stirring gently, until eggs are almost set, about 3 minutes. Pour chili over eggs and stir gently. Cook until eggs are set and chili is heated through, 6 minutes.

4. Remove skillet from heat and sprinkle cheese over eggs. Cover skillet with lid to melt cheese, 1 minute. Sprinkle with tomato, if desired. Serve with flour tortillas.

> **NOTE:** *To warm flour tortillas, place as many in your microwave as it can hold without overlapping. Microwave on High about 20 seconds. If tortillas are just warm and pliant, they're ready. Avoid overcooking. To warm 2 tortillas at a time, sandwich them between paper towels and microwave on High for 30 seconds.*

209 MIGAS OMELET WITH AVOCADO, GREEN CHILE, AND SOUR CREAM
Prep: 25 minutes   Cook: 8 to 9 minutes   Serves: 2 to 3

1 ripe avocado, peeled and diced
½ cup sour cream
2 poblano or Anaheim green chiles, roasted, peeled, seeded, and chopped (page 53), or ¾ cup canned chopped green chiles
1 scallion, sliced

1 tablespoon lemon juice
¼ teaspoon salt
Dash of Tabasco sauce
2 tablespoons butter
2 corn tortillas, torn into pieces
6 eggs
¼ pound Monterey Jack cheese, shredded (about 1 cup)

1. Preheat oven to 325°F. In a medium bowl, combine avocado, sour cream, chiles, scallion, lemon juice, salt, and Tabasco. Stir gently to mix.

2. In a 10-inch skillet with ovenproof handle, melt butter over medium-high heat. When foamy, add tortilla pieces. Cook, stirring, until soft, about 1 minute.

3. Whisk eggs to blend. Pour over tortilla pieces. Reduce heat to medium and cook, lifting edges as they begin to set to let uncooked egg flow under, until edges are set but center is still moist, about 3 minutes. Top with cheese. Transfer to oven and bake 3 to 4 minutes, until cheese melts. Remove from oven. Spread avocado mixture down one side of omelet. Return to oven for 1 minute longer, just to set mixture.

4. Fold plain side of omelet over avocado filling. Cut into portions and serve immediately.

210   EGGS REFRITOS CHALUPA-STYLE
Prep: 5 minutes   Cook: 6 minutes   Serves: 1

A chalupa is a corn tortilla fried crisp and used as a platform for various goodies.

1 corn tortilla	1 poached egg (page 116)
1 tablespoon butter	Salt and pepper
½ cup canned refried beans	Red or green salsa
½ avocado, mashed	

1. In a small skillet, fry tortilla in butter until slightly puffed, about 1 minute. Turn and fry second side 1 minute longer, until golden and crisp. Drain on paper towels.

2. In a small bowl, stir refried beans with 1 tablespoon water. Microwave, covered tightly with microwave-safe plastic, on High about 45 seconds, or just to heat through. Stir well.

3. Spread beans on crisp tortilla. Top with avocado, then poached egg. Season with salt and pepper to taste. Spoon salsa on top. Serve immediately.

---

211   HUEVOS REVUELTOS WITH GRILLED SALSA
Prep: 15 minutes   Cook: 4 minutes   Serves: 6

Huevos revueltos are Mexican scrambled eggs. Here they are jazzed up with fresh cilantro and chile powder and served in flour tortillas with a freshly made grilled salsa.

1 medium tomato, diced	¼ teaspoon pepper
3 tablespoons butter	½ teaspoon pure chile powder
8 eggs	or chili powder
¼ cup milk	12 (10-inch) flour tortillas,
1 tablespoon chopped fresh	warmed
cilantro	Grilled Salsa (page 137)
½ teaspoon salt	

1. In a large skillet, cook tomato in butter over medium-high heat for 1 minute.

2. Whisk eggs, milk, cilantro, salt, pepper, and chile powder until blended. Pour eggs over tomatoes. Move eggs slowly with spatula until eggs are set but still moist, about 3 minutes.

3. Spoon eggs into serving bowl. Take to table with stack of flour tortillas and grilled salsa.

4. To eat, scoop eggs into center of tortilla. Spoon a line of salsa down eggs, roll up, and eat.

212   GRILLED SALSA

Prep: 10 minutes   Cook: 20 minutes   Makes: 3 cups

A grill is great to prepare the ingredients for this salsa. In winter, I use a cast-iron griddle set over two burners of my stove.

1 red onion, cut into thick rings	4 garlic cloves, minced
3 ripe tomatoes, halved and seeded	2 tablespoons chopped cilantro or parsley
1 fresh poblano or Anaheim chile (see Note)	2 tablespoons lime juice
	½ teaspoon salt
	¼ teaspoon pepper

1. Arrange onion rings, tomato halves, and chile on an outdoor grill over medium-hot coals or on a cookie sheet if broiling indoors. Grill onions 4 minutes on each side; tomatoes about 3 minutes on each side, or until charred and soft; and chile until entire surface blackens, which could take up to 20 minutes. Remove each vegetable when done.

2. Chop onion and tomatoes. Place in a mixing bowl.

3. Peel poblano, cut open, and discard stem and seeds. Add to onion and tomatoes. Stir in garlic, cilantro, lime juice, salt, and pepper. Serve at room temperature.

NOTE: *If fresh chiles are unavailable, use canned whole green chiles, cut into strips. Add directly to the salsa in the mixing bowl.*

213   CHILE RELLENO CASSEROLE

Prep: 10 minutes   Cook: 50 to 60 minutes   Serves: 8

This is a more custardy version than the previous one. It uses more milk and flour.

8 to 10 whole fresh green chiles, roasted, peeled, and seeded (page 53), or 2 (8-ounce) cans whole green chiles	3 eggs
	2 cups milk
	1 cup flour
	½ teaspoon salt
1 pound Monterey Jack cheese, shredded	¼ teaspoon pepper

1. Preheat oven to 350°F. Butter bottom of a 9 x 13-inch baking dish.

2. Slit chiles. Layer half in bottom of casserole. Cover with cheese. Top cheese with remaining chiles.

3. Whisk eggs, milk, flour, salt, and pepper vigorously. Pour slowly into casserole.

4. Bake 50 to 60 minutes, or until top is golden and a toothpick inserted 1 inch from edge comes out clean.

214 BLUE CORN TORTILLA COMPANY PIE
Prep: 15 minutes   Cook: 45 to 50 minutes   Serves: 6 to 8

Lynn Winter of the Paradise Cafe in Louisville, Kentucky, has created a shrine to eggs in her restaurant. In this dish Lynn honors the Southwest. If there are no blue corn tortillas in your market, use regular corn tortillas.

12 eggs
1 cup cream or milk
½ cup shredded Monterey Jack cheese
½ cup shredded Cheddar cheese
1 tablespoon vegetable oil
½ cup diced onion
½ cup coarsely chopped red and green bell peppers
½ cup canned diced green chiles
½ cup sliced black olives
½ cup diced seeded tomatoes

½ cup frozen corn kernels, thawed
1 (16-ounce) can black beans, rinsed and drained
2 tablespoons chopped cilantro
1 teaspoon ground cumin
¼ teaspoon salt
¼ teaspoon pepper
6 blue corn tortillas, cut into wedges
Chunky Salsa (recipe follows)
Sour cream

1. Preheat oven to 400°F. Grease a 9 x 13-inch baking dish.

2. In a large bowl, whisk eggs and cream until blended. Stir in Jack and Cheddar cheeses.

3. In a large skillet, heat oil over medium-high heat. Add onion, bell peppers, and chiles. Cook until onions are tender, about 3 minutes. Add vegetables to egg-cheese mixture. Fold in olives, tomatoes, corn, black beans, cilantro, cumin, salt, and pepper.

4. Pour egg mixture into prepared baking dish. Poke tortilla wedges into mixture, leaving a few points sticking out.

5. Bake about 45 minutes, until top is slightly browned and center of pie no longer jiggles if shaken. Cut into squares. Serve hot or warm, topped with salsa and sour cream.

215 CHUNKY SALSA
Prep: 5 minutes   Cook: none   Makes: 1½ cups

1 cup canned whole tomatoes, well drained
4 whole pickled jalapeño peppers, cut into chunks
¼ cup chopped parsley

2 tablespoons chopped cilantro
1 tablespoon minced onion
Salt

In a food processor, combine tomatoes, jalapeño peppers, parsley, cilantro, and onion. Pulse to chop and blend, but leave chunks. Season with salt to taste. Use at once or refrigerate in a covered container for up to 3 days.

216   EL PASO GREEN CHILE CASSEROLE
Prep: 10 minutes   Cook: 1 hour   Serves: 8

No other dish says "party" in El Paso like Green Chile Casserole. You can find it at luncheons, cocktail parties, and bar mitzvahs, plain or with tomato sauce on top. This is the cheater's chiles rellenos—you get chiles, cheese, and eggs without having to stuff or fry the chiles.

10 to 12 whole fresh green
      chiles, roasted, peeled,
      and seeded (page 53), or
      2 (8-ounce) cans whole
      green chiles, drained
½ pound Monterey Jack
      cheese, shredded
½ pound Longhorn or
      Cheddar cheese,
      shredded

4   eggs, separated
⅔ cup evaporated milk
1   tablespoon flour
¼ teaspoon salt
⅛ teaspoon freshly ground
      pepper

1. Preheat oven to 350°F. Butter bottom of a 9 x 13-inch baking dish.

2. Arrange chiles over bottom of dish. Sprinkle a layer of Monterey Jack cheese over chiles. Top with a layer of Longhorn cheese.

3. In a medium bowl, whisk egg yolks with evaporated milk, flour, salt, and pepper until thick and light colored.

4. In another bowl, beat egg whites to stiff peaks. Fold beaten whites into egg yolk mixture. Spread over cheese. Run a spatula through eggs to fill air pockets.

5. Bake 1 hour, or until top is golden and a toothpick inserted 1 inch from the edge comes out clean.

Variation:

217   GREEN CHILE CASSEROLE
WITH CHORIZO

In a small skillet, fry ⅓ pound Mexican chorizo, breaking up pieces, until fully cooked, about 10 minutes. Strain off fat in a wire strainer; reserve drained chorizo. Prepare Green Chile Casserole as described in recipe 216, sprinkling chorizo over Longhorn cheese.

218   AVOCADO STUFFED WITH EGGS AND SALSA

Prep: 10 minutes   Cook: 1 minute   Serves: 2

Anyone who can eat an entire avocado would do well to perfect this recipe.

2 avocados	4 poached eggs (page 116)
1 lime	Salt
1 (15-ounce) can refried beans	½ cup sour cream
½ teaspoon ground cumin	Salsa
½ fresh jalapeño pepper, seeded and finely minced	

1. Preheat broiler. Halve, peel, and pit avocados. Halve lime and squeeze juice all over avocado.

2. In a medium microwave-safe bowl, mix refried beans with 1 tablespoon water, cumin, and jalapeño pepper. Cover tightly. Microwave on High about 1 minute just to warm. Stir well.

3. Spoon beans into 2 ovenproof soup bowls. Nestle 2 avocado halves in beans, cavities up. Using a slotted spoon, set poached eggs in cavities. Season lightly with salt.

4. Top with sour cream and salsa. Serve immediately.

Chapter 9

Stratas Various

The strata is a sort of savory bread pudding, a fabulous creation consisting of layers of eggs, buttered bread, and fillings often created at whim the night before you serve it, making it the easiest brunch idea ever. I love the way you just wake up and shove it in the oven in the morning, *then* make the coffee.

The strata is a relatively new contrivance for American cooks. Looking at books and pamphlets about eggs from 30 to 40 years ago, you would be hard-pressed to find a recipe for a strata. Be happy it came along. Think of it as the dump cake of egg cookery (once you've gotten the fillings prepared, of course). It's the best way to get the lushness and creativity of a quiche, a frittata, or omelet without the careful cooking or last-minute preparation.

Fairly well known are the simple stratas with cheese, typically Cheddar or Swiss cheese. Some stratas are made with white bread, others with French or sourdough bread or whole wheat bread. One classic is based on potato chips. In Mexican cooking, tortillas are used to make a stratalike dish called chilaquiles.

If you haven't had time to allow your bread to become stale, put the slices out on wire racks so air can circulate around them. They'll be "stale" in an hour. You can also crisp the bread if you have a gas oven with a pilot light by leaving the slices in the turned-off oven for about 20 minutes.

When you fill the strata layers with an egg-milk custard, it's important to pour the batter slowly and evenly so it seeps in and doesn't overflow the baking dish. Some stratas need to bake for an hour or so, some only 45 to 50 minutes. For the moistest and most richly textured strata experience, eat the strata hot from the oven. Serve right from the baking dish.

219   CINNAMON TOAST STRATA
Prep: 10 minutes   Chill: overnight   Cook: 45 minutes   Serves: 6

1 stick (4 ounces) butter,
   softened
3 tablespoons cinnamon
8 slices of whole wheat or
   other bread, such as
   sourdough or raisin bread

¼ cup sugar
6 eggs
1½ cups milk
3 tablespoons maple syrup or
   sorghum syrup

1. In a small bowl, mash butter with cinnamon. Spread on bread. Arrange 4 slices of bread in bottom of a 2-quart baking dish, buttered side-up, trimming to fit. Sprinkle with 2 tablespoons sugar. Top with remaining bread, buttered side down. Sprinkle with remaining sugar.

2. In a medium bowl, whisk eggs, milk, and maple syrup, blending very well. Pour slowly over bread. Cover with foil and refrigerate overnight.

3. Preheat oven to 350°F. Bake strata, uncovered, 45 minutes, or until puffed, golden, and set. Serve with additional maple syrup on the side.

220   GOUDA-SPINACH STRATA WITH ITALIAN SAUSAGE
Prep: 10 minutes   Chill: overnight   Cook: 1¼ hours   Serves: 4 to 6

¾ pound bulk Italian sausage
4 tablespoons butter, at room
   temperature
6 slices of French sourdough
   bread
1 (10-ounce) package frozen
   chopped spinach, thawed

½ pound Gouda cheese,
   shredded
6 eggs
1½ cups milk
¼ teaspoon salt
¼ teaspoon pepper

1. In a medium skillet, fry sausage over medium heat, stirring to break up lumps, until no longer pink, 12 to 15 minutes. Drain off fat.

2. Butter an 8- or 9-inch square baking dish. Butter slices of bread. Fit 3 slices into pan, buttered side up, trimming if necessary. Layer with half of the spinach, sausage, and cheese. Arrange remaining bread over cheese, buttered side down. Top with remaining spinach, sausage, and cheese.

3. In a medium bowl, whisk eggs, milk, salt, and pepper until blended. Pour evenly and slowly over strata. Cover with foil and refrigerate overnight.

4. Preheat oven to 350°F. Bake strata, uncovered, 1 hour, or until risen, puffed, and nicely browned.

221 HERBED COTTAGE CHEESE STRATA WITH ROASTED RED PEPPER

Prep: 10 minutes   Chill: overnight   Cook: 1½ hours   Serves: 4 to 6

2 red bell peppers
1 (16-ounce) container large-curd cottage cheese
2 tablespoons chopped fresh parsley
2 scallions, thinly sliced
1 tablespoon chopped fresh oregano or 1 teaspoon dried
1 tablespoon chopped fresh thyme or 1 teaspoon dried

6 tablespoons butter
1 tablespoon Dijon mustard
8 slices of firm-textured white or sourdough bread
6 eggs
1½ cups milk
½ teaspoon salt
¼ teaspoon pepper

1. Preheat oven to 400°F. Roast peppers on a baking sheet, turning with tongs, until skin loosens and shrivels but does not blacken, about 30 minutes. Drop roasted peppers into a plastic or brown paper bag; steam 10 minutes, or until cool to touch. Peel and discard seeds and stems; cut each pepper into 4 big squares.

2. Meanwhile, in a medium bowl, stir cottage cheese, parsley, scallions, oregano, and thyme just until blended. In a 1-cup glass measure, microwave butter with mustard on High 20 seconds to melt. Stir to mix well.

3. Butter an 8- or 9-inch square baking dish. Brush bread with mustard-butter. Arrange 3 slices, buttered side up, to fit in baking dish, trimming if necessary. Top with a layer of red peppers, then half of the herbed cottage cheese. Arrange remaining bread, buttered side down, over cottage cheese, to fit. Top with remaining peppers and cottage cheese.

4. In a medium bowl, whisk eggs, milk, salt, and pepper until blended. Pour slowly and evenly over strata. Cover with foil and refrigerate overnight.

5. Preheat oven to 350°F. Bake strata, uncovered, 1 hour, or until puffed, golden, and set.

222   GORGONZOLA, CELERY, AND WALNUT STRATA

Prep: 10 minutes   Chill: overnight   Cook: 50 minutes
Serves: 4 to 6

2 cups minced celery	6 eggs
1 stick (4 ounces) butter	1½ cups milk
1½ cups walnut halves or pieces	¼ teaspoon salt
6 slices of French or	½ teaspoon freshly ground
sourdough bread	pepper
5 ounces gorgonzola or other	
blue cheese, crumbled	

1. In a large skillet, cook celery in 2 tablespoons of the butter over high heat 1 minute. Reduce heat to medium-high and cook 3 minutes longer, until slightly softened. Add walnuts and toss. Remove from heat and let cool. Melt remaining butter.

2. Butter an 8- or 9-inch square baking dish. Brush butter over bread. Arrange 3 slices on bottom, buttered sides up. Top with half of celery-walnut mixture, then half of gorgonzola. Place remaining bread, buttered side down, over cheese. Top with remaining celery-nut mixture and gorgonzola.

3. Whisk eggs, milk, salt, and pepper, blending very well. Pour slowly and evenly over strata. Cover with foil and refrigerate overnight.

4. Preheat oven to 350°F. Bake strata, uncovered, 45 minutes, or until puffed and richly browned. Serve hot.

223   SAUSAGE CHEESE STRATA WITH WHITE WINE

Prep: 10 minutes   Chill: 6 hours or overnight   Cook: 1¼ hours
Serves: 4 to 6

This is a classic that was often requested by readers of the *Louisville Courier-Journal* when I worked there in the 1980s. It was very popular at parties during the week of the Kentucky Derby.

6 breakfast link sausages	1½ cups milk
3 tablespoons butter, softened	¼ cup dry white wine
6 slices of day-old bread	1 teaspoon powdered
1 cup shredded Cheddar	mustard
cheese	¼ teaspoon salt
6 eggs	¼ teaspoon pepper

1. In a medium skillet, cook sausages over medium heat until browned, about 12 to 15 minutes. Drain on paper towels, then crumble.

2. Butter bread and cut into small cubes. Alternate layers of bread cubes and cheese in a buttered 9 x 13-inch baking dish. Top with cooked sausage.

3. In a medium bowl, lightly whisk eggs, milk, wine, mustard, salt, and pepper until blended. Pour over bread-cheese-sausage mixture. Cover with foil and refrigerate at least 6 hours or overnight.

4. Preheat oven to 350°F. Bake, uncovered, 1 hour, or until puffed and golden.

---

224 THANKSGIVING STRATA WITH LEFTOVER TURKEY AND SOME OF YOUR GRAVY

Prep: 15 minutes   Chill: overnight   Cook: 50 minutes   Serves: 6

Easier than hash and other turkey contrivances after a Thanksgiving feast, strata can go together after you finish the main dinner, then head for the refrigerator for eating the next day. This works with stuffings made of bread, corn bread, or rice containing mushrooms, celery, nuts, or dried fruit.

8 **slices of bread, stale or dried** **on racks or in oven**	2 **cups shredded Monterey** **Jack or Cheddar cheese**
2 **tablespoons melted butter**	6 **eggs**
1 **cup leftover cranberry sauce** **(optional)**	1½ **cups milk**
2 **to 3 cups diced cooked** **turkey**	½ **cup leftover gravy or** **skimmed pan juices**
1 **cup leftover stuffing** **(optional)**	¼ **teaspoon salt**
	¼ **teaspoon pepper**
	3 **scallions, sliced**

1. Butter a 9 x 13-inch baking dish. Arrange 4 slices of bread in bottom of dish, cutting to fit. Brush with butter. Spread cranberry sauce, if available, over bread. Top cranberry sauce with half of turkey, stuffing, if available, and cheese. Brush remaining bread with butter and place, buttered side-down, on cheese. Top with remaining turkey, stuffing, and cheese.

2. In a medium bowl, whisk eggs, milk, gravy, salt, and pepper until well blended. Stir in scallions. Pour slowly over strata, allowing to soak in. Cover tightly with foil and refrigerate overnight.

3. Preheat oven to 350°F. Bake strata, uncovered, 50 minutes, or until puffed and golden.

225 ENCHILADA STRATA WITH GREEN SAUCE

Prep: 10 minutes   Chill: overnight   Cook: 53 minutes
Serves: 4 to 6

1 medium onion, minced	12 corn tortillas
1½ teaspoons butter	6 eggs
1 (14-ounce) can green enchilada sauce	1¼ cups milk
	¼ cup sour cream
1 tablespoon minced garlic	1 to 2 fresh jalapeño or serrano peppers, seeded and minced
¼ teaspoon ground cumin	
¼ teaspoon dried oregano	
2 tablespoons minced fresh cilantro	1 teaspoon salt
	½ teaspoon pepper
¾ pound Monterey Jack cheese, shredded	

1. In a medium nonstick skillet, cook onion in butter over medium-high heat until softened, about 3 minutes. Transfer onion to a mixing bowl. Stir in enchilada sauce, garlic, cumin, oregano, and cilantro. Gently stir in cheese.

2. Butter a 9-inch square baking dish. Arrange 4 tortillas, overlapping, in a dish. Spoon a third of the cheese mixture over tortillas. Repeat layering twice more.

3. In a medium bowl, whisk eggs, milk, sour cream, jalapeño, salt, and pepper. Pour slowly over layers, making sure top tortillas are submerged. Cover with foil and refrigerate overnight.

4. Preheat oven to 350°F. Bake, uncovered, 50 minutes, or until puffed and richly browned.

226 LONGHORN STRATA WITH RED CHILES

Prep: 10 minutes   Chill: overnight   Cook: 1 hour 20 minutes
Serves: 4 to 6

Little effort produces the authentic flavors of the American Southwest.

3 ancho chiles	6 eggs
5 garlic cloves	1¼ cups milk
1 pound Longhorn, Cheddar, or Colby cheese, shredded	¼ cup buttermilk, sour cream, or yogurt
6 slices of white bread	¼ teaspoon salt
4 tablespoons butter, melted	¼ teaspoon pepper

1. Soak ancho chiles in a medium saucepan with water to cover 30 minutes. Cover with a lid and bring to a boil. Reduce heat to medium-low and simmer 20 minutes. Let cool, covered. Remove chiles; reserve about ¼ cup cooking liquid.

2. Discard seeds and stems. In a food processor or blender, puree anchos with garlic and 3 to 4 tablespoons cooking liquid until smooth. Mix ¼ cup ancho puree with shredded cheese.

3. Butter an 8- or 9-inch square baking dish. Brush bread with melted butter. Arrange 3 slices, buttered side up, to fit in dish. Top with half of ancho-cheese mixture. Arrange remaining bread over it, buttered side down. Top with rest of ancho-cheese mixture.

4. In a medium bowl, whisk eggs, milk, buttermilk, salt, and pepper just until blended. Pour slowly over bread. Let soak in. Cover with foil and refrigerate overnight.

5. Preheat oven to 350°F. Bake strata, uncovered, 50 minutes, or until puffed and richly browned.

---

227 ENCHILADA STRATA WITH RED CHILE, CHEESE, AND ONION

Prep: 10 minutes   Chill: overnight   Cook: 45 minutes   Serves: 6

1 **(14-ounce) can red enchilada sauce**	1 **medium onion, finely minced**
4 **garlic cloves, finely minced**	6 **eggs**
¼ **teaspoon ground cumin**	¾ **cup milk**
¼ **teaspoon dried oregano**	½ **cup sour cream**
8 **corn tortillas**	¼ **teaspoon salt**
¾ **pound Monterey Jack cheese, shredded**	¼ **teaspoon pepper**

1. Butter a 9-inch square baking dish. In a mixing bowl, combine enchilada sauce with garlic, cumin, and oregano. Mix well. Ladle about ½ cup sauce onto bottom of baking dish. Arrange 4 tortillas, overlapping, in sauce.

2. Spoon half of remaining sauce over tortillas. Top with half of cheese and all of onion. Repeat with a layer of tortillas, then remaining sauce and cheese.

3. In a medium bowl, whisk eggs, milk, sour cream, salt, and pepper. Slowly pour over layers, making sure top tortillas and cheese are submerged. Cover with foil and refrigerate overnight.

4. Preheat oven to 350°F. Bake strata, uncovered, 45 minutes, until puffed and richly browned.

228 CHILAQUILES BRUNCH CASSEROLE

Prep: 10 minutes   Stand: overnight   Cook: 1 hour 10 minutes
Serves: 8

No two recipes for chilaquiles are alike. Along the border it's a beautiful mass of cheese, tortillas, green or red sauce, cilantro, and sour cream. By arranging the layers with a light egg custard, the dish becomes a fabulous brunch casserole (a.k.a. strata). You'd better like your house to smell like garlic because it will twice—the day you make it and the day you bake it.

1 **medium onion, chopped**	**Dash of white pepper**
4 **garlic cloves, minced**	8 **(7-inch) flour tortillas**
2 **tablespoons butter**	**Vegetable oil**
1 **(10-ounce) can tomatoes and**	1 **pound Monterey Jack**
green chiles, with their	**cheese, shredded**
liquid	8 **eggs**
1 **(16-ounce) can plum**	2 **cups milk**
tomatoes, with their	½ **teaspoon pepper**
liquid	2 **cups sour cream**
¼ **cup chopped cilantro**	2 **teaspoons chili powder**
½ **teaspoon salt**	

1. In a large skillet or flameproof casserole, cook onion and garlic in butter over medium heat until golden, 6 to 8 minutes. Add canned tomatoes with chiles and plum tomatoes, both with their liquid. Bring to a boil, reduce heat, and simmer, uncovered, stirring now and then to break up tomatoes, until sauce thickens, about 15 minutes.

2. Stir in cilantro, ¼ teaspoon of salt, and white pepper.

3. Meanwhile, stack tortillas 4 at a time and cut into fourths. In a deep-fat fryer or large saucepan, heat 2 inches oil to 350°F. Add tortilla wedges in batches without crowding and fry until golden, 30 to 60 seconds per batch. Remove with strainer or slotted spoon and drain on paper towels.

4. Ladle a little sauce on bottom of a 9x13-inch baking dish. Cover bottom with half of the fried tortilla chips. Top with half of remaining sauce and half of cheese. Repeat with chips, then rest of sauce and cheese.

5. In a medium bowl, whisk eggs, milk, remaining ¼ teaspoon salt, and pepper. Slowly pour into casserole. Cover well with foil and refrigerate overnight.

6. Preheat oven to 350°F. Bake, uncovered, 35 minutes. Mix sour cream and chili powder. Spread over casserole. Return to oven and bake 10 minutes longer, until puffed and lightly browned.

229   GOVERNOR'S EGGS

Prep: 10 minutes   Cook: 45 to 51 minutes   Serves: 8

This is *the* Kentucky Derby weekend breakfast specialty. I suppose it's as old as potato chips, which are the traditional source of this casserole's crunch. With its béchamel base, hard-cooked eggs, sausage, and cheese, it's a winner at brunch even for losers at the race: a strata-type dish without the overnight wait.

6 **breakfast sausage links**
1 **small onion, finely chopped**
2 **tablespoons butter**
2 **tablespoons flour**
1 **cup warm milk**

¼ **cup dry white wine**
6 **hard-boiled eggs, sliced**
1½ **cups coarsely crushed potato chips**

1. Set rack in middle of oven and preheat to 350°F.

2. Remove sausage from casings. In a medium skillet, cook sausage over medium heat until browned, 10 to 15 minutes. Drain on paper towels, then crumble. Discard fat.

3. In same skillet, cook onion in butter over medium heat until softened, about 3 minutes. Add flour and cook, whisking constantly, 1 full minute. Slowly whisk in milk and wine. Bring to a boil, stirring until sauce thickens, 1 to 2 minutes. Remove from heat and stir cheese into sauce until melted.

4. Arrange half of egg slices in a layer in a 9 x 13-inch baking dish. Cover with half of cheese sauce, then half of the chips and sausage. Repeat layers, ending with sausage.

5. Bake 30 minutes or until puffed and golden brown.

Chapter 10

Egg White Cuisine

In these days of fat and cholesterol vigilance, it has become fashionable to waste food. Experts say it's okay to throw away egg yolks in pursuit of a cuisine using only egg whites. This chapter is just for egg whites, but if you are not on a fat-free regimen, then I believe it wise to save the yolks for a cake or a custard.

Some of the recipes using egg whites are very low in fat and high in flavor. Some of the richness normally supplied by yolks is missing. However, not every recipe using egg whites is low in calories or low in fat. Some recipes rely on egg whites for their ability to pouf up a recipe, such as Angel Food Cake. In the Brie Herb Mousse, sufficient fat is provided by the cheese and a little cream. It's the egg whites' job to air out the mousse for a pleasant lightness.

I must admit that after making a number of soufflés with no yolks, I am sold. Soufflés using cheese, vegetables, or seafood really don't need yolks in the white-sauce base. As for baked meringue, it would not exist were it not for the egg white. That said, watch the egg white work.

---

230 EGG WHITE CHEESE FRITTERS
Prep: 5 minutes   Cook: 4 minutes   Serves: 6

I like to serve these as one of several hot hors d'oeuvres at a cocktail party. The fritters can be formed in advance, which is convenient, but they are best served as soon as they are fried.

2 **egg whites**
¼ **teaspoon salt**
⅛ **teaspoon pepper**
¾ **cup shredded Swiss cheese**

1 **cup Italian-seasoned bread crumbs**
Pinch of cayenne
Vegetable oil, for frying

1. In a small bowl, beat egg whites, salt, and pepper to stiff peaks. Fold in cheese, bread crumbs, and cayenne.

2. Form mixture into walnut-size balls. If prepared ahead, arrange on wax paper–lined cookie sheet. May be refrigerated for up to 2 hours.

3. In a large saucepan or deep-fat fryer, heat 1 inch vegetable oil to 350°F. Fry balls in 2 batches until golden brown, about 2 minutes per batch. Drain on paper towels. Serve hot.

231   CORN CLOUD SOUP
Prep: 10 minutes   Cook: 9 to 10 minutes   Serves: 6 to 8

This is a dazzling company dish that's light and tasty. The soup comes to the table with light-as-a-cloud poached egg whites bobbing on top.

⅓ **pound ground pork**
2 **egg whites**
1 **tablespoon plus 1 teaspoon Chinese oyster sauce**
4 **cups chicken stock**
2 **cups fresh or frozen corn kernels**

2½ **tablespoons cornstarch**
2 **tablespoons finely minced cilantro**
1 **tablespoon minced scallion**

1. In a small skillet, cook pork over medium heat, stirring to break up lumps, until no longer pink, about 8 minutes. Drain on paper towels.

2. In a small bowl, beat egg whites with 1 teaspoon of the oyster sauce until stiff. Set aside.

3. In a medium saucepan, bring chicken stock to a boil. Add cooked pork, remaining 1 tablespoon oyster sauce, and corn. Return to a boil. Dissolve cornstarch in 3 tablespoons cold water until smooth. Pour slowly into soup, stirring to blend. Boil until thickened and clear, 1 to 2 minutes. Remove from heat. Fold beaten egg whites into soup. They'll break up, become smooth, and bob on top.

4. Garnish with cilantro and scallion and serve immediately, making sure each portion gets some whites.

232   EGG WHITE OMELET WITH TOMATO, HERBS, AND PARMESAN CHEESE
Prep: 10 minutes   Cook: 6 minutes   Serves: 2

1 **tablespoon chopped parsley**
1 **tablespoon chopped basil**
¼ **cup grated Parmesan cheese**
3 **egg whites**
Pinch of salt

Pinch of pepper
1 **tablespoon olive oil**
1 **small shallot, minced**
1 **medium tomato, seeded and chopped**

1. In a small bowl, mix parsley, basil, and Parmesan. Have convenient to stove. In another small bowl, beat egg whites, salt, and pepper until frothy.

2. In a medium nonstick skillet, heat olive oil over medium-high heat. Add shallot and tomato. Cook, stirring, until tomato is slightly softened, 1 to 2 minutes. Reduce heat to medium. Pour in egg whites, spreading evenly. Cook until edges are firm and center is barely runny, about 3 minutes.

3. Spoon herb-Parmesan mixture over 1 side of omelet. Fold plain side over filling. Cook about 30 seconds longer to set.

4. Slide onto a serving platter. Divide in half and serve hot.

233   BRIE HERB MOUSSE

Prep: 15 minutes   Cook: none   Chill: 4 hours   Serves: 10 to 12

Brie and herbs are formed into a beautiful ring mold perfect at holiday tables to serve as a spread with toasted bread or crackers. This recipe just won't be quite the same with dried herbs, but you can use them in a pinch.

6 scallions
1 envelope plain gelatin
3 tablespoons lemon juice
¾ cup boiling water
½ pound Brie, softened
8 ounces cream cheese,
    softened
½ cup finely chopped fresh
    herbs, such as parsley,
    tarragon, rosemary, basil,
    thyme, and chervil, or
    ¼ cup chopped parsley
    and 2 teaspoons dried
    herbs

¾ cup dry white wine
¼ teaspoon salt
⅛ teaspoon white pepper
4 egg whites
½ cup heavy cream

1. Chop white and green parts of scallions separately. Sprinkle chopped green parts over bottom of a 10-inch tube pan.

2. In a large bowl, soften gelatin in lemon juice, about 5 minutes. Pour in boiling water and stir to dissolve.

3. In a food processor, blend white parts of scallion with Brie, cream cheese, and herbs. Add to gelatin, stirring to blend well. Mix in wine, salt, and pepper.

4. In a medium bowl, beat egg whites to stiff peaks. Fold into herbed cheese mixture.

5. In another medium bowl, whip cream to soft peaks. Fold into mousse. Pour into mold. Cover and refrigerate until set, at least 4 hours.

6. To serve, invert onto a round serving platter.

234 MUSHROOM AND SWISS CHEESE EGG WHITE OMELET

Prep: 10 minutes   Cook: 15 minutes   Serves: 2

1 small onion, chopped	⅛ teaspoon pepper
1 tablespoon butter	⅛ teaspoon turmeric
6 to 8 fresh mushrooms, sliced	⅓ cup shredded Swiss or
6 egg whites	Monterey Jack cheese
¼ teaspoon salt	

1. In a medium nonstick skillet, cook onion in butter over medium-high heat until softened, about 3 minutes. Add mushrooms and cook until lightly browned, 3 to 5 minutes longer.

2. In a medium bowl, whisk egg whites, 2 tablespoons water, salt, pepper, and turmeric until they begin to foam. Pour into skillet. Reduce heat to medium-low and cook until omelet is opaque and barely set, 3 to 4 minutes.

3. Sprinkle cheese over top and cook until omelet is firm, 1 to 2 minutes longer. Fold in half and cook 30 seconds longer. Remove to a serving plate. Cut into 2 pieces and serve at once.

235 RICOTTA EGG WHITE OMELET

Prep: 5 minutes   Cook: 4 to 5 minutes   Serves: 4

Ricotta adds body—as well as calcium and extra protein—with little fat. The one egg yolk included here contributes structure and color, while the crispy bread crumbs on top provide a pleasing contrast of texture with the smooth omelet.

8 ounces ricotta cheese	1 tablespoon butter
6 egg whites	½ cup toasted bread crumbs
1 whole egg	2 tablespoons chopped
3 tablespoons milk	parsley
¼ teaspoon salt	½ teaspoon dried Italian
⅛ teaspoon pepper	seasoning

1. Empty ricotta into a strainer to drain while you pull rest of omelet together. Preheat broiler.

2. In a large mixing bowl, whip egg whites, whole egg, milk, salt, and pepper just until whites billow softly. Don't overwhip.

3. In a large nonstick skillet with ovenproof handle, melt butter over high heat. When bubbly, pour in eggs. Let set a few seconds, then reduce heat to medium-low and cook, lifting edges to let uncooked egg flow underneath, until edges are set but center is still runny, about 3 minutes.

4. Spoon ricotta evenly over entire surface of eggs. Mix bread crumbs, parsley, and Italian seasoning and sprinkle on top. Quickly transfer skillet to broiler and broil 1 to 2 minutes, until omelet puffs and turns golden. Slide onto a serving platter. Serve hot, cut into wedges.

236 EGG WHITE RICOTTA FRITTATA WITH MUSHROOMS AND SUN-DRIED TOMATOES

Prep: 10 minutes   Cook: 8 to 10 minutes   Serves: 2 or 3

6 sun-dried tomato halves	Pinch of salt
½ medium onion, sliced	Pinch of pepper
3 to 4 large mushrooms, sliced	½ cup ricotta cheese
1 tablespoon butter	3 tablespoons grated
6 egg whites	Parmesan cheese
½ teaspoon dried Italian seasoning	

1. Soak tomatoes in very hot tap water to plump, 10 to 15 minutes. Drain and slice into thin strips.

2. Preheat broiler. In a medium nonstick skillet with ovenproof handle, cook onion and mushrooms in butter over medium-high heat until soft, about 5 minutes. Add dried tomato strips.

3. In a medium bowl, whisk egg whites, Italian seasoning, salt, and pepper until frothy. Pour over mushrooms. Reduce heat to medium-low and cook until bottom is set and edges puff a little, 2 to 3 minutes.

4. Spread ricotta over frittata. Run under broiler until frittata is puffed and cheese softens, 1 to 2 minutes. Slide out of pan onto a serving plate. Sprinkle Parmesan cheese on top. Serve hot, cut into wedges.

237 SAFFRON-MUSHROOM EGG WHITE SCRAMBLE

Prep: 10 minutes   Cook: 11 to 13 minutes   Serves: 2

Saffron not only tastes heavenly, it tints egg whites yellow to fool you into believing yolks are present. Remember, keep the heat on low.

⅛ teaspoon saffron threads	¼ teaspoon salt
1 tablespoon butter	⅛ teaspoon pepper
1 small onion, chopped	6 egg whites
6 to 8 fresh mushrooms, sliced	⅓ cup fresh bread crumbs

1. In a small bowl, soak saffron in 2 tablespoons water. Set aside.

2. In a medium nonstick skillet, melt butter over medium-high heat. Add onion and cook until softened, about 3 minutes. Add mushrooms and cook 3 to 5 minutes, until lightly browned.

3. In a medium bowl, whisk egg whites with saffron and water to very light foam. Pour into skillet. Reduce heat to medium-low and cook, stirring with flat edge of a spatula, until eggs are almost set, about 4 minutes.

4. Sprinkle on bread crumbs. Fold and stir gently once or twice until egg whites are set, about 1 minute. Serve at once.

238 WHITE-MAKES-LIGHT GRUYÈRE SOUFFLÉ
Prep: 10 minutes   Cook: 34 to 40 minutes   Serves: 4

A basic white sauce base is kept yolkless but gets fluffed with beaten whites for one of the richest soufflé experiences ever. You'll wonder if you'll ever again make cheese soufflé with yolks. If you can't find real Gruyère, use a good imported Swiss cheese.

¾ cup plus 2 tablespoons
   grated Parmesan cheese
3 tablespoons butter
¼ cup flour
1½ cups warm milk
   Pinch of grated nutmeg
   Pinch of cayenne

   Pinch of salt
4 ounces Gruyère or Swiss
   cheese, shredded (about
   1¾ cups)
6 egg whites
¼ teaspoon cream of tartar

1. Set rack in lower third of oven and preheat to 375°F. Wrap folded length of wax paper around outside of a 6-cup soufflé dish, making a collar 3 inches higher than dish. Tie tightly with string. Butter inside of dish and collar. Sprinkle 2 tablespoons of the Parmesan cheese all over inside of dish and collar. Set aside.

2. In a medium saucepan, melt butter over medium heat. When bubbly, add flour and cook, stirring, until the resulting paste is lightly browned, 2 to 2½ minutes. Immediately whisk in warm milk, which will sputter. Bring to a boil, whisking until sauce is very thick, 1 to 2 minutes. Reduce heat to low and simmer, stirring, 1 minute longer.

3. Remove from heat and stir in ½ cup of remaining Parmesan cheese, nutmeg, cayenne, and salt. Scrape sauce into a large mixing bowl. Fold in Gruyère cheese.

4. In a medium bowl, beat egg whites and cream of tartar to firm peaks. Fold a scoop of whites into sauce until blended to lighten. Fold rest of whites into sauce base, blending completely.

5. Pour into soufflé dish. Sprinkle remaining ¼ cup Parmesan over top. With a knife, cut a deep circle into center of batter; this will help to form a raised crown.

6. Bake 30 to 35 minutes, until soufflé is puffed, golden brown, and still slightly jiggly. Serve now!

239 WHITE-MAKES-LIGHT SALMON SOUFFLÉ

Prep: 10 minutes   Cook: 35 to 40 minutes   Serves: 4

This is a high-calcium, high-protein main-course soufflé. Serve, if you like, with rice and buttered asparagus.

¾ cup plus 2 tablespoons
   grated Parmesan cheese
3 tablespoons butter
¼ cup flour
1⅓ cups warm milk
   Pinch of cayenne
¼ teaspoon powdered
   mustard

¼ teaspoon pepper
1 (7-ounce) can sockeye
   salmon, drained well
6 egg whites
   Pinch of salt
¼ teaspoon cream of tartar

1. Set rack in lower third of oven and preheat to 375°F. Wrap folded length of wax paper around a 6-cup soufflé dish, making a collar 3 inches higher than dish. Tie tightly with string. Butter inside of dish and collar. Sprinkle 2 tablespoons Parmesan cheese all over inside of dish and collar. Set aside.

2. In a medium saucepan over medium heat, melt butter. When bubbly, add flour and cook, stirring, until resulting paste is pale, 1 to 2 minutes. Whisk in warm milk, which will sputter. Bring to a boil, whisking until sauce is smooth and very thick, 1 to 2 minutes. Reduce heat and simmer 1 minute longer, stirring.

3. Remove from heat and stir in ½ cup of remaining Parmesan cheese, cayenne, mustard, and pepper. Scrape sauce into large mixing bowl. Fold in salmon; set aside.

4. In a large bowl, beat egg whites, salt, and cream of tartar to firm peaks. Fold a scoop of whites into salmon base until blended to lighten. Fold in rest of whites, blending completely.

5. Pour into prepared soufflé dish. With a knife, cut a deep circle into center of batter to form a raised crown. Sprinkle remaining ¼ cup Parmesan on top.

6. Bake 30 to 35 minutes, until soufflé is puffed, golden brown, and still slightly jiggly. Serve at once.

240 WHITE-MAKES-LIGHT SPINACH SOUFFLÉ

Prep: 10 minutes   Cook: 30 to 35 minutes   Serves: 4

¾ cup plus 2 tablespoons
   grated Parmesan cheese
1 pound fresh spinach, well
   washed and stemmed, or
   1 (10-ounce) package
   frozen chopped spinach,
   thawed
3 tablespoons butter
¼ cup flour

1⅓ cups warm milk
¼ teaspoon powdered
   mustard
Pinch of grated nutmeg
Pinch of cayenne
Pinch of salt
6 egg whites
¼ teaspoon cream of tartar

1. Set rack in lower third of oven and preheat to 375°F. Wrap folded length of wax paper around side of a 6-cup soufflé dish, making a collar 3 inches higher than dish. Tie tightly with string. Butter inside of dish and collar. Sprinkle 2 tablespoons Parmesan cheese all over inside of dish and collar.

2. In a wok or large pot, wilt fresh spinach just in water left on its leaves from washing, over high heat. Cook 1 to 1½ minutes. Drain in a colander. When cool, squeeze out excess moisture. Coarsely chop. If using frozen spinach, press out moisture.

3. In a medium saucepan, melt butter over medium-high heat. When bubbly, add flour and cook, stirring, 1 to 2 minutes, until pale. Whisk in warm milk, which will sputter. Bring to a boil, stirring, until very thick, 1 to 2 minutes. Reduce heat and simmer 1 minute, stirring.

4. Remove from heat and stir in ½ cup Parmesan cheese, mustard, nutmeg, cayenne, and salt. Scrape into a large mixing bowl. Fold in chopped spinach.

5. In another large bowl, beat whites and cream of tartar to firm peaks. Fold a scoop of whites into spinach mixture until blended to lighten. Fold in rest of whites, blending completely. Pour into prepared soufflé dish. With a knife, cut a deep circle into center of batter to form a raised crown. Sprinkle remaining ¼ cup Parmesan on top.

6. Bake 25 to 30 minutes, until soufflé is puffed, golden brown, and still slightly jiggly. Serve right away.

241   GINGER-PEACH EGG WHITE SOUFFLÉ
Prep: 15 minutes   Cook: 31 to 36 minutes   Serves: 4

1 tablespoon butter, softened
1 cup plus 1 tablespoon sugar
1½ cups milk
½ cup cornstarch
4 to 5 peaches, peeled, pitted, and coarsely chopped (see Note), or 1 (16-ounce) package frozen peach slices, thawed and coarsely chopped

¼ teaspoon ground ginger
½ teaspoon almond extract
4 egg whites
¼ teaspoon cream of tartar

1. Set rack in center of oven and preheat to 400°F. Wrap a folded length of wax paper around side of a 6-cup soufflé dish, making a collar 3 inches higher than dish. Tie tightly with string. Butter inside of dish and collar. Sprinkle bottom and sides with 2 tablespoons of sugar, tapping out any excess.

2. In a medium saucepan, combine milk, ½ cup of remaining sugar, and cornstarch. Whisk until smooth. Bring to a boil over medium heat, whisking. Boil 1 minute, whisking constantly, until very thick. Remove from heat.

3. In a food processor, puree peaches with 3 tablespoons of sugar, ginger, and almond extract. Fold puree into milk base. Transfer mixture to large mixing bowl.

4. In another bowl, beat egg whites and cream of tartar until frothy. Keep beating while adding 2 tablespoons of sugar. Beat to stiff peaks. Fold a scoop of whites into peach base until blended to lighten. Fold in rest of whites, blending completely.

5. Pour into prepared soufflé dish. With a knife, cut a deep circle into center of batter; this will help to form a raised crown. Sprinkle remaining 2 table-spoons sugar over top.

6. Bake 30 to 35 minutes, until soufflé is puffed, golden brown, and still slightly jiggly. Serve at once.

NOTE: *To peel peaches easily, place peaches in a heatproof bowl. Pour boiling water over peaches. Let stand 30 seconds, then peel peaches under cold running water.*

242   BANANA EGG WHITE SOUFFLÉ FOR ONE
Prep: 10 minutes   Cook: 15 to 18 minutes   Serves: 1

My own weakness for bananas and caramelly brown sugar is exhibited in this easy egg white soufflé. You'll love the top, middle, and the scrapings from the sugary sides.

2 **tablespoons butter, softened**	2 **egg whites**
2½ **tablespoons granulated sugar**	2 **tablespoons powdered sugar**
1 **banana, sliced**	½ **teaspoon vanilla extract**
2½ **tablespoons brown sugar**	

1. Set rack in center of oven and preheat to 400°F. Use 1 tablespoon of butter to grease a 2-cup ramekin or soufflé dish. Sprinkle bottom and sides with ½ tablespoon of granulated sugar, tapping out any excess.

2. In a small skillet, melt remaining 1 tablespoon butter over medium-high heat. Quickly add bananas and brown sugar. Cook, tossing and stirring quickly, to coat slices on both sides, about 20 seconds. Transfer to a plate and let cool.

3. In a medium bowl, beat egg whites until frothy. Continue beating while adding remaining 2 tablespoons granulated sugar and powdered sugar. Beat until egg whites form stiff, glossy peaks. Fold in vanilla, bananas, and any cooking liquid from skillet. Transfer to buttered soufflé dish.

4. Bake 15 to 18 minutes, until soufflé is well browned and a knife inserted in center comes out clean. Eat immediately.

243   STRAWBERRY EGG WHITE SOUFFLÉ FOR ONE
Prep: 10 minutes   Cook: 16 to 18 minutes   Serves: 1

My friend Dana Jacobi makes this whenever she is in danger of reaching for a more high-volume dessert. Egg whites and strawberries give her just enough sweetness for this interlude, and with almost no fat.

½ **pint strawberries**	2 **egg whites**
3½ **tablespoons granulated sugar**	2 **tablespoons powdered sugar**
1 **tablespoon butter, softened**	½ **teaspoon vanilla extract**

1. Place strawberries and 1 tablespoon of granulated sugar in a blender or food processor. Puree until smooth. Set aside.

2. Set rack in center of oven and preheat to 400°F. Generously butter a 2-cup ramekin or soufflé dish. Sprinkle bottom and sides with ½ tablespoon of remaining granulated sugar, tapping out any excess.

3. Beat egg whites with remaining 2 tablespoons granulated sugar and powdered sugar to soft peaks. Add vanilla and beat to stiff but still glossy peaks. Fold in strawberry puree. Transfer to buttered soufflé dish.

4. Bake 16 to 18 minutes, until soufflé is puffed and lightly browned and a knife inserted in center comes out clean. Eat immediately all by yourself!

---

244 MERINGUE PIE WITH JEWELS OF SUMMER

Prep: 10 minutes   Cook: 80 to 90 minutes   Stand: 2 hours
Chill: 2 hours 20 minutes   Serves: 10

Make a meringue shell and fill with a colorful assortment of some of the most precious of the summer fruits: raspberries, blackberries, and strawberries. The best equipment is a 13½-inch deep-dish pizza pan with removable sides, or a flat pizza pan.

6 **egg whites**	1 **envelope plain gelatin**
½ **teaspoon cream of tartar**	2 **cups raspberries**
1¾ **cups superfine sugar**	2 **cups blackberries**
2 **teaspoons vanilla extract**	2 **cups strawberries**

1. Set rack in center of oven and preheat to 250°F. Butter bottom of a deep-dish pizza pan or flat pizza pan and line with parchment or wax paper.

2. In a large mixing bowl, beat egg whites to soft billows. Stop and sprinkle with cream of tartar. Continue beating while gradually adding sugar and vanilla until peaks are glossy and hold a stiff peak.

3. Spread half of meringue over bottom of prepared pan. Then drop tufts of meringue around sides, touching, to create a shell.

4. Bake 80 to 90 minutes, until meringue is lightly browned on tips. Turn off oven. Allow to dry in the oven at least 2 hours or overnight. Slide off pan and remove parchment. You may return meringue to this pan or another large platter for serving.

5. While meringue is baking, soften gelatin in ½ cup cold water, about 5 minutes.

6. In a nonreactive medium saucepan, combine ½ cup water and ½ cup of each berry. Bring to a boil over medium-high heat, mashing to extract juice. Strain and return juice to saucepan. Let stand until lukewarm. Add gelatin mixture to warm juice and stir until smooth.

7. Add remaining berries to juice and stir gently, taking care not to crush fruit. Refrigerate about 20 minutes, stirring 3 times to be sure gelatin sets evenly. Transfer berries to meringue shell. Refrigerate at least 2 hours. Cut into wedges to serve.

245   CAMILLE'S TUILES
Prep: 10 minutes   Cook: 8 to 10 minutes   Makes: about 20

The recipe for this delicate cookie is from cookbook author Camille Glenn's first book of desserts, a privately published collection. Camille is author of *Heritage of Southern Cooking* and is Louisville, Kentucky's best and most famous cook. Because she is from an age of graceful language, she says these cookies keep "exquisitely for days in a tight tin box."

½ **cup sugar**
½ **teaspoon vanilla extract**
2 **egg whites**
⅓ **cup sifted flour**

Pinch of salt
4 **tablespoons butter, melted**
½ **cup sliced almonds**

1. Set rack in lower third of oven and preheat to 375°F. Line a cookie sheet with aluminum foil, dull side up.

2. In a medium bowl, beat sugar, vanilla, and egg whites until foamy. With a large spoon, stir in—don't beat—flour, salt, melted butter, and almonds.

3. Drop batter by tablespoons onto cookie sheet, spacing cookies 2 inches apart. Spread into even circles with back of a metal spoon.

4. Bake 8 to 10 minutes. Working quickly, lift hot cookies off baking sheet and bend each over a rolling pin so it takes on shape of a curved roof tile. Leave on pin until set, about 15 seconds. Slide off and repeat. Store in an airtight container.

246   CHOCOLATE TUILES
Prep: 10 minutes   Cook: 10 minutes   Makes: about 20

Here's another cookie from Camille Glenn, this one from her book *The Fine Art of Delectable Desserts*. Eat these with poached fruit or vanilla ice cream.

½ **cup sugar**
3 **egg whites**
½ **teaspoon vanilla extract**
1 **tablespoon unsweetened cocoa powder, preferably Dutch process**

5 **tablespoons flour**
Pinch of salt
4 **tablespoons butter, melted**

1. Set rack in lower third of oven and preheat to 375°F. Line a cookie sheet with aluminum foil, dull side up.

2. In a medium bowl, beat sugar, egg whites, and vanilla to glossy soft peaks. Add cocoa, flour, salt, and melted butter. Stir well with a spoon until completely blended.

3. Drop batter by tablespoons onto cookie sheet, spacing cookies 2 inches apart. Spread into even circles with back of a metal spoon.

4. Bake about 10 minutes. Working quickly, lift hot cookies off baking sheet and bend each over a rolling pin so it takes shape of a curved roof tile. Leave on pin until set, about 15 seconds. Slide off and repeat. Store in an airtight container.

---

247 CHOCOLATE CHIP–STUDDED MINI MERINGUES
Prep: 10 minutes   Cook: 35 to 40 minutes   Makes: about 48

These are made small because they're too rich to make big.

4 egg whites	**½ teaspoon lemon juice**
Pinch of salt	**6 ounces (1 cup) semisweet**
1 cup granulated sugar	**chocolate chips**
1½ teaspoons vanilla extract	**½ cup powdered sugar**

1. Set rack in center of oven and preheat to 275°F. Line a cookie sheet with aluminum foil, dull side up.

2. In a medium bowl, beat whites until foamy. Add salt. Beat to stiff peaks while slowly adding granulated sugar, vanilla, and lemon juice. Fold in chocolate chips.

3. Drop batter onto cookie sheet by tablespoonfuls—no larger—spaced 2 inches apart. Sift powdered sugar over tops.

4. Bake 35 to 40 minutes, until tops are barely pale and meringue surface is firm. Cool completely on a wire rack. Store in a tightly covered container at room temperature.

---

248 COCONUT MACAROONS
Prep: 10 minutes   Cook: 18 to 20 minutes   Makes: about 30

3 egg whites	**½ cup sugar**
¼ teaspoon salt	**1 teaspoon vanilla extract**
¼ teaspoon cream of tartar	**1½ cups flaked coconut**

1. Set rack in lower third of oven and preheat to 325°F. Lightly grease and flour 2 cookie sheets, or grease sheets and line them with parchment paper or a brown paper bag.

2. In a large mixing bowl, beat egg whites, salt, and cream of tartar on high speed until whites are frothy. Gradually beat in sugar and vanilla. Continue to beat until whites are glossy and stand in soft peaks.

3. With a large rubber spatula, fold in coconut. Drop batter by rounded heaping tablespoons onto prepared cookie sheets.

4. Bake 18 to 20 minutes, or until macaroons are very lightly browned. Remove from oven. Leave cookies on sheets for 2 minutes before lifting off with a spatula. Transfer to wire racks and let cool completely. Macaroons store well in layers separated by wax paper in an airtight container at room temperature.

249 ANGEL FOOD CAKE

Prep: 15 minutes   Cook: 35 minutes   Stand: 2 hours   Serves: 10

The amazing voluming of egg whites continues during baking as the batter crawls up the sides of the baking pan. Low in fat (but high in sugar), angel food is an ideal light treat for child or grown-up. For a complete egg-white experience, frost with Brown Sugar Fluff Frosting (page 165) or Peppermint Mountain Frosting (page 165).

1 cup sifted cake flour	1¼ teaspoons cream of tartar
1½ cups sugar	½ teaspoon salt
1½ cups egg whites, at room temperature (12 to 13 whites from large eggs)	2 teaspoons vanilla extract

1. Set rack in lower third of oven and preheat oven to 375°F. Mix flour with ½ cup of sugar. Sift together 3 times.

2. In a large mixing bowl, beat egg whites, cream of tartar, and salt to medium-stiff peaks. Continue to beat while gradually adding remaining 1 cup sugar until whites form stiff, glossy peaks. Quickly beat in vanilla.

3. Fold in flour-sugar mixture ½ cup at a time, blending completely after each addition. Pour batter into an *ungreased* 10-inch angel food pan or 10-inch tube pan.

4. Bake 35 minutes, or until cake springs back if lightly pressed with a finger.

5. Place upside down on a wire rack. Let cool 2 hours in pan. Run a knife around edge. Shake gently to loosen cake. Let fall of its own accord from pan to serving plate.

Variations:

250 ESPRESSO ANGEL FOOD CAKE

Add 2 teaspoons finely ground instant espresso powder to flour-sugar mixture. Sift 4 times. Frost with Brown Sugar Fluff Frosting. Prepare as recipe directs on page 165, except use ⅓ cup very strong brewed espresso in place of water.

251 MARASCHINO CHERRY ANGEL FOOD CAKE

Add drained cherries from a 12-ounce jar maraschino cherries to batter after flour-sugar mixture is folded in. Add a few drops maraschino juice to cake batter to tint it pink. Frost with Peppermint Mountain Frosting (page 165).

252   PISTACHIO ANGEL FOOD CAKE

Instead of vanilla, use ¼ teaspoon almond extract. After folding in the flour-sugar mixture, add 1 cup coarsely chopped shelled unsalted pistachios to the batter. If desired, tint the batter light green with 1 or 2 drops green food coloring.

253   BROWN SUGAR FLUFF FROSTING
Prep: 5 minutes   Cook: 7 minutes   Frosts: 2 cake layers

Great on yellow cake as well as angel food.

**1½ cups (packed) light brown
        sugar
 ¼ teaspoon cream of tartar**

**2 egg whites
 2 teaspoons vanilla extract**

1. In a double boiler over simmering water, beat brown sugar, 1/3 cup water, cream of tartar, and egg whites until frosting stands in peaks, about 7 minutes. Remove from heat.

2. Add vanilla and beat briefly, about 30 seconds, just until spreading consistency.

254   PEPPERMINT MOUNTAIN FROSTING
Prep: 5 minutes   Cook: 7 minutes   Frosts: 2 cake layers

**2 egg whites
 ½ cup light corn syrup
 ¾ cup sugar
 ¼ teaspoon cream of tartar
 3 to 4 drops peppermint
        flavoring**

**Drops of red food coloring
or 2 teaspoons
maraschino cherry juice
(optional)**

1. With an electric hand mixer, beat egg whites, corn syrup, sugar, and cream of tartar in top of a double boiler over simmering water until frosting stands in peaks, about 7 minutes. Remove from heat.

2. Add peppermint flavoring and food coloring. Beat briefly, less than 30 seconds, just to spreading consistency.

255   ALMENDRADO
Prep: 30 minutes   Cook: none   Chill: 2 hours   Makes: 12 servings

El Charro is Tucson's funkiest and most legendary Mexican restaurant. This colorful dessert emerges regularly from the kitchen and into the jammed dining room of this old downtown building that once was a house. Almendrado is tinted red, green, and white, the colors of the Mexican flag, and uses lots of egg whites. The custard, of course, uses the yolks.

1 **envelope plain gelatin**	1 **cup blanched slivered**
¼ **cup cold water**	**almonds**
6 **egg whites**	1 **cup heavy cream**
¾ **cup sugar**	**Mexican Custard Sauce**
1 **teaspoon almond extract**	**(recipe follows)**
Red and green food coloring	

1. Oil and chill a 9 x 5 x 3-inch loaf pan. In a small bowl, soften gelatin for 5 minutes in cold water. Set in a larger pan of hot water to keep liquefied.

2. In a large bowl, beat egg whites until foamy. Gradually beat in sugar and continue beating to stiff, glossy peaks. Beat in gelatin and almond extract.

3. Divide whites into thirds. Tint 1 portion red, 1 portion green, and leave 1 portion white. Spread in loaf pan in layers in this order: red, white, green. Sprinkle ½ cup almonds on top. Wrap in plastic. Refrigerate at least 2 hours, until firm.

4. To serve, whip cream to medium-stiff peaks. Run knife around Almendrado and unmold onto a platter. Cut into ¾-inch slices. Lay each on dessert plate to show stripes like a flag. Pour custard sauce down the middle of "flag." Add a dollop of whipped cream and sprinkle with remaining almonds.

256   MEXICAN CUSTARD SAUCE
Prep: 5 minutes   Cook: 21 minutes   Makes: 2¾ cups

4 **egg yolks**	1 **cup evaporated milk**
⅓ **cup sugar**	½ **teaspoon vanilla extract**
1 **cup milk**	

1. In a double boiler, whisk egg yolks and sugar until smooth and lemon colored, about 1 minute. Stir in milk and evaporated milk.

2. Cook over simmering water, stirring constantly, until thick, about 20 minutes.

3. Remove from heat and stir in vanilla. Strain into a pitcher. Cover and refrigerate.

257   JAM WHIP
Prep: 5 minutes   Cook: none   Serves: 4 to 6

Here's an old-fashioned dessert that's unbelievably simple and good. Kids, especially, will enjoy this one. The best swirls are made with a good dark-colored jam, such as raspberry, black currant, or blackberry.

1 cup heavy cream	¼ cup sugar
¼ teaspoon vanilla extract	⅓ cup seedless jam, at room
2 egg whites	temperature

1. In a medium bowl with chilled beaters, whip cream and vanilla to stiff peaks with an electric mixer on high speed.

2. In another bowl, with clean beaters, whip egg whites until they begin to foam. Gradually beat in sugar and continue to beat until whites are glossy and hold a soft peak.

3. In a small bowl, stir jam briskly until smooth. Fold whipped cream into beaten egg whites. Fold in jam, leaving visible swirls. Spoon into dessert goblets or small bowls. Serve immediately or cover and refrigerate for up to 4 hours.

258   PERSIMMON WHIP
Prep: 5 minutes   Cook: none   Serves: 4

For this recipe, I particularly recommend the Hachiya persimmon, a plump, meaty fruit, recognized by its pointed tip. Any dark orange-red, pulpy soft persimmon will work, but not a hard pale one. A perfectly ripe persimmon is so soft that when you scoop it out of its skin, it will almost melt like jelly. Crumbled nut brittle adds a nice contrast of texture, if you'd like to sprinkle some on top.

2 very ripe persimmons,	¼ teaspoon vanilla extract
preferably Hachiya	2 egg whites
¼ cup brown sugar	2 tablespoons granulated
1 cup heavy cream	sugar

1. Halve persimmons and scoop out fruit. In a food processor, combine persimmon pulp and brown sugar. Puree until very smooth.

2. In a chilled bowl with chilled beaters, whip cream and vanilla until stiff. In another bowl with clean beaters, beat egg whites until frothy. Gradually beat in granulated sugar. Beat until whites form shiny stiff peaks.

3. Fold whipped cream into beaten whites. Fold in persimmon puree, leaving streaks and swirls. Spoon into dessert goblets or bowls. Serve at once or cover and refrigerate up to 4 hours.

259   FRESH LIME SORBET

Prep: 15 minutes   Cook: 2 minutes   Chill: 4 hours
Makes: about 1 quart

For this refreshing ice, you will need about 3 pounds of limes.

1½ cups sugar
2 tablespoons grated lime zest
2½ cups fresh lime juice

2 tablespoons lemon juice
3 egg whites

1. In a medium saucepan, combine sugar with 1½ cups water. Bring to a boil over medium heat, stirring to dissolve sugar. Boil, without stirring, 2 minutes. Remove from heat and let syrup cool. Refrigerate until cold, at least 2 hours or up to 5 days, in a tightly covered jar.

2. Combine lime zest, lime juice, lemon juice, and cold syrup. Pour into canister of an ice cream maker and process according to manufacturer's directions until slushy, about 10 minutes.

3. Add egg whites and process until ice is semifirm.

4. Transfer to a bowl or sturdy plastic container. Cover and place in freezer at least 2 hours, until firm.

NOTE: *If you don't have an ice cream freezer, pour lime syrup into a shallow metal pan and place in freezer to partially freeze, about 45 minutes. Transfer to a bowl and using an electric mixer on medium speed, beat in egg whites until frothy. Return to freezer and freeze at least 2 to 3 hours before serving.*

Chapter 11

Flans, Custards, Puddings, Creams, and Curds

Eggs and cream make custard. Sugar makes the custard sweet and also allows the custard to become hotter than egg yolks alone could withstand. The cream may be half-and-half or milk, and the eggs may come in the form of yolks-only or a combination of yolks and whole eggs. A yolks-only mixture makes the richest custards. A few whole eggs may be added for shimmy.

Custards come in many forms and under many names and guises. Some are thin for pouring. Some are thick and jiggly. Others bake around other ingredients, as in bread or rice pudding. This is a short list of what custard can be: crème Anglaise, boiled custard, stirred custard, baked custard, flan, pots de crème, crème brûlée, and pastry cream. Some custards are even savory. The only noncustard in the list is curd, which is eggs and sugar without cream. An acid, usually lemon, performs the necessary chemistry that allows yolks to boil without curdling.

Authorities say to cook a stirred custard to 160°F. for safety. This is irrelevant. If you stop there, you won't have much of a custard because it won't be hot enough to thicken. In fact, depending on other ingredients at work, you may not notice much thickening until 170° or 175°F. The point at which the custard thickens is really determined by the ratio of yolks to sugar and cream (or milk) or by the presence of starch, whether cornstarch or flour. The more starch, the hotter the custard can go. With enough starch, as for example in a pastry cream or pudding, the custard may even boil. When custard thickens, it may happen quickly, so pay attention.

The hotter the milk when added to the yolks, the quicker the custard will thicken, thus relieving it of the torture of drawn-out cooking. It's easy to warm the milk while you get the rest of the ingredients together, especially in the microwave.

When combining yolks and eggs, try not to over-beat them. Beating until the mixture is thick and pale yellow is expected, but beating longer than one minute may toughen the custard. Stir custard with a wooden spoon. The handles won't get hot while you stir patiently over heat.

260   ROASTED GARLIC FLAN
Prep: 5 minutes   Cook: 45 minutes   Serves: 6

On a driving trip through the Southwest I stopped in Tucson for lunch at Donna Nordin's Cafe Terra Cotta. This is my adaptation of Donna's incomparably smooth and rich Garlic Flan, which she served as an appetizer over greens. I also like it by itself or cut into cubes and added to chicken soup.

2 **heads of Perfect Roasted Garlic (recipe follows)**	1¾ **cups heavy cream**
3 **egg yolks**	**Pinch of salt**
2 **whole eggs**	**Pinch of white pepper**

1. Set rack in center of oven and preheat to 300°F. Butter six 6-ounce custard cups. Set cups in an oblong baking dish.

2. Squeeze roasted garlic from skins. Mash to a paste. Beat egg yolks with roasted garlic or pulse in a food processor until smooth. Whisk garlic-yolk mixture with eggs, cream, salt, and white pepper until well blended.

3. Pour custard evenly into buttered cups. Pour hot water into baking dish to reach halfway up sides of cups. Bake 45 minutes, or until custard is set.

4. Let custards cool on a wire rack. Slip a thin knife around edge and invert custard onto a plate. Serve warm or cold.

261   PERFECT ROASTED GARLIC
Prep: 2 minutes   Cook: 1 hour   Serves: 1 to 2 per head

Heads of garlic	**Olive oil**

1. Set rack in center of oven and preheat to 375°F. Slice about ¼ inch off root end of garlic heads to expose cloves.

2. Drizzle olive oil all over heads and cut surfaces. Wrap each head of garlic in heavy foil. Set on a baking sheet or in a pie plate.

3. Bake 1 hour, or until garlic cloves turn bronze and soft.

262   GARLIC FLAN WITH RED CHILE
Prep: 5 minutes   Cook: 55 minutes   Serves: 8

Pure ground red chile, not to be confused with ground hot red pepper, is flavorful and not necessarily spicy. It can be found in the Mexican food or spice section of many supermarkets.

4 **heads of Perfect Roasted Garlic (page 170)**
3 **egg yolks**
5 **whole eggs**

2 **cups heavy cream**
½ **teaspoon salt**
2 **teaspoons ground red chile powder**

1. Set rack in center of oven and preheat to 300°F. Butter eight 6-ounce custard cups. Set cups in an oblong baking dish.

2. Squeeze garlic out of skin into a food processor. Add egg yolks and pulse until smooth. Scrape garlic-yolk mixture into a mixing bowl. Add whole eggs, cream, and salt. Whisk until well blended. Stir in chile powder, leaving some streaks.

3. Pour custard into buttered cups, dividing evenly. Pour hot water into baking dish to come halfway up sides of cups. Bake 55 minutes, or until custard is set.

4. Remove custards to wire rack. Slip a thin knife around edge and invert custard on to a plate or serve in cups. Serve warm or cold.

263   SAFFRON FLAN
Prep: 5 minutes   Cook: 45 to 50 minutes   Serves: 6

This lightly scented savory flan is delicious in rich broth or on salad greens with cold shreds of cooked beef or chicken.

3 **egg yolks**
½ **teaspoon saffron threads**
⅛ **teaspoon ground cumin**
1½ **cups heavy cream**

½ **cup plain yogurt**
5 **eggs**
Pinch of salt
Pinch of white pepper

1. Set rack in center of oven and preheat to 325°F. Butter six 6-ounce custard cups. Set cups in oblong baking dish.

2. In a medium bowl, whisk yolks, saffron, and cumin until smooth. Add cream, yogurt, eggs, salt, and pepper. Whisk until well blended.

3. Pour custard into buttered cups, dividing evenly. Pour hot water into baking dish to reach halfway up sides of cups. Bake 45 to 50 minutes, or until custard is set and knife inserted near center comes out clean.

4. Remove custards to a wire rack. Slip a thin knife around edge and invert onto a plate or serve in cups. Serve warm or cold.

264 SWEET POTATO PUDDING WITH RUM
Prep: 10 minutes   Cook: 1½ hours   Serves: 4

This is almost like sweet potato pie without the crust. It makes a wonderful holiday side dish.

2 medium sweet potatoes
   (about ½ pound each)
4 tablespoons butter, melted
1 cup (packed) light brown
   sugar
¼ cup orange juice

3 tablespoons dark rum
¼ teaspoon grated nutmeg
1 tablespoon vanilla extract
½ cup heavy cream
3 egg yolks
4 whole eggs

1. Butter a 6-cup soufflé dish or 8-inch square baking dish. Preheat oven to 400°F.; set rack in lower third.

2. Prick sweet potatoes and bake 1 hour, or until soft. Reduce oven temperature to 325°. Cut open and scrape sweet potatoes into a medium bowl.

3. Add butter, brown sugar, orange juice, rum, nutmeg, vanilla, cream, egg yolks, and eggs. Beat with an electric mixer until very smooth. Transfer to baking dish, smoothing top gently.

4. Bake 30 to 35 minutes, or until a light crust forms on top. Serve immediately.

265 PUMPKIN RICE PUDDING SENSAS!
Prep: 25 minutes   Cook: 1 hour 45 minutes   Serves: 8

2½ cups canned solid-pack
   pumpkin
¾ cup sugar
1 teaspoon cinnamon
½ teaspoon ground ginger
½ teaspoon ground cloves

2 egg yolks
3 whole eggs
3 cups milk
¼ cup bourbon or dark rum
2 cups cooked rice
1 cup dark raisins

1. Set rack as low as possible in oven and preheat to 350°F. Generously butter a 9 x 13-inch baking dish. Have ready another, larger shallow baking pan.

2. With an electric mixer or in a food processor, blend pumpkin, sugar, cinnamon, ginger, cloves, and egg yolks until smooth. Lightly beat whole eggs, then add slowly in 3 additions to pumpkin batter, blending just until absorbed each time.

3. Transfer to a mixing bowl. Whisk in milk and bourbon. Stir in rice and raisins. Pour into prepared baking dish. Set in larger pan. Place on oven rack. Fill larger pan with very hot tap water to come halfway up sides of dish.

4. Bake, uncovered, 15 minutes. Open oven and stir gently. Continue to bake 1½ hours longer, or until a knife inserted into center comes out clean.

266   CHINESE STEAMED EGG CUSTARD
Prep: 5 minutes   Cook: 15 to 20 minutes   Serves: 4

Luxurious texture comes from oil, water, and slow steaming. What seems to be a large amount of water makes the custard very silky. This silkiness is more important than a Western concept of richness, because this custard is to be immediately spooned over rice.

4 **eggs**	1 **scallion, minced**
½ **teaspoon salt**	2 **cups steamed white rice**
1 **tablespoon vegetable oil**	
1 **tablespoon Chinese oyster**	
sauce	

1. In a heatproof bowl or dish, beat eggs well. Slowly whisk in 1½ cups water, salt, oil, and oyster sauce.

2. Set dish inside a steamer basket over a wok filled with boiling water or on a trivet in a large saucepan, holding about 2 inches boiling water. Cover and steam 15 to 20 minutes, or until knife inserted into center of custard comes out clean.

3. Remove from steamer. Top custard with scallion. Serve hot, spooned over rice, which will absorb extra liquid.

Variation:

267   CHINESE STEAMED EGGS WITH CLAMS

Add 1 (8-ounce) can drained chopped clams to eggs, using canning liquid as part of the measurement for the water, in recipe 266. Steam and garnish as directed.

268 PRESIDENT GRANT'S RICE PUDDING
Prep: 10 minutes   Cook: 1 hour 17 minutes   Serves: 8

If you have a rice cooker, use it to cook the rice, then use the rice while it's hot. If using leftover rice that has been refrigerated, reheat it with steam. Put the rice in a bowl and set on a rack inside a wok or saucepan over a little simmering water and cover. Steam until very warm to the touch. Or add a little water to the bowl of rice, cover with plastic, and microwave on Medium until rice softens, about 2 minutes.

1½ cups hot cooked long-grain white rice	2 cups milk
½ teaspoon salt	1 tablespoon finely minced lemon zest
1 tablespoon butter	1 teaspoon vanilla extract
4 eggs, separated	Lemon Curd Sauce (recipe follows)
½ cup sugar	
2 cups half-and-half	

1. Set rack in middle of oven and preheat to 350°F. Butter a 2-quart baking dish.

2. Bring 3 cups water to a boil in a medium saucepan. Add rice and salt. Cover, reduce heat to low, and cook 17 minutes. Stir butter into hot rice.

3. In a large mixing bowl, whisk egg yolks and sugar until smooth and pale, about 1 minute. Whisk in half-and-half, milk, lemon zest, and vanilla. Stir in buttered rice.

4. In another mixing bowl, beat egg whites to medium-stiff peaks. Fold into rice base. Transfer to baking dish. Set in a larger pan and add very hot tap water to come halfway up sides of dish.

5. Bake, uncovered, 1 hour, or until knife inserted near center comes out clean. Serve warm with Lemon Curd Sauce.

269 LEMON CURD SAUCE
Prep: 3 minutes   Cook: 3 minutes   Makes: about 1⅔ cups

Just because this sauce comes with President Grant's Rice Pudding doesn't mean you can't pour it over fruit or bread pudding.

1 egg	¼ cup fresh lemon juice
1 cup sugar	4 tablespoons butter
½ teaspoon grated nutmeg	
2 tablespoons finely grated lemon zest	

1. In a medium saucepan, beat egg, sugar, nutmeg, and lemon zest until smooth. Stir in lemon juice and 3 tablespoons water.

2. Set over high heat and bring to a boil, stirring constantly. Add butter and cook, stirring, until butter is blended into sauce, about 3 minutes. Serve hot.

270 BUBBLING BROWN SUGAR BREAD PUDDING

Prep: 10 minutes   Cook: 1½ hours   Serves: 8

Brown sugar instead of white sugar and fresh bread instead of stale bread makes this a very special bread pudding indeed. Dress it up by serving portions from tall goblets.

4 to 5 cups fresh French bread,
    cut into 1-inch cubes
4 whole eggs
1 egg yolk
1 cup (packed) dark brown
    sugar
2 teaspoons cinnamon

2 teaspoons vanilla extract
½ teaspoon salt
4½ cups milk
1 cup golden raisins
    Warm Bourbon Sauce
    (recipe follows)

1. Preheat oven to 350°F. Butter a 9 x 13-inch baking dish. Place bread cubes in a large mixing bowl.

2. In a large bowl, beat whole eggs, egg yolk, and brown sugar until thick and smooth. Blend in cinnamon, vanilla, salt, and milk. Pour over bread cubes and mix gently.

3. Transfer to prepared baking dish. Sprinkle raisins over top. Set bread pudding in a roasting pan filled with very hot tap water reaching two-thirds up side of baking dish.

4. Bake 1½ hours. To serve, spoon into wine glasses or goblets. Ladle Warm Bourbon Sauce over each serving.

271 WARM BOURBON SAUCE

Prep: 5 minutes   Cook: 9 to 10 minutes   Makes: 3½ cups

2 cups sugar
2 sticks (8 ounces) butter
½ teaspoon cinnamon
¼ teaspoon grated nutmeg

½ cup bourbon, rum,
    whiskey, or Amaretto,
    Grand Marnier, or coffee-
    flavored liqueur

1. In a medium saucepan, combine sugar and butter over medium heat. Cook, stirring constantly, until syrup reaches soft-ball stage (243°F. on a candy thermometer), about 9 to 10 minutes.

2. Remove from heat. Whisk in cinnamon, nutmeg, and bourbon. Serve sauce warm over warm bread pudding.

272 RICE PUDDING CUSTARD MOLD

Prep: 10 minutes   Cook: 25 to 30 minutes   Chill: 6 hours
Serves: 16

Here rice pudding is lightened with the addition of whipped cream, which is folded into the mixture at the end. Gelatin added to the custard makes this more like a rice Bavarian than an ordinary pudding. It's very creamy, very rich, very comforting. Taste for vanilla or other flavoring once the mixture is cooled, but before it is placed in the mold. You may find that as it loses heat, it may need more oomph.

¾ cup raw medium-grain rice, such as Calrose or sushi rice, or short-grain rice, such as pearl or Arborio
4 cups milk
1 vanilla bean or 2 teaspoons vanilla extract
½ cup plus 3 tablespoons sugar

2 envelopes plain gelatin
Crème Anglaise, cooled (recipe follows)
1 cup heavy cream
Caramelized Strawberry Sauce (page 213) or fresh fruit

1. Add rice to a large saucepan of boiling water and cook 5 minutes. Drain and return rice to saucepan. Add milk, vanilla bean, and ½ cup of the sugar.

2. Bring to a simmer, reduce heat so milk barely bubbles, and cook, stirring often, 20 to 25 minutes, or until rice is tender but fully cooked. Remove from heat and stir to cool down. Remove vanilla bean from rice. If using vanilla extract, add it now.

3. Meanwhile, soften gelatin in ½ cup cold water, about 5 minutes. Add gelatin to cooled Crème Anglaise, stirring until smooth. Fold Crème Anglaise into rice.

4. Whip cream with remaining 3 tablespoons sugar to medium-stiff peaks. Fold into pudding. Wet a 10- to 12-cup ring mold. Spoon pudding into mold, cover well with plastic wrap, and refrigerate 6 hours or overnight, until set.

5. To unmold, dip into hot water 10 to 15 seconds. Invert onto a serving plate. If pudding does not drop out, rap gently with a spoon, but don't bang it on serving plate. It should slowly fall out. Serve in slices topped with Caramelized Strawberry Sauce or fresh fruit.

273 CRÈME ANGLAISE

Prep: 5 minutes   Cook: 12 to 14 minutes   Makes: 2¾ cups

2 cups half-and-half
1 vanilla bean or 1 tablespoon vanilla extract

6 egg yolks
⅓ cup sugar

1. In a large glass measure, combine half-and-half and vanilla bean. Microwave on High about 2 minutes, uncovered, to warm—but not boil.

2. In a double boiler, whisk yolks and sugar by hand or with an electric hand mixer until thick and smooth, about 2 minutes. Slowly stir in heated half-and-half without creating froth.

3. Cook over simmering water, stirring constantly, until custard coats a wooden spoon, 10 to 12 minutes. Remove from heat. Strain any lumps. Transfer to a bowl and stir to cool down.

---

274 CREMA CATALANA *DELICE!*

Prep: 10 minutes   Cook: 13 to 18 minutes   Chill: 6½ hours
Makes: 4 to 6 servings

The silken texture of this rich Spanish custard comes from cornstarch. The dessert typically is infused during cooking with strips of orange peel, cinnamon stick, and a whole vanilla bean. If you don't have a vanilla bean, stir in 1 tablespoon pure vanilla extract after removing custard from heat in step 3.

3½ cups heavy cream	1½ tablespoons cornstarch
1 vanilla bean	1 (2-inch) cinnamon stick
5 egg yolks	Peel of 1 orange
1½ cups sugar	Peel of 1 lemon

1. In a large glass measure or microwave-safe bowl, combine cream and vanilla bean. Microwave on High 3 minutes, to just under a boil.

2. In a heavy medium saucepan, whisk together egg yolks, ½ cup sugar, and cornstarch until smooth, about 1 minute. Slowly whisk in hot vanilla cream. Drop in cinnamon, orange peel, and lemon peel. Cook over medium-high heat, stirring, until custard begins to bubble around edges of pan, about 5 minutes.

3. Pour custard through a strainer set over a bowl. Set in a larger bowl of ice and stir until cooled. Pour into 4 large or 6 small custard cups. Set on a baking sheet, cover with plastic wrap, and refrigerate at least 6 hours.

4. In a heavy medium saucepan, combine remaining 1 cup sugar with ¼ cup water. Bring to a boil, stirring to dissolve sugar. Continue to boil, without stirring, until caramel turns a rich mahogany brown, 5 to 10 minutes, depending upon humidity. Immediately remove from heat and pour caramel over tops of cold custard, tilting each cup to make a thin layer over each. Serve at once or refrigerate, uncovered, 30 minutes longer.

275   CRÈME BRÛLÉE

Prep: 5 minutes   Cook: 48 minutes   Chill: 6 hours   Serves: 4

2 cups heavy cream	1 tablespoon vanilla extract
4 egg yolks	⅛ teaspoon salt
1 whole egg	¼ cup dark brown sugar
⅔ cup granulated sugar	

1. Preheat oven to 350°F. Arrange four 6-ounce custard cups in a baking dish or roasting pan large enough to hold cups without touching.

2. Heat cream in a microwave, uncovered, on High for 2 minutes, or on stovetop until bubbles form around edge of pan.

3. In a medium bowl, whisk egg yolks, whole egg, and granulated sugar until thick and lemon colored, 1 to 2 minutes. Gradually whisk in hot cream. Stir in vanilla and salt. Pour into custard cups, place pan in oven, and fill larger pan with enough very hot tap water to reach halfway up custard cups.

4. Bake 45 minutes. Carefully remove cups from water. Let cool on a wire rack. Cover with plastic wrap and refrigerate at least 6 hours.

5. About 2 to 3 hours before serving, preheat broiler with rack as close to heat as possible. Sprinkle 1 tablespoon brown sugar evenly over top of each custard. Broil until sugar melts, then browns, 15 to 60 seconds. Refrigerate again. Serve cold.

276   HONEY POTS DE CRÈME

Prep: 5 minutes   Cook: 37 to 42 minutes   Serves: 6

⅔ cup light honey	2 whole eggs
2½ cups heavy cream	1 teaspoon vanilla extract
4 egg yolks	

1. Set rack in center of oven and preheat to 350°F. Arrange six 6-ounce custard cups in a baking dish or roasting pan large enough to hold cups without touching.

2. Stir honey into cream. Microwave, uncovered, on High about 2 minutes, just to warm.

3. In a large bowl, preferably with a pour spout, beat egg yolks and eggs until thick and light yellow, about 1 minute. Stir in heated honey-cream and vanilla. Pour into custard cups, dividing evenly.

4. Place baking dish in oven. Fill with very hot tap water to within ½ inch of rims of cups. Bake about 35 to 40 minutes, or until center is still slightly jiggly.

5. Let custards cool on rack. Cover custard with plastic wrap and refrigerate until cold before serving.

277 ESPRESSO POTS DE CRÈME
Prep: 5 minutes   Cook: 37 to 42 minutes   Serves: 6

1 tablespoon instant espresso powder	2 whole eggs
2½ cups heavy cream	½ cup sugar
4 egg yolks	2 teaspoons vanilla extract

1. Set rack in center of oven and preheat to 350°F. Arrange six 6-ounce custard cups in a baking dish or roasting pan large enough to hold cups without touching.

2. Stir espresso powder into cream. Microwave, uncovered, on High about 2 minutes, just to warm.

3. In a large bowl, preferably with a pour spout, beat egg yolks, eggs, and sugar until thick and light yellow, about 1 minute. Stir in hot espresso-cream and vanilla. Pour into custard cups, dividing evenly.

4. Place dish or pan with cups in oven. Fill with very hot tap water to within ½ inch of rims of cups. Bake about 35 to 40 minutes, or until center is still slightly jiggly.

5. Let custards cool on rack. Cover with plastic wrap and refrigerate until cold before serving.

278 CHAMPAGNE SABAYON TARTLETS
Prep: 10 minutes   Cook: 5 to 7 minutes   Serves: 8

My friend caterer Joan Leineke of Sacramento, California, is a devoted kitchen addict with the best whipped custard sauce ever. It's made with French Champagne.

8 egg yolks	1 cup heavy cream
½ cup plus 2 tablespoons sugar	Egg Yolk Tartlet Shells (page 180)
¼ teaspoon salt	1 pint strawberries, sliced
¾ cup French Champagne or other dry sparkling wine	

1. In a double boiler, vigorously whisk egg yolks, ½ cup of the sugar, salt, and Champagne over simmering water until mixture triples in volume and custard thickens, 5 to 7 minutes. Immediately strain into a bowl set in a larger bowl of ice. Whisk to cool.

2. Whip cream to medium-soft peaks. Fold into sabayon. Cover and refrigerate until ready to fill tart shells.

3. In a medium bowl, toss strawberries with remaining 2 tablespoons sugar. If berries are tart, add a bit more sugar to taste. Pour sabayon into tartlet shells. Using a slotted spoon, set strawberries atop tartlets and serve.

279   EGG YOLK TARTLET SHELLS

Prep: 30 minutes   Chill: 1 hour   Cook: 25 to 30 minutes   Makes: 8

¼ cup heavy cream
2 egg yolks
1 teaspoon vanilla extract
2¾ cups flour
½ cup sugar

¼ teaspoon salt
2 sticks (8 ounces) cold
   unsalted butter, cut into
   pats

1. In a small measuring cup, combine heavy cream, egg yolks, and vanilla. Set aside.

2. Measure flour, sugar, and salt into a food processor. Top with pats of butter. Run machine until mixture looks like cornmeal and butter is evenly distributed. With machine on, pour cream-yolk mixture into food processor. Process just until dough forms a loose ball. Stop immediately. Gather dough into a ball, halve, and press into 2 thick disks. Wrap in plastic and refrigerate at least 1 hour.

3. Set rack in center of oven and preheat to 375°F. Have ready eight 4-inch tartlet pans with removable bottoms.

4. On a lightly floured surface, roll out 1 pastry disk ⅛ inch thick. Cut into four 6-inch circles. Fit dough into pans without stretching it. Repeat with second disk. Line each pastry shell with a circle of foil.

5. Bake 20 minutes. Remove foil and continue to bake until tartlet shells are lightly browned, 5 to 10 minutes longer.

---

280   CARAMEL CUSTARD

Prep: 5 minutes   Cook: 45 minutes   Chill: 3 to 4 hours   Serves: 6

This baked custard is taken to a sophisticated flavor level by using a thinned caramelized sugar to sweeten the cream.

¾ cup sugar
3 cups hot heavy cream

2 teaspoons vanilla extract
6 egg yolks

1. Set rack in center of oven and preheat to 350°F. Arrange six 8-ounce ramekins or custard cups in a baking dish or roasting pan large enough to hold cups without touching.

2. In a heavy medium saucepan, combine sugar and ¼ cup water. Bring to a boil, stirring to dissolve sugar. Boil, without stirring, until caramel turns a deep golden brown, about 5 minutes. Remove from heat and carefully pour in another ¼ cup water. After sputtering stops, stir until smooth. Let cool slightly.

3. Pour hot cream into a medium heatproof bowl. Whisk in hot caramel. In a large bowl, lightly beat egg yolks. Gradually stir in hot caramel cream and vanilla. Pour custard into prepared ramekins. Fill baking pan with enough hot tap water to reach halfway up ramekins.

4. Bake 40 minutes, until jiggly but not runny. Let cool on a wire rack. Cover with plastic wrap and refrigerate 3 to 4 hours. Run a thin knife around edge of each custard to loosen. Invert onto dessert plates, allowing caramel to spill out and puddle around custard.

281 CARAMEL CRUNCH CUSTARD OVER BANANAS

Prep: 20 minutes   Cook: 21 to 30 minutes   Chill: 2 hours   Serves: 6

This stove-top version of the Spanish custard *natillas* receives a pouring of hot caramelized sugar over its cold top; then the custard is poured over a platter of buttery broiled bananas.

3 bananas, sliced lengthwise	1 egg, separated
3 tablespoons melted butter	1¼ cups granulated sugar
2 tablespoons brown sugar	2 cups warm milk
2 whole eggs	1 (2-inch) cinnamon stick

1. Preheat broiler. Arrange banana slices in a 9-inch pie plate. Top with butter and brown sugar. Broil about 4 inches from heat until sugar melts, 3 to 4 minutes. Set aside or cover and refrigerate until serving.

2. In a double boiler, whisk 2 whole eggs and 1 egg yolk with ½ cup granulated sugar until thick and light yellow, 1 to 2 minutes. Gradually stir in warm milk without creating froth. Drop in cinnamon stick. Cook over simmering water, stirring, until custard thickens enough to coat a metal spoon, 15 to 18 minutes.

3. Strain custard into a bowl set in a larger bowl of ice. Stir until cool. Cover with plastic wrap directly on surface of custard and refrigerate until cold, at least 2 hours or overnight.

4. Close to serving, transfer bananas and their sugary liquid to an oval platter. Remove chilled custard from refrigerator and have convenient to stove. In a small heavy pot, heat remaining ¾ cup granulated sugar and ¼ cup water over medium-high heat until clear. Boil, without stirring, until caramel is color of iced tea, 5 to 10 minutes. Immediately drizzle hot caramel over cold custard. Caramel will sizzle and bubble up, then harden.

5. In a small bowl, beat egg white with an electric mixer or whisk until stiff. Fold into custard, crushing caramel pieces as you mix. Pour custard over broiled bananas. Serve within the hour.

282 INDIVIDUAL FLANS

Prep: 5 minutes   Cook: 35 minutes   Serves: 6

Flan originally comes from Spain, a country that uses a lot of eggs in its desserts. True flan is a yolks-only proposition, typically cooked in individual ramekins. You can continue this tradition by using custard cups, or you can make a single large flan in an oblong baking dish or glass pie plate. Either way, line the dish with caramelized sugar before the custard is added. When the flan is unmolded, the caramel is revealed as a dark glaze on top as well as a sauce to spoon up with the flan.

¾ **cup plus ⅔ cup sugar**
8 **egg yolks**

2¼ **cups warm milk**

1. Set rack in center of oven and preheat to 350°F. In a medium-size heavy saucepan, combine ¾ cup sugar and ¼ cup water. Bring to a boil over medium heat, stirring to dissolve sugar. Boil, without stirring, until syrup turns a deep golden brown, about 5 minutes. (It's best to use a light-colored pan so you can see what's happening.) Immediately and carefully pour in another ¼ cup water. After sputtering stops, stir until caramel is smooth.

2. Pour hot caramel into six 6-ounce ramekins or custard cups. Swirl to coat inside of ramekins. Place cups in a baking dish large enough to hold the custard cups without touching.

3. In a large bowl, preferably with a pour spout, whisk egg yolks and remaining ⅔ cup sugar until thick and light yellow. Gradually stir in warm milk. Pour custard into ramekins directly over caramel, which by now should be hard.

4. Place in oven. Fill larger pan with 1 inch very hot tap water. Bake about 30 minutes, or until flans are set and a knife inserted near centers comes out clean.

5. Run knife around edge of flans to loosen. Invert while hot onto serving plates. Allow caramel to spill out as you invert flans. Serve warm or cold.

Variation:

283 LARGE FLAN

Preheat oven to 350°F. Pour hot caramel into a 9-inch glass pie plate. Using pot holders or mitts, immediately swirl plate to coat bottom and sides. Prepare custard as in recipe 282 and pour over caramel. Cover with buttered foil, buttered side down. Bake inside another shallow pan filled with very hot tap water for 1 hour, or until a knife inserted near center comes out clean. Unmold onto serving plate while warm.

284   MEXICAN FLAN

Prep: 5 minutes   Cook: 1 hour 40 minutes   Chill: 3 hours
Serves: 10

I picked up this recipe in the colonial city of Guanajuato, at a hotel just off the main square. The rise of egg desserts in Mexico coincided with the presence of the conquering Spaniards, who made sure that chickens and eggs abounded so they could have their Old World favorites in the New World. Today's Mexicans like the convenience of canned milk.

¾ cup granulated sugar
¼ cup brown sugar
5 eggs
1 (14-ounce) can sweetened
   condensed milk

1 (5-ounce) can evaporated
   milk
1½ cups half-and-half
1 tablespoon vanilla extract

1. Preheat oven to 300°F. In a small heavy saucepan, bring granulated sugar and brown sugar to a boil over medium-high heat. Boil until the color of iced tea, 8 to 12 minutes. Immediately pour caramel into a 10-inch glass pie plate or 6-cup ring mold. Using potholders or mitts, swirl plate to coat bottom and sides with caramel.

2. In a large bowl, whisk together eggs, condensed milk, evaporated milk, half-and-half, and vanilla until blended. Pour over hardened caramel. Cover with buttered foil, buttered side down. Set in a roasting pan or baking dish large enough to hold pie plate and place in oven. Fill roasting pan with very hot tap water to within ½ inch of top of flan.

3. Bake 1½ hours, or until a knife inserted near center comes out clean. Remove from water bath. Let cool 10 minutes. Using potholders or mitts, carefully invert onto a large round platter. Liquefied caramelized sugar will flow out and pool around flan. Refrigerate until chilled, about 3 hours. Serve cold.

285   LEMON CURD

Prep: 10 minutes   Cook: 10 minutes   Makes: about 2½ cups

4   teaspoons grated lemon zest
⅔   cup fresh lemon juice
5   whole eggs
1   egg yolk

1   cup sugar
1   stick (4 ounces) unsalted
    butter, melted

1. In a food processor, combine lemon zest, lemon juice, whole eggs, egg yolk, and sugar. Process until smooth. With machine on, pour in melted butter.

2. Pour mixture into a nonreactive medium saucepan. Cook over medium heat, stirring constantly and quickly, until curd bubbles and thickens, a good 10 minutes. Strain into a mixing bowl. Let cool. Curd will keep, covered, in refrigerator for up to 3 days.

286   CHERRIES FLOATING IN CRÈME ANGLAISE

Prep: 5 minutes   Cook: 15 minutes   Serves: 6

Classic Crème Anglaise is flavored with vanilla, but almond is a natural with cherries. In fact, some of the finest almonds grown in California have the aftertaste of cherries. To solve this dilemma, I've given you the choice below. Because this recipe is made with pitted fresh cherries, it is highly seasonal and does require a cherry pitter.

2   pounds fresh Bing cherries,
    rinsed gently, stems
    intact
½   cup granulated sugar
4   egg yolks

1¾   cups hot milk
1   teaspoon vanilla or almond
    extract
    Powdered sugar

1. Pit cherries without disturbing stem by setting cherry in cherry pitter slightly off center. Place pitted cherries, stems up, on a rimmed serving platter

2. In a double boiler, gradually whisk granulated sugar into egg yolks. Continue to beat until very pale, about 1 minute. Slowly whisk in hot milk. Cook over simmering water, stirring constantly, until a finger drawn across back of wooden spoon leaves a bare spot, about 15 minutes.

3. Stir in vanilla. While warm, pour custard sauce over cherries. Serve immediately, dusted with powdered sugar.

NOTE: *To keep Crème Anglaise warm, place pot in a larger pot of warm water. Custard will hold for up to 30 minutes. Stir before spooning over cherries. If you want to serve the custard cold, pour Crème Anglaise into a bowl. Cover surface with plastic wrap and refrigerate for up to 3 hours.*

287 DOUBLE CHOCOLATE BAKED CUSTARD

Prep: 10 minutes   Cook: 1½ hours   Chill: overnight   Serves: 8

Plan on leaving this molded custard in refrigerator overnight to set up.

2 **teaspoons plain gelatin**
3 **cups heavy cream**
⅓ **cup plus 1 tablespoon sugar**
½ **pound semisweet chocolate, chopped**

7 **egg yolks**
3 **tablespoons unsweetened cocoa powder**
2 **teaspoons vanilla extract**

1. Preheat oven to 350°F. Dissolve gelatin in ¼ cup cold water and set aside. Place a 10-inch tube pan or 6-cup loaf pan in a baking dish or roasting pan.

2. In a large microwave-safe bowl, combine cream and ⅓ cup sugar. Microwave on High about 3 minutes, almost to boiling. Stir in chocolate and immediately cover with plastic wrap. Let stand 2 minutes. Stir briskly until chocolate cream is dark and smooth and no chocolate particles are visible. Add softened gelatin and mix very well.

3. Place egg yolks in a large bowl. In a small bowl, mix cocoa powder with remaining 1 tablespoon sugar. Whisk cocoa sugar into yolks. Add vanilla and whisk until smooth. Gradually stir hot chocolate cream into yolk mixture, mixing until very smooth. Strain custard into tube pan.

4. Place larger dish holding pan of custard in oven. Fill larger dish with 2 inches very hot tap water. Bake about 1½ hours, or until a knife inserted 1 inch from edge comes out clean. Let cool, then cover and refrigerate overnight to set completely.

5. To serve, dip bottom of mold in a bowl of hot water. Invert onto a serving platter. Cut custard into thick slices with a knife dipped in hot water, then wiped dry.

Chapter 12

Soufflé All Day

Beaten egg whites, folded into a main base are, to me, the hallmark of the many dishes we call soufflés. You can have soufflés from morning till night, from side dish to dessert. Soufflés are more than an elegant dessert of time-consuming technique that tempts failure for a short-lived performance. You can make a soufflé a little bit flat in a normal baking dish and serve it at a routine family meal. It can be a side dish at dinner, rather than the dinner itself.

Whether a puffed omelet or pancake batter or a beautiful dessert, every soufflé is sprung from a veritable launching pad of a million tiny bursts of air, thanks to the magic of beaten egg whites. In cold soufflés, they bind and create volume. Hot soufflés would not rise without them. But remember, overbeaten egg whites are the downfall of many a soufflé. Beat only to smooth, glossy peaks that just hold their shape when the beater is turned upside down.

Most soufflés call on two forms of bases—white sauce for savory soufflés and sweet custard for fruit or dessert soufflés. The white sauce may or may not contain egg yolks. Obviously, white sauce with yolks is rich, indeed.

This chapter includes all manner of soufflés—hot or cold, savory or sweet, high or flat—except those made with egg white only (see Egg White Cuisine, page 151).

Most soufflé bases can be made ahead. If you've already buttered and lightly sprinkled a soufflé dish or baking dish with flour or cheese or sugar, that leaves only the beating of the egg whites and folding them in just before baking. Truth to tell, you can complete the entire process, pour the mixture into the baking dish, and keep the uncooked soufflé refrigerated up to 3 hours before baking!

288   CORN DINNER SOUFFLÉ

Prep: 10 minutes   Cook: 17 to 24 minutes   Serves: 4 to 6

Puff isn't everything—big puff, that is. This soufflé is baked in an ordinary baking dish. It puffs lightly and can be scooped out or cut into squares to enjoy as an accompaniment with or as the main course itself.

Butter and flour for dish
3 to 3½ cups fresh or frozen
   corn kernels
2 tablespoons butter
2 tablespoons flour
1½ cups warm milk

½ teaspoon salt
⅛ teaspoon white pepper
4 egg yolks, lightly beaten
5 egg whites
⅛ teaspoon cream of tartar

1. Set rack as low as possible in oven and preheat to 400°F. Lightly butter bottom and up sides of a 9 x 13-inch baking dish or oval gratin dish. Dust with flour, tapping out excess.

2. Place corn in a food processor or blender and pulse a few times to chop very coarsely. Set aside in processor bowl.

3. In a medium saucepan, melt butter over medium-high heat. When foamy, whisk in flour. Cook, whisking, 1 to 2 minutes. Gradually whisk in warm milk. Bring to a boil, whisking until smooth and thick, 1 to 2 minutes. Stir in corn, salt, and pepper. Remove from heat and whisk in egg yolks.

4. In a large bowl, beat egg whites and cream of tartar to glossy stiff peaks. Fold corn base into whites. Gently spread in baking dish, smoothing top.

5. Bake about 15 to 20 minutes, until puffy and golden brown. Serve immediately.

289   SPOONBREAD SOUFFLÉ

Prep: 5 minutes   Cook: 21 to 26 minutes   Serves: 6

Here's a dressed-up version of a homey American classic.

Butter and flour for dish
2½ cups milk
1 cup yellow cornmeal
4 tablespoons butter
1 tablespoon sugar

1 teaspoon salt
2 egg yolks, well beaten
5 egg whites
⅛ teaspoon cream of tartar

1. Set rack on lowest level of oven and preheat to 375°F. Butter a 2-quart baking dish or soufflé dish. Dust with flour, tapping out excess.

2. In a large saucepan, heat milk until bubbles form around edge. Gradually stir in cornmeal, butter, sugar, and salt until smooth. Reduce heat to medium; cook and stir 1 minute. Remove from heat and stir about ½ cup hot cornmeal mixture into beaten egg yolks. Then add yolks to remaining cornmeal, stirring quickly. Let cool slightly.

3. In a large mixing bowl, beat egg whites and cream of tartar to stiff peaks. Fold into cornmeal base. Spread in baking dish.

4. Bake 20 to 25 minutes, until puffed and light gold. Serve immediately.

---

290   DELUXE CHEESE GRITS SOUFFLÉ
Prep: 10 minutes   Cook: 32 to 34 minutes   Serves: 6

Sharp Cheddar and Parmesan cheese turn humble grits into a luxurious soufflé, fine enough for your best company. Grits are the end of the line for kernels of corn. This dish sends them out with some formality and a richness rarely enjoyed.

Butter and flour for dish
½ **cup quick-cooking grits**
2 **tablespoons butter**
2 **tablespoons flour**
1 **cup warm milk**
½ **teaspoon salt**
⅛ **teaspoon freshly ground pepper**

3 **egg yolks**
1 **cup shredded Cheddar cheese**
¼ **cup grated Parmesan cheese**
5 **egg whites**
⅛ **teaspoon cream of tartar**

1. Set rack on lowest level of oven and preheat to 400°F. Butter and flour a 9 x 13-inch baking dish. Dust with flour, tapping out excess.

2. In a medium-size heavy saucepan, bring 2 cups salted water to a boil. Slowly stir in grits, sprinkling lightly a little at a time to prevent lumps. Return to a boil, reduce heat to low, and cook, stirring, until thick and sputtering, about 10 minutes.

3. Meanwhile, in another medium saucepan, melt butter over medium-high heat. When foamy, add flour. Cook, stirring, 1 to 2 minutes. Gradually whisk in warm milk, salt, and pepper. Bring to a boil, whisking, until sauce is smooth and thickened, 1 to 2 minutes.

4. In a small bowl, lightly whisk egg yolks. Slowly whisk about ½ cup hot sauce into yolks. Pour yolks back into sauce base, whisking to blend. Add grits to sauce. Remove from heat and stir in Cheddar and Parmesan cheese, leaving some unmixed streaks.

5. In a large bowl, beat egg whites with cream of tartar to stiff peaks. Fold about one-fourth of whites into grits base to lighten. Fold grits base back into rest of egg whites. Transfer to baking dish.

6. Place soufflé in oven and immediately reduce heat to 375°F. Bake about 20 minutes, until puffed and golden. Serve immediately.

291   POLENTA SOUFFLÉ AMERICAN-STYLE WITH CHEDDAR CHEESE

Prep: 10 minutes   Cook: 25 to 30 minutes   Serves: 6

Polenta is cornmeal ground just a little more coarsely than regular cornmeal. Here butter is melted in the microwave with the garlic, producing an aroma that will drift through the house announcing to anyone with a nose on his or her face that garlic will definitely be in this dish.

Butter and flour for dish	1 **teaspoon salt**
4 **tablespoons butter**	2 **egg yolks, lightly beaten**
1 **tablespoon minced garlic**	5 **egg whites**
2½ **cups milk**	⅛ **teaspoon cream of tartar**
1 **cup polenta or yellow**	1 **cup shredded Cheddar,**
cornmeal	**Swiss, or Jarlsberg cheese**
1 **tablespoon sugar**	

1. Set rack on lowest level of oven and preheat to 375°F. Butter and flour a 9 x 13-inch baking dish. Dust with flour, tapping out excess.

2. In a small glass measure, microwave butter with garlic on High 45 to 60 seconds, until butter melts.

3. In a large saucepan, warm milk over high heat until bubbles form around edge, 2 to 3 minutes. Gradually stir in cornmeal, garlic butter, sugar, and salt until smooth. Reduce heat to medium and cook, stirring, 30 seconds.

4. Remove from heat and stir about ½ cup hot cornmeal mixture into beaten egg yolks. Add yolks to remaining polenta, stirring quickly to mix. Let cool slightly.

5. In a large bowl, beat egg whites and cream of tartar to stiff peaks. Fold cheese into whites, then fold whites into cornmeal base. Spread in prepared baking dish.

6. Bake 20 to 25 minutes, until soufflé is puffed and very light gold. Serve immediately.

Variation:

292   POLENTA SOUFFLÉ ITALIAN-STYLE WITH GORGONZOLA CHEESE

Prepare the polenta soufflé as described in recipe 291, substituting ½ cup crumbled Gorgonzola and ½ cup shredded mozzarella or provolone for the Cheddar in step 5. Proceed as directed.

293   CRAB SOUFFLÉ

Prep: 15 minutes   Cook: 30 to 32 minutes   Serves: 6

Fresh crabmeat is an expensive proposition, I know. But this soufflé just isn't the same with fake crabmeat, also called surimi. Canned crab is my second choice; if you use that, be sure to drain it very well. Any crabmeat should be picked over well to remove any bits of shell or cartilage.

Butter and flour for dish	1½ cups warm milk
1 scallion, minced	⅛ teaspoon cayenne
3 tablespoons butter	1 teaspoon salt
2 cups (12 ounces) fresh	3 egg yolks, beaten
crabmeat, preferably	½ cup grated Parmesan cheese
fresh	4 egg whites
3 tablespoons flour	⅛ teaspoon cream of tartar
2 tablespoons tomato paste	

1. Set rack on lowest level of oven and preheat to 400°F. Butter and flour a 2-quart soufflé dish or 9 x 13-inch glass baking dish. If using soufflé dish, extend height of dish with a 4-inch-wide collar made from a folded strip of aluminum foil tied around dish. Also butter and flour foil.

2. In a medium skillet, cook scallion in 1 tablespoon butter over medium-high heat about 1 minute, just to soften. Add crabmeat and cook, stirring, 1 to 2 minutes, depending upon whether crab is canned or fresh. Layer in bottom of prepared dish.

3. In a medium saucepan, melt remaining 2 tablespoons butter over medium-high heat. When foamy, add flour and cook, stirring, 1 minute. Blend in tomato paste. Gradually whisk in warm milk. Bring to a boil, whisking until sauce is thickened and smooth, 1 to 2 minutes. Season with cayenne and salt. Remove from heat and whisk in beaten egg yolks. Stir in Parmesan cheese.

4. In a large bowl, beat egg whites and cream of tartar to stiff peaks. Fold sauce into whites with gentle wide strokes. Pour over crabmeat.

5. Place dish in oven and immediately reduce heat to 375°F. Bake 25 minutes, until soufflé is puffed, golden on top, and slightly jiggly in center. Serve right away.

294 POTATO, PEPPER, AND PEA SOUFFLÉED OMELET

Prep: 15 minutes   Cook: 21 to 28 minutes   Serves: 4 to 6

Martha Rose Shulman has been teaching me about cooking ever since we were friends in Texas and I signed up for her cooking classes. Here I've adapted her famous light touch and one of her flat omelets made essentially from egg whites. Three yolks are spread out over a very large omelet that will serve up to six.

1 pound russet (baking) potatoes, peeled and cut into ½-inch dice	1 large green bell pepper, cut into ½-inch dice
¾ teaspoon salt	3 eggs
¼ cup olive oil	8 egg whites
1 onion, chopped	¼ cup milk
3 garlic cloves, minced	½ teaspoon pepper
	1 cup thawed frozen peas

1. Place potatoes in a microwave-safe bowl. Add ¼ cup water and a pinch of salt. Cover tightly and microwave until tender,, about 5 minutes on High. Drain and set aside.

2. In a large nonstick skillet with ovenproof handle, heat 2 tablespoons olive oil over medium-high heat. Add onion, garlic, and bell pepper. Cook until softened, about 3 minutes. Scrape vegetables onto a large plate to cool slightly.

3. In a large mixing bowl, gently beat eggs, egg whites, milk, salt, and pepper. Stir in cooked vegetables. Add peas and potatoes.

4. In same large skillet, heat remaining 2 tablespoons olive oil over high heat. When hot, pour in egg mixture. Swirl to distribute. Cook, lifting edges to let some of uncooked egg flow underneath, until sides firm up, 1 to 2 minutes.

5. Reduce heat to low. Cover and cook until omelet is nearly set but still moist in center, 10 to 15 minutes. Meanwhile, preheat broiler.

6. Run omelet under broiler 2 to 3 minutes to brown top. Serve hot or at room temperature, cut into wedges or diamond shapes.

295 SOUFFLÉED PANCAKE WITH PROSCIUTTO, ARTICHOKES, AND ASPARAGUS

Prep: 15 minutes   Cook: 29 to 32 minutes   Serves: 6

One weekend in late spring, food writer Toni Allegra was loaded with leftovers from an overambitious jaunt through the farmers' market in the Napa Valley. Waiting to spill onto a puffy half omelet/half pancake were artichokes, asparagus, a whole red bell pepper, and some prosciutto—you know, the basics in a Napa Valley kitchen. Here's my simplified version of her concoction, which uses both fresh and canned vegetables. Since they are served on top of the souffléed pancake, the presentation is colorful and most attractive.

2 cups fresh asparagus tips
4 canned artichoke hearts, cut
   into 6 wedges each
1 red onion, sliced
3 tablespoons olive oil
6 tablespoons butter
½ cup diced prosciutto or ham

6 whole eggs
1 egg white
1½ cups milk
1½ cups flour
¾ cup grated Parmesan cheese
1 red bell pepper, cut into
   long thin strips

1. Preheat oven to 425°F. In a large saucepan of boiling salted water, boil asparagus 2 to 3 minutes, until just tender and still bright green. Drain, rinse under cold running water, and drain well. Return asparagus to same pot. Add artichokes to asparagus.

2. In a medium skillet, sauté onion in olive oil and 2 tablespoons of the butter over medium heat until soft but not browned, about 4 minutes. Add to asparagus-artichoke mixture.

3. Place 3 tablespoons of the remaining butter in a wide 12-inch round baking dish, skillet with ovenproof handle, or paella pan and melt in the oven. With a whisk or with an electric mixer on low speed, beat eggs and egg white. While beating, slowly pour in milk. Slowly add flour, beating until lumps dissolve. Stir in cheese.

4. Pour egg mixture into dish or pan. Place in oven and bake 20 minutes, or until sides puff.

5. While pancake bakes, in a medium skillet, melt remaining 1 tablespoon butter over medium heat. Add red pepper and cook until soft, 3 to 5 minutes. Add to asparagus and artichokes and toss to mix.

6. At last minute, heat vegetables in saucepan or in a ceramic or glass bowl in a microwave. Pile into center of baked pancake and serve at once, cut into wedges.

296 BAKED JAPANESE EGG PINWHEELS

Prep: 5 minutes   Cook: 27 minutes   Makes: 8 pieces

The Japanese sushi favorite *uzumake tamago* is a baked soufflé at heart.

5 eggs
1 cup flaked surimi (imitation crab)
3 tablespoons sugar

Pinch of salt
1 to 2 tablespoons vegetable oil

1. Preheat oven to 375°F. Separate 2 eggs. In a medium bowl, combine yolks with remaining 3 whole eggs and whisk until blended. Stir in surimi, sugar, and salt.

2. In another bowl, beat 2 egg whites until stiff. Gently fold whites into egg-surimi mixture.

3. In a 9-inch square metal baking dish, heat oil on top of stove over medium-high heat. When hot, pour in egg mixture. Cook until bottom browns, about 2 minutes.

4. Transfer to oven and bake 25 minutes, or until a knife inserted near center comes out clean. Let cool briefly on a rack. Invert to unmold omelet onto a cutting board. Roll up while hot. When cool, slice at 1-inch intervals. Present with spirals up.

297 HOT LEMON SOUFFLÉ

Prep: 40 minutes   Cook: 20 to 25 minutes   Serves: 4

Cathy Burgett is the pastry and dessert teacher at Tante Marie's Cooking School in San Francisco. Her word for what happens when eggs and sugar combine: "Enigmatic." She is especially fond of soufflés, and I've included two of her favorites, Hot Lemon Soufflé and Chocolate Soufflé.

Butter and sugar for dish
4 tablespoons butter, melted
⅔ cup granulated sugar
Grated zest of 3 lemons

⅓ cup fresh lemon juice
4 egg yolks
5 egg whites
Powdered sugar

1. Set rack on lowest level of oven and preheat to 425°F. Heavily butter a 4-cup soufflé dish. Sprinkle with sugar, tapping out excess.

2. In a double boiler, combine butter, ⅓ cup of the granulated sugar, lemon zest, lemon juice, and egg yolks. Cook over simmering water, whisking, until a sauce forms that is consistency of heavy cream, 8 to 10 minutes. Do not allow to boil. Remove from heat. Keep covered.

3. In a large bowl, beat egg whites to moderately stiff peaks. While beating, slowly add remaining ⅓ cup granulated sugar. Continue beating until whites are stiff and glossy.

4. Fold about one-fourth of beaten whites into warm lemon curd. Add lemon mixture to bowl with remaining egg whites. Fold together as lightly as possible.

5. Spoon mixture into prepared soufflé dish. Bake immediately until souffle is puffed and browned on top, 12 to 15 minutes. Sprinkle top with powdered sugar and serve at once.

---

298   CHOCOLATE SOUFFLÉ
Prep: 10 minutes   Cook: 12 to 15 minutes   Serves: 4

One of Cathy Burgett's soufflé secrets is to keep the soufflé base at a warm temperature. Here the chocolate base can be made ahead and chilled. If so, it must be warmed before the whites are folded in. If not made ahead, the chocolate base should be just warm to complete the process by the time you've beaten the whites.

Butter and sugar for dish
½ cup heavy cream
6 ounces semisweet
    chocolate, chopped
3 egg yolks

1½ teaspoons brandy
5 egg whites
3 tablespoons granulated
    sugar
Powdered sugar

1. Generously butter a 4-cup soufflé dish. Sprinkle with sugar, tapping out excess.

2. In a medium saucepan, bring cream to a boil. Remove from heat. Immediately add chopped chocolate, stirring until smooth.

3. Beat yolks into hot chocolate mixture. Stir in brandy. Keep at room temperature, covered. Soufflé base can be prepared 3 to 4 hours ahead.

4. Set rack on lowest level of oven and preheat to 400°F. Beat egg whites until stiff. Add sugar and beat again until very stiff and glossy. Stir about one-fourth of egg whites into warm chocolate base. Fold chocolate mixture back into egg whites, combining lightly but thoroughly.

5. Pour mixture into prepared dish. Quickly place in oven and bake 12 to 15 minutes, until puffed but still slightly jiggly in center. Sprinkle powdered sugar over top of soufflé and serve at once.

299   GREENBRIER COLD BOURBON SOUFFLÉ

Prep: 15 minutes   Cook: 14 to 18 minutes   Chill: 4 hours
Serves: 6 to 8

The first time I put this dessert in my mouth was in 1981 at a conference at the Greenbrier resort in West Virginia. At that time, it was called Cold Old Bourbon Soufflé. Old bourbon is a luxurious beverage, but I've found young bourbon works just as well in this soufflé and is easier on the budget. This is a big party dessert, which can be halved easily for a smaller crowd.

Butter and sugar for dish	**Pinch of salt**
1 **envelope plain gelatin**	1 **cup sugar**
¾ **cup bourbon**	1½ **cups heavy cream**
8 **eggs, separated**	¼ **cup chopped toasted pecans**
2 **teaspoons vanilla extract**	

1. Butter an 8-cup soufflé dish. Make sides of dish higher with an 8-inch-wide folded length of wax paper or aluminum foil wrapped around rim and tied with string. Butter collar and sprinkle inside of dish and collar with sugar.

2. In a double boiler, sprinkle gelatin over bourbon and let stand 5 minutes to soften. Warm over simmering water until gelatin dissolves, 2 to 3 minutes.

3. In a large mixing bowl, beat egg yolks until thick and lemon colored. Add yolks to bourbon-gelatin mixture. Stir in vanilla. Cook over boiling water, stirring constantly, until custard thickens enough to coat a metal spoon, 12 to 15 minutes. Remove from heat and let cool, stirring occasionally.

4. In a large mixing bowl, beat egg whites and salt until foamy. Gradually beat in sugar and continue to beat to stiff and glossy peaks. With a large whisk, stir one-third of egg whites into bourbon custard to lighten. Fold in remaining whites.

5. Whip 1 cup of cream to stiff peaks. Fold one-third of cream into soufflé until blended. Fold in remaining cream until no lumps remain. Pour into prepared soufflé dish. Refrigerate until set, at least 4 hours or overnight.

6. At serving time, whip remaining ½ cup cream to stiff peaks. Pipe or dollop onto soufflé. Garnish with chopped pecans.

300   CHERRY-VANILLA ICED SOUFFLÉ

Prep: 15 minutes   Cook: 25 minutes   Chill: 30 minutes
Freeze: 5 hours   Serves: 6

Fresh summer cherries are irresistible with vanilla, hence the famous ice cream flavor. Why not combine them in an airy cold soufflé? This make-ahead will ingratiate you to all your friends and guests.

1 **pound fresh Bing cherries,** **pitted, or 1 (16-ounce) can** **pitted sweet cherries,** **drained**	4 **whole eggs, separated**
	2 **egg yolks**
	1¼ **cups sugar**
	1 **cup hot milk**
¼ **cup kirsch or brandy**	½ **teaspoon vanilla extract**
1 **envelope plain gelatin**	1 **cup heavy cream**

1. In a medium bowl, soak cherries in kirsch. In a small bowl, soak gelatin in ¼ cup cold water until soft, about 5 minutes.

2. In a double boiler, beat 6 egg yolks and ¼ cup sugar until pale, about 1 minute. Gradually beat in hot milk. Stir in gelatin mixture. Cook over scarcely simmering water, stirring, until custard thickens, about 25 minutes. Strain into a large bowl.

3. Stir liquid from cherries and vanilla into custard and refrigerate until thick, about 30 minutes, stirring a couple of times for even setting.

4. Meanwhile, make sides of an 8-cup soufflé dish higher with an 8-inch-wide length of wax paper or aluminum foil folded lengthwise in half, then wrapped around rim and tied with string.

5. In a large bowl, beat egg whites until foamy. Gradually beat in remaining 1 cup sugar. Beat to fairly stiff peaks. Fold a large scoop of whites into chilled custard to lighten, blending completely. Fold in remaining whites.

6. Beat cream to stiff peaks. Fold into egg white mixture and spoon soufflé into soufflé dish. Freeze 1 hour.

7. Drop cherries into partially frozen soufflé. Cut through mixture with a dull knife to distribute cherries. Return to freezer for 4 hours or, well wrapped, for up to 4 days.

8. To serve, let soufflé stand at room temperature 10 minutes, then scoop out with a large spoon.

301   SWEET OMELET WITH DRIED FRUIT COMPOTE

Prep: 5 minutes   Cook: 32 minutes   Serves: 4 to 6

The sweet luxury of this simple, rich dish is one of my family's most eagerly awaited Sunday treats. It's covered in a thick syrup from the fruit compote and the eggs are still kind of jiggly (that's the way we like them) in the middle. But the sides are baked so high that every slice of the fork expels so much air that if we lean over the plate, we can hear the omelet go *poosh-sh-sh*. It sure beats snap, crackle, and pop.

2½ tablespoons flour	Powdered sugar
1 cup milk	Dried Fruit Compote (recipe
6 eggs, separated	follows)
3 tablespoons butter	
3 tablespoons granulated sugar	

1. Preheat oven to 350°F. In a large mixing bowl, whisk flour with ¼ cup of milk until smooth. Add rest of milk, then egg yolks. Whisk until smooth again.

2. Put butter in a large nonstick skillet with ovenproof handle. Place in oven until butter melts, about 5 minutes. Swirl to coat sides.

3. Meanwhile, in a large bowl, beat egg whites until foamy. Continue beating while gradually adding granulated sugar. Beat to stiff and glossy peaks. Blend beaten egg whites into yolk mixture, stirring gently until just 1 or 2 streaks remain.

4. Pour egg mixture into hot skillet. Bake until set, about 12 minutes. Loosen edges with a spatula and invert onto a large round plate. Dust generously with powdered sugar sprinkled through a sieve. Serve warm, topped with compote.

DRIED FRUIT COMPOTE
Makes: 1 cup

4 pitted prunes, chopped	¼ cup sugar
4 dried apricots, halved	1 teaspoon vanilla extract
4 dried pears, chopped	½ teaspoon cinnamon
4 dried apple slices	About 1 cup red wine or
2 tablespoons raisins	water

1. In a nonreactive medium saucepan, combine all ingredients, adding just enough wine to cover dried fruit.

2. Bring to a simmer over low heat. Let bubble gently until thick and syrupy, about 20 minutes. Remove from heat and let fruit cool in syrup until warm. Syrup will be consistency of honey when cooled.

302 WINTER ORANGE-VANILLA SOUFFLÉ

Prep: 15 minutes   Cook: 32 to 34 minutes   Serves: 6

Butter and sugar for dish
1 cup milk
1 vanilla bean, split
  lengthwise, or 2
  teaspoons vanilla extract
¼ cup cornstarch
½ cup sugar
  Dash of salt
5 eggs, separated

¼ cup flour
1 tablespoon grated orange
  zest
1 cup fresh orange juice
2 tablespoons Grand Marnier
  or Cointreau
  Orange Sauce (recipe
  follows)

1. Set rack on lowest level of oven and preheat to 400°F. Butter an 8-cup soufflé dish. Make sides of dish higher with an 8-inch-wide length of wax paper or aluminum foil folded lengthwise in half, then wrapped around rim and tied with string. Butter the collar. Sprinkle inside of dish and collar with sugar. Set aside.

2. Pour ¾ cup milk into a 2-cup glass measure. Scrape seeds from vanilla bean into milk. Microwave on High 1 minute, to heat to just under a boil.

3. In a medium saucepan, blend cornstarch with remaining ¼ cup milk, sugar, salt, egg yolks, and flour. Beat until smooth and pale, about 1 minute. Whisk in warm vanilla milk until smooth. Add orange zest.

4. Cook over medium heat, whisking to keep smooth, until custard boils and thickens, about 3 minutes. Scrape custard into a large mixing bowl. Whisk in orange juice and liqueur. If using vanilla extract, blend in now. Let cool for 10 minutes.

5. In a large bowl, beat egg whites to soft peaks. Gradually add remaining ¼ cup sugar and beat to stiff and glossy peaks. Fold into orange base.

6. Pour into prepared soufflé dish. Draw a deep circle in center of batter to make a top hat. Bake 25 minutes, or until top browns but soufflé is slightly runny in center. Serve immediately with Orange Sauce.

ORANGE SAUCE
Makes: about 1 cup

1 cup orange juice
½ cup sugar
1 tablespoon cornstarch

2 tablespoons butter, in pats
1 tablespoon Grand Marnier
  or Cointreau

1. In a medium saucepan, blend orange juice with sugar and cornstarch. Bring to a boil over medium heat. Cook, stirring, until thick and clear, 3 to 5 minutes.

2. Remove from heat. Add butter and liqueur. Stir until butter melts and sauce is smooth. Serve hot or warm.

303 ROTHSCHILD SOUFFLÉ STACK

Prep: 10 minutes   Cook: 23 minutes   Serves: 6

7 **eggs, separated**	1 **cup heavy cream**
½ **cup flour**	**About ⅔ cup favorite jam,**
¾ **cup sugar**	**such as blackberry**
1 **cup milk**	

1. Preheat oven to 400°F. In a medium saucepan, whisk together egg yolks, flour, sugar, and milk to a paste. Cook over medium heat, stirring, until paste boils and thickens, about 8 minutes. Transfer to a large mixing bowl.

2. In another large bowl, beat egg whites to soft peaks. Fold a scoop of whites into yolk base. Fold remaining whites into base. Divide soufflé mixture evenly among 3 generously buttered ovenproof dinner plates, spreading gently. Bake soufflés all at same time until just set, about 15 minutes.

3. Meanwhile, whip cream to stiff peaks. Remove soufflés from oven and while warm, spread one with jam. Slide second one off plate and stack on first. Spread with jam. Repeat with third one, spreading with jam.

4. Top stack with dollops of whipped cream. When it makes contact with the hot stack, it will begin to melt, creating a sauce. Serve immediately, cutting wedges and spooning them into bowls.

304 BIG BILLOWY AUSTRIAN VANILLA DUMPLINGS

Prep: 20 minutes   Cook: 5 to 6 minutes   Serves: 6

These big, billowy sweet dumplings collapse in about 5 minutes, just like a real soufflé, so be sure to serve dessert as soon as it comes out of the oven.

4 **tablespoons butter**	1 **vanilla bean**
8 **eggs, separated**	6 **tablespoons flour**
⅓ **cup sugar**	**Powdered sugar**
¼ **teaspoon vanilla extract**	

1. Set rack on lowest level of oven and preheat to 425°F. Melt butter in a 6-cup baking dish or oval gratin in oven.

2. In a large bowl, beat egg whites until foamy. Gradually beat in sugar and continue beating to firm but not stiff peaks.

3. In another bowl, blend egg yolks with vanilla extract. Scrape seeds from vanilla bean into yolks and mix well. Pour down side of bowl into whites. Use a large whisk or rubber spatula to fold together.

4. Sieve flour over top of batter. Fold until flour is incorporated and mixture is smooth, but don't overblend or batter will deflate.

5. With a large spoon, scoop up 6 even mounds of dumpling batter and drop gently into baking dish. Pull up on tips so sections become distinct.

6. Bake 5 to 6 minutes, until tips are brown and most of dumpling is pale brown outside and creamy inside. Serve immediately dusted with powdered sugar.

---

305   FROZEN MINEOLA SOUFFLÉ
Prep: 15 minutes   Cook: 18 to 21 minutes   Chill: 30 minutes
Freeze: 4 hours   Serves: 6

A Mineola is a cross between tangerine and a type of grapefruit. It is sweet and subtle, but certainly interchangeable with any juicy orange or tangerine variety. This icy dessert provides a delightful light ending to any dinner party.

Butter and sugar for dish	1½ cups fresh Mineola or
2 tablespoons plain gelatin	tangerine juice
4 whole eggs, separated	1 tablespoon tangerine or
2 egg yolks	orange liqueur
⅔ cup plus ½ cup sugar	1 cup heavy cream
1 tablespoon grated Mineola	
or tangerine zest	

1. Butter a 6-cup soufflé dish. Make dish higher with an 8-inch-wide strip of wax paper or foil folded in half lengthwise, wrapped around rim, and tied with string. Butter collar. Sprinkle inside of dish and collar with sugar, shaking to coat evenly.

2. In a small bowl, soak gelatin in ¼ cup cold water until soft, about 5 minutes.

3. In a double boiler, beat 6 egg yolks with ½ cup sugar until light yellow, about 1 minute. Add gelatin, place over simmering water, and cook, stirring, until custard is thick enough to coat back of a metal spoon, 12 to 15 minutes.

4. Scrape custard into a large bowl. Whisk in zest, juice, and liqueur until smooth. Refrigerate about 30 minutes, until base begins to gel, stirring a few times so custard sets evenly.

5. In a large bowl, beat 4 egg whites to stiff peaks, gradually adding ⅓ cup of remaining sugar. Fold into base.

6. Whip cream with remaining ⅓ cup sugar. Fold into custard. Pour mixture into soufflé dish. Freeze 4 hours or overnight, or wrap entire soufflé well in foil and freeze up to 4 days.

Chapter 13

Egging on Dessert

The structure and shape of various desserts wouldn't exist without eggs. Eggs go to work in desserts to build height, to bind and thicken, to add volume, and to make satisfying texture. Even if the egg isn't the star ingredient, it's usually there doing its job unobtrusively and effortlessly. Many old desserts were the results of leftover yolks or leftover whites being put to sweet, sinful use. A yolks-only batter can bake into a rich, golden cake as easily as a whites-only batter can become angel food. Some desserts use the yolks and whites but keep them in separate functions. An example of this is Snow Eggs in Custard Sauce (known formally as Floating Islands). The egg whites comprise the "snow" eggs and are poached in milk, and the yolks go in the poaching milk to make the custard, a true waste-not-want-not dish. The freshness of eggs is extremely important for desserts. The higher the yolk sits on its white, the better the body of your dessert will be.

Too HARD!

306 DAFFODIL CAKE WITH PINEAPPLE CUSTARD FILLING AND CREAM CHEESE–HONEY FROSTING

Prep: 10 minutes   Cook: 25 to 30 minutes   Stand: 1½ hours
Serves: 10

Daffodils are idealized in a yellow and white marbled cake, with each color contributed by either whites or yolks. I've seen this cake made as a layer cake, with the yellow layer made of sponge cake, and the white layer made of angel food. I believe the marbled look is prettier. Pineapple Custard Filling is a favorite among my friends, and the frosting continues a springtime theme by being flavored with the sweet by-product of spring's pollinator—bees.

1 cup sifted cake flour	½ teaspoon almond extract
1¼ cups sugar	2 teaspoons finely minced
8 whole eggs, separated	orange or tangerine zest
4 egg whites	Pineapple Custard Filling
1½ teaspoons cream of tartar	(page 205)
½ teaspoon salt	Cream Cheese–Honey
1½ teaspoons vanilla extract	Frosting (page 205)

1. Set rack in center of oven and preheat to 350°F. Sift flour and ¾ cup of the sugar together 3 times. Set aside.

2. In a large mixing bowl, beat 12 egg whites, cream of tartar, and salt until foamy. Gradually beat in remaining ½ cup sugar. Continue to beat until sugar is completely dissolved and whites hold medium-firm peak. Quickly beat in vanilla and almond extract. Fold flour-sugar mixture into whites ¼ cup at a time, folding in each addition until completely absorbed before adding next.

3. In a medium bowl, beat egg yolks and orange zest on very high speed until thick and daffodil yellow, at least 5 minutes. Fold about 1½ cups egg-white batter into yolks; blend well.

4. Spread half of egg white mixture in bottom of 2 *ungreased* 9-inch cake pans. Top with spoonfuls of yellow and white batter, using all of yellow and half of remaining whites. Finally, drop remaining white batter on top and spread smooth. With a table knife, cut through batter, swirling in figure 8s to marble.

5. Bake 25 to 30 minutes, until top of layers springs back when lightly touched. Let cool 1½ hours in pans and inverted on racks. Loosen cakes with a narrow spatula or table knife and gently shake onto wax paper. Transfer 1 layer to a cake plate. Spread with Pineapple Custard Filling and place second layer on top. Frost with Cream Cheese–Honey Frosting.

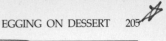

307 (PINEAPPLE CUSTARD FILLING)

Prep: 5 minutes   Cook: 1 to 2 minutes   Makes: 2 cups

1 (20-ounce) can crushed
    pineapple in syrup
3 egg yolks
½ cup sugar

2 tablespoons flour
2 tablespoons cornstarch
1 tablespoon butter

1. Drain pineapple, reserving fruit and syrup separately.

2. In a medium saucepan, beat egg yolks, sugar, flour, and cornstarch until smooth. Whisk in pineapple syrup. Cook over medium heat, stirring vigorously with a wooden spoon, until mixture thickens and pulls away from sides of pan, 1 to 2 minutes. Mixture will resemble cream puff paste. Beat hard over heat 30 seconds longer with wooden spoon. Remove from heat.

3. Transfer thick custard to a mixing bowl. Beat in butter. Let cool completely. When cool, stir in crushed pineapple. Keep cold until ready to fill cake.

---

308 CREAM CHEESE–HONEY FROSTING

Prep: 5 minutes   Cook: none   Makes: 2½ cups

1 pound cream cheese, at
    room temperature
1 stick (4 ounces) butter, at
    room temperature

½ cup mild honey

1. In an electric mixer fitted with paddle attachment, whip cream cheese and butter until smooth and fluffy.

2. Pour in honey. Beat until well combined and smooth. Cover and refrigerate until set before frosting cake.

309 BUTTERMILK POUND CAKE
Prep: 5 minutes   Cook: 1 hour   Makes: 14 to 16 slices

This pound cake is moist and very flavorful. Even served plain, it's always a hit.

Butter and flour for pan
3 cups flour
½ teaspoon salt
½ teaspoon baking soda
2 sticks (8 ounces) butter, at room temperature

3 cups sugar
6 eggs
1 tablespoon vanilla extract
1 cup buttermilk

1. Set rack in center of oven and preheat to 350°F. Generously butter 10-inch tube pan. Dust with flour, tapping out excess. Sift together flour, salt, and baking soda.

2. In an electric mixer fitted with paddle attachment, beat butter on high speed until fluffy. Gradually add sugar, beating until smooth and very well blended.

3. In a small bowl, combine eggs and vanilla. With mixer on low speed, slowly add eggs in 3 portions to butter-sugar mixture, waiting until each portion is well absorbed before adding next.

4. With mixer on low, add sifted ingredients alternately with buttermilk, beginning and ending with flour. Transfer batter to prepared pan.

5. Bake 1 hour, or until cake is golden and a toothpick inserted near center comes out clean.

6. Let cool in pan on a wire rack 10 minutes. Run a knife around cake, invert onto rack, and let cool completely before slicing.

310 JANE'S GOLD CAKE
Prep: 5 minutes   Cook: 1 to 1¼ hours   Serves: 8

My friend Jane Fleischaker remembers this as the cake her grandmother made after she made Grandpa's weekly angel food cake.

Butter and flour for pan
3 cups plus 2 tablespoons flour
1 tablespoon plus 2 teaspoons baking powder
¼ teaspoon salt

2 sticks (8 ounces) butter, at room temperature
2 cups sugar
11 egg yolks
1 tablespoon lemon, almond, or vanilla extract

1. Set rack in center of oven and preheat to 325°F. Grease or butter a 10-inch tube pan. Dust with flour, tapping out excess. Sift together flour, baking powder, and salt.

2. In an electric mixer fitted with paddle attachment, beat butter until smooth and fluffy. Gradually add sugar, beating a full 2 minutes.

3. Add egg yolks and beat 5 minutes. Add ⅓ cup of sifted flour mixture to butter-yolk mixture and beat 1 minute. Mix in extract. Stir in remaining flour and 1 cup cold water. Beat 5 minutes. Pour batter into prepared pan.

4. Bake 15 minutes. Raise heat to 375°F. Bake 45 to 60 minutes longer, until a toothpick inserted halfway between rim and pan's tube comes out clean.

5. Let cool in pan on a wire rack 10 minutes. Run a knife around cake, invert onto rack, and let cool completely before slicing.

---

311   RICHEST CHOCOLATE MOUSSECAKE
Prep: 15 minutes   Cook: 18 to 23 minutes   Serves: 12 to 14

2 **sticks (8 ounces) plus**
  2½ **tablespoons unsalted**
  butter
	10 **ounces (10 squares)**
	  unsweetened chocolate
	  About 1 cup semisweet

5 **whole eggs, separated**	**chocolate shavings or**
4 **egg yolks**	**chopped chocolate**
1¼ **cups sugar**	**(optional)**

1. Set rack in center of oven and preheat to 350°F. Use ½ tablespoon butter to grease bottom, but not sides, of an 8-inch round cake pan.

2. Place remaining butter in a glass measure or microwave-safe bowl. Microwave on High 1 to 1½ minutes. Let cool.

3. In a large mixing bowl, beat 9 egg yolks and sugar with an electric mixer on medium speed 3 to 4 minutes to dissolve sugar.

4. Melt chocolate in a double boiler over hot water or in a microwave, uncovered, on Medium, about 2 minutes. Stir until smooth and cooled.

5. Beat melted butter into egg yolk mixture. Stir in melted chocolate.

6. In another large bowl, beat egg whites to soft peaks. Fold one-fourth of whites into chocolate batter until no streaks show. Fold rest of whites into batter. Pour only two-thirds of batter into buttered pan. Refrigerate remaining batter.

7. Bake 15 to 20 minutes. Center will appear underdone. Cool cake in pan on a rack.

8. Run knife around sides of cake and invert onto serving platter. Frost with remaining batter or pipe onto cake in swirly decorations. Sprinkle all over with chocolate shavings, if using. This cake is best cut with a knife dipped in hot water, then wiped dry.

312   SUNSHINE CAKE
Prep: 10 minutes   Cook: 60 to 65 minutes   Stand: 1½ hours
Serves: 10 to 12

The technique for making this cake is similar to that used for angel food, even though beaten yolks join the beaten whites. At the end of mixing, flour is gently folded into the batter a small amount at a time. For success, be sure to sift the flour, both before the measuring and when adding to the batter. Use this cake like a sponge cake.

9 **eggs, separated**	½ **teaspoon lemon extract**
1 **teaspoon cream of tartar**	½ **teaspoon orange extract**
½ **teaspoon salt**	½ **teaspoon vanilla extract**
1¼ **cups sugar**	1½ **cups sifted cake flour**

1. Set rack in center of oven and preheat to 325°F. In a very large bowl, beat egg whites on high speed with cream of tartar and salt until foamy. Gradually beat in ¾ cup sugar and continue to beat until glossy and medium-stiff. Beat in lemon extract, orange extract, and vanilla.

2. In another bowl, beat egg yolks and ½ cup sugar until thick and very pale, at least 4 minutes. Fold yolks into whites.

3. Sift flour, ½ cup at a time, over batter, folding in gently after each addition. Pour batter into an *ungreased* 9- or 10-inch tube pan. Cut a swirl through batter with a table knife.

4. Bake 60 to 65 minutes, until top of cake springs back when lightly touched.

5. To cool, turn upside down with tube over a bottle neck or funnel. Let cake cool in pan completely, about 1½ hours. Turn right side up and loosen cake from pan with thin knife. Invert and gently shake out of pan onto serving plate.

313   ORANGE CHIFFON CAKE
Prep: 10 minutes   Cook: 60 to 70 minutes   Stand: 1 to 1½ hours
Serves: 10

7 **eggs, separated**	1 **tablespoon grated orange**
½ **cup vegetable oil**	**zest**
1 **teaspoon vanilla extract**	1 **tablespoon baking powder**
2 **cups flour**	1 **teaspoon salt**
1½ **cups sugar**	¾ **teaspoon cream of tartar**

1. Set rack in lower third of oven and preheat to 325°F. In a 4-cup glass measure or medium bowl, whisk together egg yolks, oil, vanilla, and ¾ cup water.

2. In a large bowl, combine flour, sugar, orange zest, baking power, and salt. Stir or whisk gently to mix.

3. In a large bowl, beat egg whites and cream of tartar on high speed until beaters dipped into foam and turned upside-down hold a firm peak.

4. Make a well in center of flour. Pour in egg yolk–oil mixture and stir vigorously until smooth and well blended. Fold into beaten egg whites. Turn batter into an *ungreased* 10-inch tube pan.

5. Bake 60 to 70 minutes, until edges have begun to pull away from sides of pan and top of cake is golden brown and feels springy if touched lightly.

6. Invert cake in pan on a funnel or bottle neck and let cool completely, 1 to 1½ hours. Run a thin knife around edge of cake to loosen it and let fall gently onto a serving plate.

---

314   SNOW EGGS IN CUSTARD SAUCE

Prep: 20 minutes   Cook: 12 to 15 minutes   Chill: 2 hours
Serves: 6 to 8

Also known as Floating Islands, this is the ultimate egg recipe because it exhausts all that an egg has to give. Snowy meringues are made of the eggs' whites; they are formed into ovals that cook in milk ultimately destined for a custard made with the eggs' yolks. This dish is reputed to have been among the favorites of Thomas Jefferson, and it's still popular in France, where it's known as *oeufs à la neige*.

4 **cups milk**	8 **eggs, separated**
1½ **cups sugar**	
1 **teaspoon vanilla extract or**	
1 vanilla bean	

1. Pour milk into a Dutch oven or other large pot. Stir in ¼ cup sugar and vanilla. Heat over medium heat until bubbles form around edge of pan.

2. Meanwhile, beat egg whites on high speed until foamy. Continue beating while slowly pouring in 1 cup sugar. Beat to very stiff, glossy peaks.

3. Stir hot milk a few times. Using 2 large spoons, form about one-fourth of meringue into 3 ovals and add to hot milk. Poach, turning gently, 30 to 40 seconds per side, until lightly firmed. Remove with a slotted spoon to drain on a towel-lined cookie sheet. Repeat with remaining meringue to make 12 ovals altogether. Strain cooking milk into a large glass measure with a pour spout.

4. In a medium saucepan, beat egg yolks with remaining ¼ cup sugar until thick and light yellow. Set over medium heat. Gradually stir in milk. Cook, stirring, until custard thickens enough to coat a metal spoon, about 12 to 15 minutes. If necessary, strain again. Cover and refrigerate custard until cold, at least 2 hours. Lightly cover meringues and refrigerate separately.

5. To serve, pour custard into a large serving bowl and float ovals on top. Or spoon custard into individual bowls with 1 or 2 meringues on top.

315   NO FINER BUTTERSCOTCH PIE
Prep: 10 minutes   Cook: 17 to 20 minutes   Chill: 6 hours
Serves: 8

The best butterscotch pudding is needed to satisfactorily fill this pie. That means you need a strong arm to stir the butterscotch filling until it's thick enough to set up.

6 **egg yolks**	1 **cup milk, warmed**
4½ **tablespoons unsalted butter**	1 **teaspoon vanilla extract**
¾ **cup (packed) dark brown**	**Egg Pie Crust, baked and**
sugar	**cooled (page 215)**
3 **tablespoons flour**	

1. Have egg yolks ready in a medium bowl, preferably with a pour spout.

2. In a medium saucepan, cook butter over medium-high heat until golden brown but not burned, 2 to 3 minutes. Immediately reduce heat to medium and add brown sugar and flour. Cook, stirring, 2 minutes. Carefully and slowly whisk warm milk into brown sugar mixture (it may splatter). Cook, whisking, over medium heat until thick, 10 to 12 minutes.

3. Whisk about ½ cup pudding into egg yolks. Whisk yolks back into pudding. Cook, whisking, 3 minutes longer, until pudding is very thick. Remove from heat and mix in vanilla.

4. Pour pudding into a bowl, straining if not smooth. Let stand until cool but pourable. Pour filling into cooled pie crust. Wrap pie in plastic. Refrigerate until set, about 6 hours.

316   APPLE-RUM CUSTARD CAKE (I)
Prep: 15 minutes   Cook: 65 to 67 minutes   Serves: 10

From Germany comes an apple cake baked with a custard filling, which I made richer and thicker with heavy cream and additional eggs. Use Granny Smiths, Gravensteins, or any other tart apple. If you don't have any, I always say you won't throw the world order out of balance if you use a sweet apple in something sweet. I've made this with Fuji apples, about the sweetest apple ever, with the grand result of a sweeter cake.

⅓ cup raisins	2½ **pounds Granny Smith**
¼ cup rum or apple brandy	**apples, peeled and sliced**
¾ cup fresh white bread	¼ inch thick (about 5)
crumbs	Thick Custard Filling
6 tablespoons butter, melted	(recipe follows)
Rich Yolk Crust, prebaked	3 tablespoons sugar
in a 9-inch springform	
pan (page 211)	

1. Set rack in center of oven and preheat to 350°F. Soak raisins in rum.

2. In a small bowl, combine bread crumbs and 3 tablespoons of the melted butter. Mix with your fingers to moisten evenly. Sprinkle over partially baked Rich Yolk Crust in springform pan.

3. Arrange apples on crumbs. Drain raisins, reserving rum for Thick Custard Filling. Sprinkle raisins over apples. Set pan on a baking sheet. Bake 12 minutes.

4. Pour half of the custard sauce slowly over apples. Bake 20 minutes. Pour on rest of custard filling and bake 25 minutes longer. Remove from oven but do not turn it off. Raise oven rack to highest level.

5. In a small bowl, mix sugar with remaining melted butter. Sprinkle over top of cake. Bake cake 8 to 10 minutes, until lightly browned. Some topping may drip onto baking sheet.

6. Let cool completely on a wire rack. Remove sides of pan. Slice with a knife dipped in hot water, then wiped dry.

THICK CUSTARD FILLING
Makes: about 4 cups

2 **whole eggs**	2½ **cups heavy cream**
4 **egg yolks**	¼ **cup rum or apple brandy**
⅓ **cup sugar**	

Whisk whole eggs, egg yolks, and sugar until thick and light yellow. Beat in cream and rum.

---

317 RICH YOLK CRUST
Prep: 10 minutes   Cook: 12 minutes   Makes: one 9-inch crust

1 **vanilla bean**	1 **stick (4 ounces) plus**
3 **tablespoons sugar**	6 **tablespoons butter,**
2 **teaspoons grated lemon zest**	**softened**
2¼ **cups flour**	4 **egg yolks**

1. Set rack in center of oven and preheat to 350°F. Split vanilla bean lengthwise in half and scrape out seeds. Place seeds in a food processor with sugar and lemon zest. Pulse until blended. Add flour and pulse to mix. Place butter pieces on top of flour. Pulse to mealy mixture.

2. With machine on, add egg yolks, one at a time, until dough forms. It won't leave sides of the bowl, so don't overmix. Press over bottom and halfway up sides of a 9-inch springform pan.

3. Prebake 12 minutes, or until light gold. Remove from oven and let cool.

318 BUTTERMILK PIE WITH CARAMELIZED STRAWBERRY SAUCE

Prep: 10 minutes   Cook: 50 to 63 minutes   Serves: 6 to 8

Take care: This pie will toughen and shrink if it's overbaked.

3 **eggs, separated**
¾ **cup sugar**
¼ **cup flour**
1¾ **cups buttermilk**
2 **teaspoons vanilla extract**
5 **tablespoons butter, melted**

Lemon Butter Pie Crust,
   baked and cooled (recipe
   follows)
Caramelized Strawberry
   Sauce (page 213)

1. Set rack in center of oven and preheat to 425°F. In a large bowl, whisk egg yolks, sugar, and flour until smooth. Stir in buttermilk, vanilla, and melted butter. Stop stirring as soon as ingredients are blended.

2. In a medium bowl, beat egg whites to stiff peaks. Stir gently into buttermilk base. Pour mixture into prepared crust.

3. Bake 10 minutes. Reduce oven temperature to 325°F. and bake 15 to 20 minutes longer. Top may wiggle, but if a knife dipped into pie near center comes out clean, pie is done.

4. Serve at room temperature with Caramelized Strawberry Sauce.

319 LEMON BUTTER PIE CRUST

Prep: 10 minutes   Chill: 30 minutes   Cook: 20 to 25 minutes
Makes: one 9-inch pie shell

1½ **cups flour**
2 **teaspoons finely minced**
   lemon zest
½ **teaspoon salt**
1 **stick (4 ounces) cold butter,**
   in pats

2 **tablespoons solid vegetable**
   shortening, very cold
About 3 tablespoons ice
   water

1. Set rack in center of oven and preheat to 425°F. Place flour, lemon zest, and salt in a food processor. Pulse to mix.

2. Top flour with butter pieces and shortening. Pulse until evenly crumbly. With machine on, slowly pour in ice water, pouring when dough forms a ball that knocks around sides of machine. Flatten into a disk, wrap in plastic, and refrigerate 30 minutes.

3. Roll out dough to a thin 12-inch circle. Set in pie plate and cut overhang so dough extends ¾ inch beyond rim. Fold overhang under and crimp large flutes. Prick all over with a fork. Cover bottom with foil and fill with pie weights or dried beans or rice.

4. Bake 15 minutes. Remove foil and weights. Return to oven and bake 5 to 10 minutes longer, or until pale gold. Let cool before filling.

CARAMELIZED STRAWBERRY SAUCE
Makes: about 1¾ cups

1 pint fresh strawberries, rinsed and hulled	1 tablespoon lemon juice ⅔ cup sugar

1. Slice half of strawberries and set aside. Puree other half with lemon juice.

2. Place sugar in a heavy, medium saucepan. Slowly pour in ¼ cup water. Bring to a boil over medium-high heat without stirring. Boil until sugar turns color of iced tea, 3 to 6 minutes. Immediately remove from heat and pour in ¼ cup more water. Stir out lumps.

3. Add strawberry puree. Cook, stirring, until heated through, about 2 minutes. Add strawberry slices. Heat 30 seconds, just to soften. Let cool before serving. Serve at room temperature or slightly chilled.

---

320   PERSIMMON CUSTARD PIE
Prep: 15 minutes   Cook: 60 to 70 minutes   Serves: 8 to 10

Use large persimmons—the kind with the teardrop shape—for this recipe. It ripens until it's ugly, shriveled, and feels perfectly rotted. That's when it's best. The earthy orange color and season conveniently coincide with Thanksgiving, which is when I always make this pie.

1½ to 2 cups persimmon pulp (5 to 6 persimmons)	2 whole eggs 4 egg yolks
1½ cups heavy cream	1 teaspoon vanilla extract
3 tablespoons flour	Egg Pie Crust, unbaked
1 cup sugar	(page 215)
4 tablespoons unsalted butter, melted	

1. Set rack in center of oven and preheat to 450°F. In a food processor, puree persimmon until smooth.

2. In a large bowl, whisk cream, flour, sugar, and melted butter until well blended.

3. In a medium bowl, lightly beat whole eggs, egg yolks, and vanilla. Whisk into cream mixture. Add persimmon pulp, swirling gently and leaving some streaks. Pour into pastry shell. Set on a baking sheet.

4. Bake pie 10 minutes. Reduce heat to 350°F. Bake 50 to 60 minutes longer, until bubbling. Rotate pie if spotty browning occurs. Let cool before serving.

321   LILLIE TOMLIN'S FROZEN LEMON PIE

Prep: 10 minutes   Cook: none   Freeze: 1 hour   Serves: 6

Lillie, mother of comedienne Lily Tomlin, gave me this recipe for the dessert her daughter requested most during the holidays. It's a very old-fashioned recipe from the glory days of eggs, when all you needed to finish a dish was eggs, sugar, some flavoring—in this case, lemon—and no cooking.

3 **eggs, separated**
½ **cup sugar**
5 **tablespoons lemon juice**

1 **cup heavy cream**
   About 22 vanilla wafers
   Mint leaves

1. In a medium bowl, beat egg whites until stiff. Add ½ cup sugar, then egg yolks and beat again until glossy. Stir in lemon juice.

2. In another medium bowl, whip cream to stiff peaks. Fold into lemon mixture. Set aside.

3. Between sheets of wax paper, roll enough vanilla wafers into crumbs to measure 1 cup. Press over bottom and up sides of a buttered 9-inch pie plate or square baking dish. Pour in lemon filling. Freeze at least 1 hour or overnight.

4. Before cutting, leave out a few minutes to soften. Garnish each serving with 1 or 2 mint leaves.

---

322   CARAMELIZED BANANA CREAM PIE

Prep: 10 minutes   Cook: 7 to 9 minutes   Chill: 3 hours   Serves: 8

Not content to simply slice bananas raw into a crust, I cook them in brown sugar and rum, then arrange them on the bottom of the pie.

1 **tablespoon flour**
3 **tablespoons cornstarch**
½ **cup plus 2 tablespoons granulated sugar**
2½ **cups milk**
4 **egg yolks**
1 **teaspoon vanilla extract**
2 **tablespoons butter**

¼ **cup light brown sugar**
3 **medium bananas, sliced**
1 **tablespoon cognac or brandy**
   Egg Pie Crust, baked and cooled (recipe follows)
1½ **cups heavy cream**

1. In a large heavy saucepan, whisk flour, cornstarch, ½ cup of the sugar, and milk until smooth. Cook over medium-high heat, stirring constantly, until mixture comes to a boil, 2 to 3 minutes. Boil 2 minutes. Remove from heat.

2. In a small bowl, whisk about ½ cup hot milk mixture with egg yolks, then whisk yolks back into base. Cook another 1 to 2 minutes, stirring constantly, until custard is very thick. Pour into a medium bowl set in another bowl of ice and water. Stir in vanilla. Set aside, stirring now and then, to cool.

3. In a large skillet, melt butter over medium-high heat. Add brown sugar and bananas and cook quickly, turning, about 2 minutes, until bananas just begin to soften. Immediately increase heat to high. Add brandy and ignite carefully. As soon as flames subside, pour bananas onto a plate to cool.

4. Line pie shell with caramelized bananas and any juices on plate. Pour custard filling over bananas. Cover with plastic wrap and refrigerate until chilled and set, at least 3 hours.

5. In a medium bowl, whip cream and remaining 2 tablespoons sugar to medium-firm peaks. Pipe or swirl over top of pie. Pie slices best with a smooth knife warmed in hot water, then wiped dry.

323 EGG PIE CRUST
Prep: 10 minutes   Chill: 30 minutes   Cook: 23 to 25 minutes
Makes: one 9-inch pie shell

1¼ **cups flour**
 1 **tablespoon sugar**
    Pinch of salt
 5 **tablespoons cold butter, cut**
      into pieces

 2 **tablespoons solid vegetable**
      shortening
 1 **egg**
 2 **to 3 tablespoons ice water**

1. Set rack in lower third of oven and preheat to 425°F. In a food processor, combine flour, sugar, and salt. Mix with a few pulses. Place butter and shortening on top of flour mixture. Pulse until dough is uniformly crumbly. Add egg. Pulse to blend.

2. With machine on, pour in ice water. Run machine just until dough collects itself into a loose ball, then stop immediately. By hand, press dough into well-shaped ball. Flatten into a disk, wrap, and refrigerate at least 30 minutes.

3. Roll out pastry into a 12- or 13-inch circle. Fit into a 9- or 10-inch pie plate. Cut overhang to ¾ inch and fold under. Crimp rim. If not baking right away, cover and refrigerate.

4. To bake, prick pastry all over with a fork. Line bottom with foil and fill with pie weights or dried beans or rice. Bake 15 minutes. Remove foil and weights. Bake 8 to 10 minutes longer, or until crust is pale brown. Let cool before filling.

324 MERINGUE NESTS FILLED WITH HONEYED CREAM CHEESE
Prep: 10 minutes   Cook: 1½ to 2 hours   Stand: 1 hour
Chill: 2 hours   Makes: 12

This elegant desert is luscious and creamy. For a touch of color, top with a few fresh berries.

4 **whole eggs, separated**	1 **pound cream cheese**
2 **egg whites**	4 **teaspoons lemon juice**
1¼ **cups sugar**	⅓ **cup mild honey**
1 **cup heavy cream**	

1. Set oven rack in center of oven and preheat to 200°F. Line a baking sheet with parchment paper cut to fit. Trace twelve 2½-inch circles on paper, using a cup or glass. Turn paper over.

2. In a large mixing bowl, beat 6 egg whites, gradually adding sugar, until fairly stiff peaks form. Fill a pastry bag with mixture and pipe nests, filling each circle and making side walls 1 inch high. Or form with a spoon.

3. Bake 1½ to 2 hours, until shells are crisp and dry. Turn oven off and leave nests in oven for 1 hour.

4. While meringues bake, whisk yolks and cream in top of a double boiler. Cook and stir gently over simmering water about 6 to 8 minutes, until thick enough to coat spoon heavily. Color will darken. Let cool.

5. In a large mixing bowl, beat cream cheese, lemon juice, and honey until fluffy. On low speed, beat in cooked yolk mixture. Let cool.

6. Pour filling into nests while still on baking sheet. Set sheet in refrigerator for 2 hours, or until filling sets.

7. To serve, lift each filled nest with a spatula to a dessert plate.

---

325 LEMON CURD CREAM PIE
Prep: 10 minutes   Cook: none   Chill: 2 hours   Serves: 8

1 **cup cream**	**Egg Pie Crust, baked and**
⅓ **cup sugar**	**cooled (page 215)**
1 **teaspoon vanilla**	
Lemon Curd (page 184) or	
1⅔ **cups jarred lemon**	
curd	

1. In a medium bowl, whip cream while slowly adding sugar and vanilla to stiff peaks. Fold into lemon curd.

2. Pour into prepared pie shell. Wrap well in plastic. Refrigerate until chilled and set, at least 2 hours, before serving.

326   HEAVENLY LEMON PIE

Prep: 10 minutes   Cook: 10 minutes   Chill: 8 hours   Serves: 6 to 8

This is a four-egg pie. The whites make the crust and the yolks enrich the filling. It's a bit messy, but it packs an awfully big wow factor.

4 egg yolks	2 cups heavy cream
½ cup sugar	**Meringue Coconut Crust,**
1 tablespoon grated lemon	**baked and cooled (recipe**
zest	**follows)**
3 tablespoons lemon juice	

1. In a double boiler, whisk egg yolks, sugar, lemon zest, and lemon juice until smooth and light in color, about 2 minutes. Cook over simmering water, stirring, until thickened, about 10 minutes. Transfer custard to a bowl and let cool.

2. Whip 1 cup cream to stiff peaks. Fold into cooled custard. Pour into prepared Meringue Coconut Crust. Refrigerate at least 8 hours or, preferably, overnight.

3. When ready to serve, whip remaining cream. Pipe decoratively over surface of pie.

327   MERINGUE COCONUT CRUST

Prep: 5 minutes   Cook: 1 hour 10 minutes
Makes: one 10-inch pie shell

1 cup sugar	4 egg whites
¼ teaspoon cream of tartar	3 tablespoons flaked coconut

1. Set rack on lowest level of oven and preheat to 275°F. Sift sugar and cream of tartar together.

2. In a medium bowl, beat egg whites to stiff peaks. Continue beating while slowly adding sugar. Beat until glossy and very stiff. Spread meringue in a buttered 10-inch pie plate so bottom is ¼ inch thick and side wall is 1 inch thick. Sprinkle coconut over rim.

3. Bake 1 hour 10 minutes, or until golden and crisp. Turn off oven and leave crust in it to cool.

328   BOURBON CREAM PIE

Prep: 10 minutes   Cook: 6 to 8 minutes   Chill: 4 hours
Serves: 8

Bourbon and eggs have always found companionship in Southern desserts. Here is a cream pie with a definite spirited quality.

¾ **cup sugar**	1 **teaspoon vanilla extract**
5 **tablespoons cornstarch**	**Egg Pie Crust, baked and**
¼ **cup bourbon**	**cooled (page 215)**
2¼ **cups milk**	**Whipped cream**
3 **eggs yolks, lightly beaten**	**Chocolate shavings**
1 **tablespoon butter**	

1. Sift sugar and cornstarch into a medium saucepan. Slowly whisk in bourbon and milk until smooth. Bring to a boil over medium-high heat, stirring constantly, 3 to 5 minutes. Boil and stir the thickened pudding 1 full minute.

2. Stir half of hot pudding into egg yolks, then pour yolk mixture into pudding base in saucepan. Bring to a simmer. Cook 2 minutes longer, stirring, until even thicker.

3. Remove from heat. Stir in butter and vanilla. Pour filling into pie shell. Cover and refrigerate until set, 4 to 6 hours or overnight.

4. Serve topped with dollops of whipped cream and a sprinkling of chocolate shavings. This cuts best with a knife dipped in hot water, then wiped dry.

329   LEMON MERINGUE PIE

Prep: 10 minutes   Cook: 10 to 15 minutes   Serves: 8 to 10

Considered one of the most difficult of all the pies, this one is worth the project. A friend from Liverpool says the lemon curd in this pie is better than any he can remember his mum made in England. This is a big, impressive pie that cuts into tall wedges.

1⅔ **cups sugar**	4 **teaspoons finely grated**
½ **cup cornstarch**	**lemon zest**
Pinch of salt	**Egg Pie Crust, baked and**
⅔ **cup lemon juice**	**cooled (page 215)**
6 **egg yolks**	**Lofty Pie Meringue (recipe**
3 **tablespoons butter**	**follows)**

1. Preheat oven to 350°F. In a heavy saucepan, combine sugar, cornstarch, and salt. Slowly stir in lemon juice and 1⅔ cups water.

2. Beat egg yolks until smooth. Add to saucepan with butter. Cook over medium heat, stirring constantly, until mixture thickens and just boils. Boil 1 minute, stirring. Remove from heat and add zest. Pour custard into baked crust.

3. Spread meringue around edges first, making sure to seal it well to crust. Fill in center with rest of meringue, making swirls.

4. Bake 10 to 15 minutes, until tips are lightly brown. Let cool to room temperature. Pie cuts best with a knife dipped in hot water, then wiped dry.

---

330   LOFTY PIE MERINGUE

Prep: 5 minutes   Cook: none   Makes: enough to cover one 9-inch pie

Make just before using.

6 **egg whites**
¼ **teaspoon cream of tartar**

½ **teaspoon pure vanilla extract**
¾ **cup sugar**

In a large bowl, beat egg whites, cream of tartar, and vanilla to stiff peaks. Keep beating while slowly adding sugar. Beat until glossy and very stiff.

---

331   CHOCOLATE BANANA CREAM PIE

Prep: 1 hour   Cook: 6 minutes   Chill: 6 hours   Serves: 8

4 **ounces semisweet chocolate**
⅓ **cup plus ¼ cup sugar**
3 **tablespoons cornstarch**
6 **egg yolks**
2¾ **cups hot milk**
2 **teaspoons vanilla extract**
   **Egg Pie Crust, baked and
   cooled (page 215)**

2 **bananas, sliced**
   Lemon juice (optional)
1 **cup heavy cream**
2 **tablespoons unsweetened
   cocoa powder**

1. Place chocolate in a small glass dish and microwave, uncovered, on Medium 45 seconds to melt. Stir until smooth.

2. Sift together ⅓ cup of the sugar and cornstarch onto a piece of wax paper or plate. In a medium bowl, beat egg yolks and sugar-cornstarch mixture until thick and pale, about 2 minutes. Stir in melted chocolate. Whisk in hot milk.

3. Transfer to a heavy saucepan and cook over medium-high heat, stirring constantly, until pudding boils and thickens, about 2 minutes. Reduce heat and simmer 1 minute, stirring. Remove from heat. Stir in vanilla. Transfer pudding to a bowl set in a larger bowl of ice and water. Stir to cool somewhat.

4. Line pie shell with bananas. If desired, sprinkle lightly with lemon juice to prevent darkening. Top with warm chocolate filling. Wrap pie in plastic. Refrigerate until filling sets, about 6 hours.

5. Shortly before serving, beat cream with remaining ¼ cup sugar and cocoa until stiff peaks form. Decorate top of pie with chocolate cream. Serve soon or keep cold until serving. For the cleanest slices, use a knife dipped in hot water, then wiped.

332   MILE-HIGH LIME PIE
Prep: 15 minutes   Cook: 16 to 22 minutes   Freeze: 4 hours
Serves: 8 to 10

I like to serve this after a light fish dinner. Take the zest off the limes before you squeeze them for juice.

5 eggs, separated
1¼ cups sugar
1 cup strained lime juice
    (about 5 limes)
1 envelope plain gelatin
    Grated zest of 3 limes plus
    strips for garnish

Chocolate Crumb Crust,
    baked and cooled (recipe
    follows)
Lofty Pie Meringue
    (page 219)

1. In a double boiler, beat egg yolks and sugar until thick and pale, about 2 minutes. Add lime juice and cook, stirring, until custard thickens enough to coat a metal spoon, 8 to 12 minutes. Transfer to a bowl and let cool slightly.

2. Meanwhile, dissolve gelatin in ¼ cup cold water, about 5 minutes. Add softened gelatin and grated zest to lime custard, whisking well to combine.

3. In a medium bowl, beat egg whites until foamy. Gradually beat in sugar. Beat to stiff peaks. Fold into lime custard. Pour into crust. Wrap well in foil and freeze at least 4 hours.

4. Preheat oven to 400°F. With a dampened metal spatula, spread meringue over pie to edges, building up tips. Bake 8 to 10 minutes, until tips are browned. Serve or store in refrigerator for up to 4 hours. This pie cuts best with a smooth knife dipped in a tall glass of hot water, then wiped dry.

333   CHOCOLATE CRUMB CRUST
Prep: 10 minutes   Cook: 10 minutes   Makes: one 9-inch shell

10 double graham crackers
    (1 wrapped package from
    box)
1 round tablet Mexican
    chocolate or 2 ounces
    semisweet baking
    chocolate, chopped into
    small pieces

2 teaspoons cinnamon
3 tablespoons brown sugar
4 tablespoons butter, melted

1. Heat oven to 400°F. In a food processor, grind graham crackers to crumbs. Add chocolate pieces and process until chocolate is pulverized into crumbs. Stir in cinnamon and brown sugar. Pour crumbs into bottom of a 9-inch springform pan.

2. Pour melted butter directly over crumbs in pan. Using your fingers, quickly mash mixture until crumbs hold together. Press crust over bottom and up sides of pan.

3. Bake 10 minutes. Let cool before filling.

---

334 NO-BAKE LEMON CHEESECAKE
Prep: 30 minutes   Cook: 14 to 17 minutes   Chill: overnight
Serves: 10 to 12

2 envelopes plain gelatin
6 egg yolks
2 cups sugar
1½ cups warm milk
2 teaspoons vanilla extract
2 pounds cream cheese

¼ cup lemon juice
Zest of 2 lemons, finely minced or grated
4 egg whites
1 cup heavy cream

1. Soak gelatin in ¼ cup cold water 5 minutes to soften.

2. In a double boiler, whisk egg yolks and ½ cup of sugar until thick and pale yellow, about 2 minutes. Gently stir in warm milk without creating any foam. Cook over simmering water, stirring, until custard thickens enough to coat a metal spoon, about 12 to 15 minutes. Strain into a medium bowl. Stir in vanilla. Let cool until just warm.

3. Warm gelatin in microwave 10 seconds on High just to liquefy. Stir gelatin into cooled custard.

4. In a large bowl, beat cream cheese, remaining 1½ cups sugar, lemon juice, and lemon zest with an electric mixer on high speed until smooth. Slowly stir in gelatin-custard.

5. In a medium bowl, beat egg whites to stiff peaks. Fold into cheesecake base. In another medium bowl, whip cream until stiff. Fold into cheesecake.

6. Pour into a 10-inch springform pan. Refrigerate overnight.

7. At serving, slide warm knife around edge of cake. Remove springform collar. Serve cut in wedges.

335   CRUSTLESS EGG AND CREAM CHEESE PE

Prep: 10 minutes   Cook: 1¼ hours   Serves: 8

1 **pound cream cheese, softened**	1 **teaspoon vanilla extract**
4 **eggs**	8 **ounces sour cream**
2 **egg yolks**	1 **tablespoon brown sugar**
1 **cup granulated sugar**	3 **tablespoons powdered sugar**

1. Preheat oven to 325°F. In an electric mixer fitted with paddle attachment, beat cream cheese until smooth.

2. In another bowl, whip eggs, egg yolks, and granulated sugar until thick. Combine cream cheese and egg mixture, beating just until smooth. Stir in vanilla. Pour batter into a 9-inch springform pan. Set on baking sheet.

3. Bake 1 hour, or until a knife inserted halfway between edge and center comes out clean. Leave oven on. Let pie cool 20 minutes on wire rack.

4. In a medium bowl, whisk sour cream, brown sugar, and powdered sugar until smooth. Pour over pie. Return to oven 15 minutes to set and lightly brown. Let cool before serving.

336   COFFEE BAVARIAN CREAM

Prep: 5 minutes   Cook: 12 to 14 minutes   Chill: 2½ hours Serves: 6 to 8

The Bavarian cream, or *bavarois*, was not known in French cooking until the early nineteenth century, when it was popularized by French chef Antonin Carême. It brings a new life to Crème Anglaise, which is flavored, lightly stiffened with gelatin, and lightened in texture by folding in whipped cream. The enhancements and flavor possibilities are in the hundreds.

2 **tablespoons instant espresso powder**	½ **teaspoon vanilla extract**
½ **cup boiling water**	2 **cups heavy cream**
1 **tablespoon plain gelatin**	**Chocolate-covered coffee beans**
Warm Crème Anglaise (page 176)	

1. Dissolve coffee in boiling water. Let cool.

2. Soften gelatin in ¼ cup cold water for 5 minutes. Microwave on High 10 seconds to liquefy.

3. Stir gelatin into Crème Anglaise until smooth. Gently stir in coffee and vanilla. Refrigerate about 30 minutes to set up, stirring now and then to prevent spotty gelling.

4. In a medium bowl, whip cream to stiff peaks. Fold into coffee-gelatin base. Pour into individual dessert goblets. Cover and refrigerate until set, at least 2 hours. Garnish with coffee beans before serving.

337 WHITE CHOCOLATE–GUAVA MOUSSE

Prep: 20 minutes   Cook: 5 to 7 minutes   Chill: 2 hours
Serves: 6 to 8

9 ounces white chocolate,
    evenly chopped
5 eggs, separated
½ cup plus ⅓ cup sugar
½ cup undiluted guava
    concentrate

¾ cup heavy cream
Mint sprigs
Bittersweet chocolate
    shavings

1. In a double boiler over barely simmering water, melt white chocolate pieces. Stir to make smooth. Scrape chocolate into a glass or stainless steel bowl. Place in a larger pan of hot water and set aside. Wash double boiler.

2. In a clean double boiler, beat egg yolks and ⅓ cup of sugar until thick and pale, about 1 minute. Whisk in guava concentrate. Cook over simmering water, stirring, until slightly thickened, 5 to 7 minutes. Stir in white chocolate and remove from heat.

3. In a medium bowl, beat egg whites and ¼ cup of remaining sugar to medium-stiff peaks. Fold into guava base. In another medium bowl, whip cream and remaining ¼ cup sugar to stiff peaks. Fold into mousse. Cover and refrigerate until set, at least 2 hours.

4. To serve, mound in goblets and garnish with mint or bittersweet chocolate shavings, or both.

338 CHOCOLATE-KAHLÚA MOUSSE

Prep: 10 minutes   Cook: 1 or 2 minutes   Chill: 2 hours   Serves: 8

12 ounces semisweet
     chocolate, coarsely
     chopped
 6 tablespoons butter
 4 eggs, separated
½ cup sifted powdered sugar

¼ cup Kahlúa or other coffee-
     flavored liqueur
 1 teaspoon instant coffee
     powder
¼ cup granulated sugar
 2 cups heavy cream

1. In a glass measure, combine chocolate and butter and microwave, uncovered, on Medium for about 1 minute. Stir. Repeat melting in 20-second intervals, as needed, until just a small piece of chocolate remains. Stir until the last piece melts.

2. In a large bowl, whisk egg yolks, powdered sugar, Kahlúa, and coffee powder until very smooth. Stir in melted chocolate-butter.

3. In a medium bowl, beat whites, gradually adding granulated sugar, to stiff peaks. Fold into chocolate mixture. In a medium bowl, whip cream to stiff peaks. Fold into mousse.

4. Pour into a serving bowl or divide among individual goblets. Cover and refrigerate at least 2 hours or overnight.

339   DEEP CHOCOLATE MOUSSE
Prep: 15 minutes   Cook: 12 to 14 minutes   Chill: 2 hours
Serves: 6

½ cup plus 3 tablespoons
  sugar
5 egg yolks
8 ounces semisweet
  chocolate, coarsely
  chopped

7 tablespoons butter
3 egg whites
½ cup heavy cream

1. In a medium saucepan, bring ½ cup sugar and ⅓ cup water to a boil, stirring to dissolve sugar. Boil 5 minutes.

2. In a double boiler over barely simmering water, whisk yolks lightly. Beat in hot syrup. Cook, stirring, 5 to 8 minutes, until yolks are creamy and thick. Transfer to a mixing bowl. Stir to cool down.

3. Place chocolate in a medium microwave-safe bowl and microwave, uncovered, on Medium for about 1 minute. Stir. Repeat at 20-second intervals, as needed, until just a small piece of chocolate remains. Stir until the last piece melts. Whisk butter, pat by pat, into chocolate. Stir yolk mixture into chocolate base.

4. In a medium bowl, beat whites until foamy. Keep beating while adding remaining 3 tablespoons sugar. Beat to medium-firm peaks. Fold a scoop of whites into chocolate base until completely smooth. Fold in remaining whites until no white streaks show. In a small bowl, whip cream. Fold into mousse.

5. Divide among individual goblets or transfer to a serving bowl. Cover and refrigerate to firm up, about 2 hours.

340   CHOCOLATE DACQUOISE
Prep: 20 minutes   Cook: 60 to 70 minutes   Chill: overnight
Serves: 8

The meringue layers and strips can be prepared one day ahead.

3½ tablespoons unsweetened
  cocoa powder
1 cup powdered sugar
5 egg whites

⅔ cup granulated sugar
Warm Deep Chocolate
  Mousse (page 224)
Powdered sugar, for dusting

1. Set rack in center of oven and preheat to 300°F. Line 2 large baking sheets with parchment paper or butter and flour sheets.

2. Sift cocoa and powdered sugar together twice. In a large bowl, beat egg whites until foamy. Keep beating while gradually adding granulated sugar. Beat to glossy stiff peaks. Fold in cocoa-sugar mixture.

3. Draw three 5-inch circles on 1 baking sheet. Turn over paper. Fill a pastry bag and pipe two-thirds of meringue to fill circles. Pipe remaining third in ½-inch-wide strips across second baking sheet. Lacking a pastry bag, you can do this with a spoon.

4. Bake meringue strips 30 to 45 minutes, circles 60 to 70 minutes, until firm but not browned. Let cool until meringues harden. Carefully lift off sheets. Break strips into 1-inch pieces.

5. Use half of Deep Chocolate Mousse to frost 2 meringue disks. Stack one on the other and set third disk on top. Frost top and sides of dacquoise with remaining mousse. Press meringue pieces onto sides in all directions. Refrigerate overnight.

6. At serving, dust top with powdered sugar. Dessert cuts best with a smooth knife dipped in hot water, then wiped dry.

---

341 CLASSIC RICH VANILLA ICE CREAM
Prep: 10 minutes   Cook: 16 to 20 minutes   Chill: overnight
Makes: about 1½ quarts

2 cups heavy cream	6 egg yolks
2 cups milk	1 cup sugar
1 vanilla bean, split and scraped, or 1 tablespoon vanilla extract	4 tablespoons butter, in pats

1. In a 2-quart glass measure with pour spout, microwave cream, milk, and vanilla bean and seeds on High for 4 to 5 minutes to heat without boiling. Or steep in a medium saucepan over medium-low heat. If using extract, heat cream and milk, then stir in vanilla.

2. In a double boiler, beat egg yolks and sugar until thick and pale, about 1 minute. Lightly whisk in hot cream mixture. Cook over simmering water, stirring, until thick enough to coat a metal spoon, 12 to 15 minutes. Remove from heat. Stir in butter, pat by pat.

3. Transfer to canister of an ice cream maker. Cover and refrigerate. Ice cream is best if allowed to ripen overnight. It will keep up to 3 or 4 days.

4. Remove vanilla bean. Place canister in ice cream maker. Finish according to manufacturer's instructions.

T. RICHE! ? ? ?

342 (RICH AND DARK CHOCOLATE ICE CREAM)

Prep: 10 minutes   Cook: 17 to 20 minutes   Chill: overnight
Makes: about 1½ quarts

2 cups heavy cream	5 egg yolks
2 cups half-and-half	1 cup sugar
8 ounces (8 squares)	4 tablespoons butter, in pats
unsweetened chocolate,	2 teaspoons vanilla extract
chopped evenly	

1. In a glass measure, combine cream, half-and-half, and chocolate pieces and microwave, uncovered, on High for 5 minutes to just under a boil. Or heat in a large saucepan over medium-low heat. Stir a few times to melt chocolate completely.

2. In a double boiler, beat egg yolks and sugar until thick and pale, about 1 minute. Whisk in chocolate mixture without causing mixture to foam. Cook custard over simmering water, stirring, until thick enough to coat a metal spoon, 12 to 15 minutes. Remove from heat. Stir in butter, pat by pat, until melted, then vanilla.

3. Transfer to canister of ice cream maker. Cover and refrigerate. Ice cream is best if allowed to ripen overnight. It will keep up to 3 or 4 days.

4. Place canister in ice cream maker and freeze according to manufacturer's directions.

Variations:

343 (MOCHA LATTE ICE CREAM)

Dissolve 1 tablespoon instant espresso powder into the heated chocolate mixture in step 1 of recipe 342. Continue as directed.

344 CHOCOLATE–CHOCOLATE CHIP ICE CREAM

Freeze ice cream in recipe 342 just until mushy in step 4. Stop machine and add 2 cups semisweet chocolate chips or ½ pound semisweet chocolate, roughly shaved. Continue as directed.

345 CHOCOLATE-ALMOND ICE CREAM

Freeze ice cream in recipe 342 until it becomes slushy and clings to paddle in step 4. Stop machine and sprinkle in 1½ cups slivered almonds. Continue as directed.

346 CHOCOLATE–MACADAMIA NUT ICE CREAM

Add 1 cup coarsely chopped unsalted macadamia nuts in step 4 of recipe 342. Continue as directed.

347 FIG KAHLÚA ICE CREAM
Prep: 15 minutes   Stand: 2 hours   Chill: 8 hours
Cook: 15 to 20 minutes   Makes: about 1½ quarts

The sultry backdrop of figs makes for a remarkably compatible flavor for Kahlúa. Use black Mission figs for richest color. Brown Calimyrna figs are a good substitute.

3 cups chopped dried figs	1 cup sugar
½ cup Kahlúa	2 tablespoons butter, in pats
6 cups hot milk	1 teaspoon vanilla extract
5 egg yolks	

1. In a big bowl, soak figs in Kahlúa 2 to 3 hours. Pour hot milk over figs. Cover and refrigerate 5 hours or overnight.

2. Strain fig milk into a 2-quart glass measure or medium saucepan. Heat in microwave or on stovetop just to warm it through, 3 to 5 minutes. In a food processor or blender, puree figs with remaining 1 cup milk, leaving some visible pieces.

3. In a double boiler, beat egg yolks and sugar until thick and pale yellow, about 1 minute. Slowly stir in warm fig milk without causing mixture to foam. Stir in reserved fig puree. Cook over simmering water, stirring, until custard is thickened enough to coat a metal spoon, 12 to 15 minutes. Remove from heat. Stir in butter until melted, then vanilla.

4. Transfer to canister of an ice cream maker and cover with piece of plastic wrap laid directly on surface of custard. Refrigerate 3 to 4 hours or overnight. Custard will keep up to 3 or 4 days.

5. Place canister in ice cream maker and freeze according to manufacturer's directions.

348   STRAWBERRY ICE CREAM

Prep: 20 minutes   Cook: 16 to 20 minutes   Chill: overnight
Makes: about 1½ quarts

2½ **pints strawberries, rinsed**   ¾ **cup sugar**
   and hulled
   Classic Rich Vanilla Ice
   Cream (page 225)

1. Place half of strawberries in a food processor or blender and puree until smooth. Make ice cream through step 2. Stir puree into ice cream base and pour into canister of an ice cream maker. Cover and refrigerate overnight.

2. Slice remaining strawberries. In a medium bowl, toss sliced strawberries with sugar.

3. Begin freezing ice cream in canister according to manufacturer's instructions. When ice cream becomes slushy and clings to paddle, add sliced strawberries along with any juices in bowl. Finish freezing according to manufacturer's directions.

349   CARAMEL ICE CREAM

Prep: 10 minutes   Cook: 15 to 20 minutes   Chill: 3 to 4 hours
Makes: about 1 quart

1½ **cups sugar**   6 **egg yolks**
 2 **cups warm milk**   1½ **cups heavy cream**

1. Pour 1 cup of sugar evenly into a large saucepan. Set over medium-high heat and let sugar cook until it liquefies, then boils. Without stirring, let sugar boil until it turns dark amber. Remove from heat.

2. Immediately pour in warm milk, which will spatter and boil. Let settle, then stir until caramel smooths out. Return to heat, if necessary, to warm through.

3. In a double boiler, beat egg yolks and remaining ½ cup sugar until thick and light yellow, about 1 minute. Slowly stir in warm caramel-milk mixture without causing foaming. Cook over simmering water, stirring, until custard is thick enough to coat a wooden spoon (at least 160°F. on a candy thermometer), 10 to 12 minutes. Remove from heat. Stir to cool down.

4. Pour caramel custard into canister of ice cream freezer. Add cream and stir well. Cover and refrigerate 3 to 4 hours or overnight. Custard will keep up to 3 days.

5. Place canister in ice cream maker and freeze according to manufacturer's directions.

350 SOUR CREAM BLINTZES

Prep: 10 minutes   Cook: 42 minutes   Chill: 1 hour if baked
Serves: 6 to 8

The best blintzes are filled with a dry-curd fresh cheese known as pot cheese or farmer cheese, which is common in the Northeast. To approximate it elsewhere, let small-curd cottage cheese drain overnight through a strainer set over a bowl in the refrigerator.

12 ounces farmer cheese or
   well-drained cottage
   cheese
½ cup sour cream
2 egg yolks
2 tablespoons butter,
   softened, plus 2
   tablespoons more if
   frying

2 tablespoons sugar
½ teaspoon vanilla extract
   Sour Cream Blintz Crepes
   (page 230)

1. In a medium bowl, combine farmer cheese, sour cream, egg yolks, butter, sugar, and vanilla. Stir with a fork until smooth and well blended.

2. Place a small amount of filling on cooked side of a crepe. Fold sides toward center, then roll up to close.

3. If frying, heat about 2 tablespoons butter in a large skillet. When foaming, add blintzes about 4 or 5 at a time and fry until golden brown, about 2 to 3 minutes per side. Repeat with remaining blintzes and butter as needed.

4. If baking, place assembled blintzes in a well-buttered oblong baking dish as you go. Refrigerate at least 1 hour. Preheat oven to 350°F. Bake blintzes 30 minutes, uncovered, until browned and bubbly.

351   SOUR CREAM BLINTZ CREPES
Prep: 5 minutes   Cook: 12 minutes   Makes: about 12

4 eggs
¾ cup milk
¼ cup sour cream
3 tablespoons sugar

Pinch of salt
1 cup flour
Butter

1. In a 2-quart measure with a pour spout or in a medium bowl, whisk together eggs, milk, sour cream, sugar, and salt until smooth. Stir in flour in 3 portions, mixing until smooth after each addition.

2. Pour about 2 tablespoons batter into a 6-inch crepe pan or nonstick skillet over medium heat, swirling and tipping to coat entire surface thinly.

3. Fry crepe on one side only until set, about 1 minute. Slide out of pan. Stack on a plate with crepes separated by wax paper. If sticking occurs, add butter to pan as needed.

352   HARD SAUCE
Prep: 5 minutes   Cook: none   Chill: 1 hour   Makes: about ⅔ cup

This dessert sauce isn't really hard, it's easy. With no cooking and an electric mixer, you can whip it up in about 5 minutes, though it wants to chill out for about an hour in the fridge. Serve it as a spread over toasted pound cake or warm poached fruit or, in its more traditional pairing, over plum pudding.

4 tablespoons unsalted butter,
    at room temperature
1 cup powdered sugar
1 egg

2 teaspoons brandy or dark
    rum
½ teaspoon vanilla extract

1. In a mixing bowl, beat butter until light and fluffy. Gradually beat in powdered sugar. Beat on high speed until smooth and creamy. Add egg, brandy, and vanilla. Beat until light and fluffy, 2 to 3 minutes.

2. Scrape into a jar or container, cover, and refrigerate until fairly solid, about 1 hour or up to 2 days.

Chapter 14

Shake It Up, Baby

As acts of raw egg consumption go, few impress more than celluloid Sylvester Stallone as Rocky, who guzzled raw eggs every morning while training for The Fight. Despite that portrayal, eggs in drinks are a lovely tradition at holiday time. They were integral in power breakfast drinks just a few decades ago. And they were the foundation for many nutritious beverages through the ages, when simply sneaking an egg into one concoction or another added nutritional power that was hardly noticed in the taking.

Eggnog is by far the most popular egg beverage. It comes in lots of flavors with all kinds of spirits added. If you are worried about raw eggs in eggnog, make it from a cooked custard base.

---

353 OLD-STYLE SOUTHERN EGGNOG
Prep: 10 minutes   Chill: 1 hour plus 1 day   Cook: none   Serves: 24

This is the old way to make eggnog. The yolks and whites, while treated separately, remain uncooked. It is important to add the alcohol slowly, or the yolks may curdle.

12 egg yolks	**6 egg whites**
2 cups sugar	**Pinch of salt**
3 cups bourbon	**4 cups heavy cream**
1 cup brandy or rum	**Freshly grated nutmeg**

1. In a large mixing bowl, beat yolks and sugar with an electric mixer until thick, about 2 minutes. Cover and refrigerate 1 hour.

2. Return to mixer. On very low speed, drizzle in bourbon and brandy while beating constantly but gently. Refrigerate, covered, 1 to 3 days to ripen.

3. When ready to serve, in a large bowl, beat egg whites and salt to fairly stiff peaks. Slowly pour chilled eggnog base into whites, folding until blended. Transfer to a big punch bowl.

4. In a large bowl, beat cream to stiff peaks. Fold into eggnog; some tufts may float. Grate nutmeg over top. Wipe sides of bowl clean. Serve immediately.

354 WILDFLOWER HONEY–EGG SHAKE
Prep: 3 minutes   Cook: none   Serves: 1

1 **egg**	1 **tablespoon orange flower**
¾ **cup milk**	**water or lemon juice**
2 **to 3 tablespoons wildflower**	4 **to 6 ice cubes**
honey	

1. In a blender, blend egg a few seconds, until foamy.

2. Stop machine. Add milk, honey, and orange flower water. Turn on blender and blend while adding ice, until thick and frothy. Serve immediately.

355 SHAKER LEMONADE
Prep: 10 minutes   Cook: none   Serves: 2

Most Shaker villages in America saw an extremely high use of lemons. In this drink, besides the lemons, the two most important ingredients are fresh raw eggs and shaved ice. Then they'd sip it through a "straw" cut from the hollow stems of the lovage plant.

2 **eggs**	**Ice, preferably shaved**
1½ **tablespoons sugar**	2 **long lovage stems (optional)**
2 **tablespoons ice water**	
Juice of 2 large lemons	
(about ½ cup)	

1. Beat eggs and sugar until very pale yellow and somewhat thickened, about 1½ minutes. Stir in ice water and lemon juice.

2. Fill 2 glasses two-thirds full of shaved or well-hammered ice. Pour egg-lemonade over ice.

3. Sip through a lovage stem or plastic straw.

356 QUICK SHERRY EGGNOG
Prep: 5 minutes   Cook: none   Serves: 6

4 **eggs**	3¼ **cups very cold milk**
¼ **cup sugar**	½ **cup heavy cream**
½ **cup cream sherry**	**Freshly grated nutmeg**

1. In a medium bowl, beat eggs and sugar on high speed until thick and pale, about 1 minute. With mixer on very slow speed, drizzle in sherry, then milk. Keep cold until serving.

2. When ready to serve, in a medium bowl, whip cream to stiff peaks. Ladle eggnog into 6 tall glasses. Top with whipped cream and a dusting of grated nutmeg. Don't forget to offer long spoons!

357 ESPRESSO EGGNOG

Prep: 10 minutes   Cook: 14 to 20 minutes   Chill: overnight
Serves: 10 to 15

2 **cups milk**	1 **cup bourbon**
2 **tablespoons instant espresso**	½ **cup Kahlúa**
powder	2 **teaspoons vanilla extract**
6 **egg yolks**	4 **egg whites**
1 **cup plus 2 tablespoons**	2 **cups heavy cream**
sugar	**Freshly grated nutmeg**
½ **cup dark rum**	

1. In a 1-quart glass measure, microwave milk with espresso powder, uncovered, on High about 2 minutes until warm. Or heat in a small saucepan on top of stove.

2. In a double boiler, beat egg yolks and 1 cup sugar until light colored and fluffy, about 1 minute. Slowly whisk in warm coffee-milk. Cook over simmering water, stirring, until custard is thick enough to coat spoon, 12 to 18 minutes. Transfer to a mixing bowl. Cool slightly, stirring occasionally.

3. Slowly whisk in rum, bourbon, Kahlúa, and vanilla. Cover with plastic wrap placed directly on surface of custard. Refrigerate overnight or up to 3 days to ripen.

4. When ready to serve, pour custard into a large punch bowl. In a medium bowl, beat egg whites with remaining 2 tablespoons sugar to fairly stiff peaks. Fold into custard.

5. In a large bowl, beat cream to stiff peaks. Fold into eggnog. Let some tufts of cream and egg whites float on surface. Sprinkle with nutmeg. Serve immediately.

Variations:

358 CHOCOLATE EGGNOG

Add 1 cup chocolate syrup to milk as it warms for recipe 357. When serving, omit nutmeg. Top with shaved chocolate instead.

359 MOCHA EGGNOG

Add 1 cup chocolate syrup plus 2 tablespoons instant espresso powder to milk as it warms for recipe 357. When serving, omit nutmeg. Sprinkle with cinnamon instead.

360   PARTY EGGNOG
Prep: 15 minutes   Cook: 16 to 19 minutes   Chill: overnight
Serves: 30

This eggnog has a cooked base, which some people may be more comfortable with. It's loaded with liquors and is designed for a large gathering. The recipe can be halved easily.

12 egg yolks
2 cups plus 3 tablespoons
    sugar
4 cups warm milk
1 vanilla bean, split and
    scraped, or 2 teaspoons
    vanilla extract

1 cup dark rum
2 cups bourbon
1 cup Cognac or other brandy
8 egg whites
4 cups heavy cream
    Freshly grated nutmeg

1. In a double boiler, whisk egg yolks and 2 cups sugar until fluffy and pale yellow, about 1 minute. Whisk in warm milk. Add vanilla bean. Cook over simmering water, stirring, until custard is thick enough to coat back of a spoon, 15 to 18 minutes. Transfer to a mixing bowl. Lay plastic wrap directly on surface of custard. Let cool slightly.

2. Slowly whisk in rum, bourbon, and Cognac. If using vanilla extract, add it now. Cover and refrigerate overnight or up to 3 days to ripen.

3. When ready to serve, remove vanilla bean. Pour custard into a large punch bowl. In a large bowl, beat egg whites to foamy stage. Keep beating while slowly adding remaining 3 tablespoons sugar. Beat to fairly stiff peaks. Fold egg whites into custard.

4. In a large bowl, beat cream to stiff peaks. Fold into eggnog, letting some tufts of cream and egg whites float. Sprinkle with nutmeg. Serve immediately.

361   EGG FLIP
Prep: 5 minutes   Cook: none   Serves: 1

3 tablespoons Cognac or
    brandy
3 tablespoons heavy cream
1 egg

1 teaspoon powdered sugar
3 or 4 ice cubes
    Freshly grated nutmeg

In a blender, combine Cognac, cream, egg, powdered sugar, and ice cubes. Cover and blend on high speed until ice is coarsely chopped. Strain flip into a whiskey sour or other cocktail glass. Sprinkle nutmeg on top and serve at once.

362   EGG CREAM
Prep: 5 minutes   Cook: none   Serves: 2

Contrary to what you might assume, a classic egg cream does not contain any eggs. A real New York egg cream is made from chocolate syrup, milk, and seltzer. If made right, the beverage looks as if it has eggs, because the froth on top resembles beaten egg white. The American Egg Board gave the Egg Cream an egg so it could live up to its name.

2 **eggs**	2 **tablespoons chocolate syrup**
¾ **cup cold milk**	1 **cup cold club soda or seltzer**
3 **tablespoons coffee liqueur**	

In a blender or food processor, combine eggs, milk, coffee liqueur, and chocolate syrup. Blend at least 20 seconds, until silky smooth. Divide chocolate base between 2 tall glasses. Pour ½ cup club soda into each glass, stirring hard to create a head of foam. Serve at once.

---

363   TROPICAL EGGNOG
Prep: 10 minutes   Cook: 13 to 19 minutes   Chill: overnight
Serves: 10 to 15

This makes a thick, mousselike nog. Add the liqueurs slowly—rough treatment and impatience could curdle the custard.

6 **egg yolks**	¾ **cup dark rum**
½ **cup plus 2 tablespoons**	¾ **cup Cognac or other brandy**
granulated sugar	4 **egg whites**
¼ **cup dark brown sugar**	1½ **cups heavy cream**
2 **cups warm half-and-half**	**Pineapple wedges on**
2 **cups pineapple juice**	**toothpicks**

1. In a double boiler, whisk egg yolks, ½ cup granulated sugar, and brown sugar until fluffy, about 1 minute. Slowly whisk in warm milk until blended but not too frothy. Stir in pineapple juice. Cook over barely simmering water, stirring, until custard is thick enough to coat a spoon, 12 to 18 minutes. Transfer to a mixing bowl. Let cool somewhat.

2. Slowly whisk in rum and Cognac. Cover with plastic wrap placed directly on surface of custard. Refrigerate overnight or up to 3 days to ripen.

3. When ready to serve, pour custard into a punch bowl. In a medium bowl, beat egg whites with remaining 2 tablespoons sugar to moderately stiff peaks. Fold into custard.

4. In a large bowl, beat cream to stiff peaks. Fold into eggnog. Let some tufts of cream and egg whites float on surface. Garnish with pineapple wedges on toothpicks.

364   MINT JULEP EGGNOG

Prep: 10 minutes   Steep: 2 hours   Cook: 20 to 23 minutes
Chill: overnight   Serves: 6 to 8

1¾ cups plus 2 tablespoons
    sugar
1 cup packed mint leaves
1 cup warm milk
6 egg yolks
1 vanilla bean or 2 teaspoons
    vanilla extract

2 cups bourbon
4 egg whites
2 cups heavy cream
   Sprigs of mint

1. In a medium saucepan, bring 1 cup sugar and 1 cup water to a boil, stirring to dissolve sugar. Reduce heat and simmer 5 minutes, without stirring. Remove from heat and add mint, bruising it with a wooden spoon. Cover pot. Let steep 2 hours. Strain, reserving mint syrup and discarding leaves.

2. In a glass measuring cup, combine warm milk and mint syrup. Microwave on High for 1 minute. In a double boiler, whisk egg yolks and ¾ cup sugar until light and fluffy, about 1 minute. Slowly beat in warm mint milk. Cook over simmering water, stirring, until custard is thick, 12 to 15 minutes. Transfer to a bowl. Lay plastic wrap directly on surface of custard. Let cool.

3. Slowly whisk in bourbon. Cover and refrigerate overnight or up to 3 days to ripen.

4. When ready to serve, pour custard into a large punch bowl. In a medium bowl, beat egg whites with remaining 2 tablespoons sugar until stiff peaks form. Fold into custard.

5. In a large bowl, beat cream to stiff peaks. Fold into eggnog, letting some tufts of cream and egg whites float on surface. Garnish with mint sprigs.

365   TOM AND JERRY

Prep: 8 minutes   Cook: none   Serves: 4

2 eggs, separated
1 tablespoon sugar
¼ to ½ teaspoon ground
    allspice

¼ cup light rum
⅛ teaspoon cream of tartar
1½ cups milk, warmed
   Freshly grated nutmeg

1. In a small mixing bowl, beat egg yolks, sugar, and allspice with an electric hand mixer on high speed until very thick and light yellow, 3 to 5 minutes. Blend in rum.

2. In another small mixing bowl, with clean, dry beaters, beat egg whites and cream of tartar on high speed until stiff but not dry, just until whites no longer slip when bowl is tilted. Fold yolks into whites.

3. Pour ½ cup of egg mixture into each of 4 warmed 8-ounce mugs.

4. Into center of each mug, pour ⅓ cup hot milk directly over egg froth. Sprinkle each serving with grated nutmeg and serve immediately.

Index

Acknowledgments

The author gratefully acknowledges the following people for permission to use or adapt their recipes: Cathy Burgett, for chocolate and lemon soufflés; Janet Fletcher, for Oven Ratatouille from *More Vegetables, Please* (Berkeley: Harlow & Ratner, 1992); Camille Glenn, for chocolate and almond tuiles from *The Fine Art of Delectable Desserts* (Camille Glenn, Louisville, 1982); the Greenbrier resort, for Greenbrier Quiche and Cold Old Bourbon Souffle from *The Greenbrier Cookbook: Favorite Recipes from America's Resort* (White Sulphur Springs, WV: The Greenbrier, 1992); Maggie Oster, for Fresh-Herb Pickled Eggs and Spiced Pickled Eggs from *Herbal Vinegar* (Pownal, VT: Storey Communications, Inc., 1994); and Scripps-Howard and *The Cincinnati Post* for Pickled Beets and Eggs—By: Joyce Rosencrans, *The Cincinnati Post*. Used with permission.

Also thanks to: Kathleen Abraham, Hilary Abramson, Antonia Allegra, Brenda Bell, Leslie Bramlage, Martha Casselman, Vivienne Corn, Dotty Griffith, Cindy Indorf, Dixie Jew, Linda Jew, Marcie Rothman, Ellie Brecher (for not cooking), and to David and Robert.